GREAT MORNING

GREAT MORNING

Left Hand, Right Hand! Volume III
An Autobiography

Q————————————————————

OSBERT SITWELL

QUARTET BOOKS
LONDON   MELBOURNE   NEW YORK

Published by Quartet Books Limited 1977
A member of the Namara Group
27 Goodge Street, London W1P 1FD

First published by Macmillan London Limited, 1948

Copyright © 1975 by Frank Magro

ISBN 0 7043 3156 x

Printed and bound in Great Britain by
Hazell Watson & Viney Ltd,
Aylesbury, Bucks

ACKNOWLEDGEMENTS

As in former volumes of this work, there are several persons whose kindness I must take the first opportunity to acknowledge. My thanks are due to Miss Mary Mills, the literary executor of Archbishop Lord Davidson, for allowing me to reproduce a letter he wrote to me, and similarly I must express gratitude to my friend the Hon. Anthony Asquith for sanctioning the appearance here of a letter to me from his mother, the late Countess of Oxford and Asquith. I owe a great debt to Mr. Hamilton Temple Smith for his illuminating description of a visit to Renishaw and for giving leave to make it public, and to Mrs. C. Maxwell for sending me, by kind permission of Colonel Mackenzie Smith, Mrs. Horatia Ewing's account of my father as a very young man. I am also indebted to the Editor of *Truth* for his kindness in allowing me to reprint the article on " The Frauds of Julian Field " which forms the main part of Appendix E. Finally, I have again to thank my friend Mr. Thomas Mark, who has seen *Great Morning* through the press.

OSBERT SITWELL

CONTENTS

BOOK V

MARS VICTORYALL

BOOK VI

THE ROSE AND THE THORN

> *Delio:*
> Hark! the dead stones seem to have pity on ye
> And give you good counsel.
>   *Antonio:*
> Echo, I will not talk with thee
> For thou art a dead thing.
>   *The Duchess of Malfi*, Act V, Scene iii

Chapter One
THE HOUS OF MARS VICTORYALL

I⊤ was a brief winter's walk, a brisk turn of a special kind, against a background familiar to me, because my sister and I, when we were children, had visited it, and I had never forgotten its wintry vastness, solemnity and gloom. At times the place seemed a toy fort that had become real, and swollen stonily to enormous proportions, its walls and castellations assuming ample material substance, just as the toy soldiers in their scarlet tunics had acquired life; at others, it appeared to be a terrace levelled among stone mountains or, again, a piazza in a small hill town, high up, but under a smoky sky. It was ten minutes to eight in the morning — and when I say eight, I mean eight, and not, as in these lying times, six or seven; a fact which, owing to the relative degrees of light, makes a difference to my scene; it was ten minutes to eight, and, swinging our arms smartly, six of us had to walk up and down in twos, at a pace full of winter's zest. The stone mountains that framed this stage gave evidence in their texture, a few of them, of extreme antiquity, but most, on the other hand, displayed a Victorian primness and hard precision, seeming to be the realisation in stone of a drill-sergeant's dream. Everything was spick and span, and even the roughest, oldest of these

I

mountains, even the most uncouth in bulk, even Julius Caesar's Tower itself, had been trimmed and clipped, as it were, to provide a fitting background for parades. One or two old trees alone, though they too had been pruned and pared, made for this place some obstinate claim to kinship with Nature and the world outside. And occasionally a very large old raven would croak loudly and walk across the frosty ground in front of us, lifting its claws high, as if the stone burned them. I would have liked to stop and watch this bird, because it had an air of immense age, of being, indeed, although it carried its years so well, as old as anything in this setting; causing one to wonder whether it could be — as no doubt in fact it was — a living representative of the collection [1] of beasts and birds that, in the eighteenth and early nineteenth centuries, had drawn hither, to the side of the now destroyed Lion Tower, all visitors to London.

The raven still stalked slowly and at its will, flapping and croaking, but we had to walk rapidly up and down in a straight line, our swords knocking a little and clanking as we moved. We would glance from time to time at the ranks of men, clad in long grey coats, and now standing at ease. They were drawn up facing the White Tower, and we paced up and down between this massive building and the men. Inside that tower, among much else to be seen, was King Henry VIII's steel suit — feared yet, the custodian once told me, by tourists; these peering crowds of little men still scrupled to touch it, in case some morbid influence from the tomb should communicate to them the maladies of the dead giant.

It was a very clear morning, with a berry-bright frostiness

[1] The menagerie had originated, many centuries earlier, in a gift to King Henry III of three leopards. This monarch resided much in the Tower of London and the beasts were sent him there, as a present and a compliment to the arms of the Plantagenets, by the Emperor Frederick. Soon after receiving these heraldic beasts, the king acquired a bear from Norway ; for which animal the City Sheriffs were held responsible, being commanded to provide a muzzle and chain for him when out of the water, and a strong rope to hold him " when fishing in the Thames ". The king subsequently added to this nucleus an elephant ; while Edward II augmented it with a lion. . . . The kings kept their wild animals in a semi-circular sunken area, adjoining the now demolished Lion Tower, by the Middle Gate.

that matched the rooster's music of the bugles sounding their calls, and the stones crackled as we walked over them. But at this season and this hour, more often fog enclosed us and the whole of the vast area of city stretching round us, beyond these towers and bounding walls — for this, the Tower of London, was the very citadel of the fog. Here night could reign for forty-eight hours at a stretch. Then the naked electric-light globes that, as part of the traditional pipe-clayed bareness of barrack-rooms, swung in the draught from open windows of a winter's evening, burnt all day, yet seemed to have no more power than a match would have, if it were lighted in this elephantine and engulfing darkness. For these hours, the barrack-rooms themselves became mysterious. . . . There are — or were — so many different varieties of fog, and all of them lived here, and crept out when occasion offered. There was the night darkness, or prevalence of a perpetual dusk, black but clear, in which figures could still be seen moving and ordinary life could still be carried on; there was the transparent yellow fog, the most boding of all, which turned the world sullen and filled it with a gloomy, suppressed excitement, seeming to make the clatter of the men's rifles on the ground more pronounced, and the raven's croakings more frequent and more cracked; there were the thick yellow fogs, made of yellow wool, and the white, made of white wool, when every activity came to a standstill, and everyone choked, and eyes and ears ached, and nothing could be seen; and a great number of less deleterious fogs in chalk-grey and dove-grey and amber.

At any moment of day or night, though, and even when swathed in layers of fog, the Tower of London remained a place of mystery, beautiful and, at the same time, because of its stoniness and crenellation, ugly. The neatness that recent centuries had striven to impose upon these shapes that appeared to have been hacked out of primeval chaos, the accretions, only served to make it more tremendous. After the manner of Maiden Castle or Stonehenge, its origins stretched so far back that no glimpse of them could be obtained. It was a system of life, a city, more than a building; a forgotten palace, from days still dimly to be apprehended in the folds of tapestries, a

3

forgotten church, a forgotten — no, a remembered — prison.
Rivalling Windsor Castle as the chief repository of English
history and tradition, this formidable fortified mount was not
only a world in itself, but the heart, now a little atrophied, of
the greatest of English cities, the centre from which it had
grown, the centre from which it had been governed. For
hundreds of years — ever since, indeed, Gundulph the Weeper,
Bishop of Rochester, had, at the command of William the
Conqueror, supervised the building of the White Tower —,
this stone mountain had typified its city.

> Upon thy lusty Brigge of pylers white
> Been merchauntis full royall to behold ;
> Upon thy stretis goth many a semely knyght
> In velvet gownes and cheynes of fyne gold.
> By Julyus Cesar thy Tour founded of old
> May be the hous of Mars victoryall,
> Whose artillary with tonge may not be told :
> London, thou art the floure of Cities all.[1]

Though never touched as, for example, was the Capitol, by
great art or world-renowned legend, nevertheless it is scarcely
less romantic, and countless myths attend it. It remains the
place beyond all others, except Windsor, where the local colour
of every age in English history lingers and has still a meaning.
Outside these walls, the Beefeaters, perhaps, may look obsolete,
an anachronism, but here, within, they are plainly the warders
of the Tower of London, faithful to Tudor masters. At eleven
each night the Ceremony of the Keys, when their royal owner-
ship is challenged and declared, brings back the memory of
many monarchs, and relates especially to the epoch when the
Pretenders threatened the English throne ; just as the Crown
Jewels, near-by, in their tower, epitomise the whole of our
history, down to the days of which I write. In the fires of ruby
and emerald, you can perceive, as though portrayed by the
monks illuminating their missals with the pure tones and pig-
ments of Norman and Gothic times, the early marriages of
our kings with members of the royal houses of France and
Spain. Dead princesses, whose effigies lie in the Abbey beside

[1] *To the City of London*, by William Dunbar.

4

those of their husbands — princesses with the slender necks, oval faces and long-fingered hands of the Gothic Age, with delicate features and narrow eyes filled with wonder, as though they opened and shut them upon a world full of inspired marvels and transcendent beauty — brought with them as their dowry these splendid jewels. In certain gems, again, is yet reflected the Renaissance magnificence of the Tudor princes, while the Koh-i-Noor focuses in the brilliant strangeness of its lights the romance of the English conquest of India, in the same way that the more material fires of the Cullinan Diamond symbolise and recall the war in South Africa. These stone cliffs, which surround them, are nearly a millennium old; but how much more ancient was not the original fortification, the palisade on this sacred mount; what Saxon kings, what Roman warriors, what British princes and chieftains of the neolithic age may not have lived here, are not buried here, or on Tower Hill, the exhalations from their bones adding their impalpable contribution to the general atmosphere of the Tower!

Behind these walls, threefold, of palace, fortress and prison, long lay captive the innocent and the guilty; to take a few names at random of those who forfeited, through unsuccessful war, their freedom, or were accused of treason or of undeclared crimes: Gruffydd ab Llywelyn, who broke his neck in trying to escape from here — what manner of Celtic prince was he, clad in what armour or diadem and tartan robes? —, David II of Scotland, Charles, Duke of Orleans — captured at Agincourt —, Henry VI, the Duke of Clarence, Perkin Warbeck, Edward V and his brother, the Duke of York — perhaps the most celebrated victims of any crime within these precincts —, Anne Boleyn, Catherine Howard, Thomas Cromwell, the Protector Somerset, Cranmer, Essex, Sir Walter Raleigh, Thomas Wentworth, Lord Strafford, the Duke of Monmouth, and Lord Lovat the Jacobite. Death and imprisonment, however, were not the only fortunes pertaining to this place. Several of the Plantagenet kings dwelt here of their own choice, and illustrious princes and princesses were born here, bearing in consequence throughout their lives the proud title *de la*

Tour . . . And a lovely appendage it is, too, carrying with it in the mind the music of the names — laden with the associations of medieval history — of the component parts of this great building. Let us call the roll : the White Tower — so termed because King Henry III caused it to be whitewashed in 1241 —, the Lion Gate, the Galleyman's Tower, the church of St. Peter-ad-Vincula and the chapel of St. John, the Salt or Julius Caesar's Tower, the Constable Tower, the Brick Tower, the Flint Tower, the Lanthorn Tower, the Wardrobe Tower, the Bloody Tower, the Wakefield Tower, the Beauchamp Tower, the Martin or Jewel Tower, the Brass Mount and Legge's Mount, the Cradle Tower, the King's House, the Well Tower, the Traitor's Gate, Sir Walter Raleigh's Walk, the Byward Tower, the Bell Tower, the Broad Arrow Tower, the Bowyer Tower, the Devereux and Devil's or Develin Tower.

In accordance with the best taste of their time, generations have done their utmost to spoil the aspect of this mount, tearing down its gates, selling its very stones [1] — but you can no more spoil the Tower of London, rooted in the imagination of the race which created it, than a man can dent the Himalaya Mountains with the palm of his hand. . . . The place is ugly in its way, as I have said, but also beautiful at all times ; beautiful and strange on such a morning as I have described ; beautiful, too, in how remote and desolate a manner, in the later hours, dominated by the melancholy hooting of steamers rather than, as before noon, by the smell of fish wafted from Billingsgate, near-by, and when the towers and buttresses and

[1] Augustus Hare, in *Walks in London* (Allen & Unwin), states that in the restorations at the end of the nineteenth century, the Traitor's Gate was particularly maltreated. The original stone steps, worn down by the feet of so many personages famous in English history, were ripped away from their setting, together with the stone upon which Elizabeth sat, when, as a princess of twenty-one, she was landed here to be imprisoned in the Tower. These steps were replaced by what was contemporarily described as " a neat staircase of Bath stone ". The gates themselves, though buffeted by the ten thousand tides that had washed them green as the stone rafts of Venice, were still stout and able to stand for centuries : but neither this nor the history attaching to them prevented the authorities from allowing them to be sold for fifteen shillings to a Whitechapel shopkeeper. Eventually, Barnum, the showman, hearing of them, bought them from their new proprietor for fifty pounds, and transported them to New York, where they formed for some years the chief attraction among his exhibits.

walls and battlements show distinctly as in a Hoxton print every line of cement, every roughness of the stone — not that the light is strong, but that it plays on everything with a peculiar grey clearness —, and the men, no longer clad in scarlet or in long grey coats, but dressed in white shorts and thick, striped jerseys, kick footballs higher, along the now dry and dusty moat, than the walls that shut it in ; beautiful at dusk when the wind seems almost to hold up the tide, bringing the Pool of London to the very edge of the terrace, lapping and flapping and bumping at it with, to my ears, an echo of Venetian waves, curly and playful as dolphins ; most beautiful of all at night, when the castle walls become the walls of Dunsinane or Elsinore, stony, bereft, loaded with the burden of crimes and tragedies, and with the mystery of the ultimate plight of man. Then the sentry, as he stamps on the pavement, makes with iron heels a sound that suggests the clanking of a knight in armour, and Roman ghosts too, Roman centurions and traders, disappear, as you watch, into the dim, greenish light of the Victorian gas-lamps, surmounted with their gold crowns. In the dungeons the victims of the Plantagenet kings still cry out to the darkness, and in the higher chambers necromancers and sorcerers peer through slits at the sky ; (one of them has inscribed his name, together with a globe and the signs of the Zodiac, on an inner wall of the Salt Tower : " Hew Draper made thys spheer, the 30 daye of Maye anno 1561 "). . . . Such was the Tower, some thirty years ago, when I lived there, and such, no doubt, it is today.

Returning to it at a late hour, after an evening's pleasure, its majesty cooled youthful blood. False and obvious as sounded by daylight the story that at night you could sometimes see in an open space the shadow, thrown by the moon, of the Axe, it was impossible on a moonlit night not to look for it as you passed under vast arches, along the dark green alleys carved by the icy light among these stony ways. All round, the stout and buttressed walls showed their crenellated circuit. . . . And the drive in a taxi-cab through a deserted City, that led up to arrival at the Tower, aided the impression ; drives through length upon illumined length of emptiness, where only from time to time a cat howled, and never a human being stirred, past spires and domes and monuments, past Wren churches that are now a memory (though it may be we still breathe their dust), through streets and past buildings the names of which men will never allow to die, so that they will rise again, as did the great monuments of Rome, with each succeeding age — and of these names the most famous is the Tower of London.

When we reached it, if the time was past two o'clock in the morning, before we could enter under the portcullis to find ourselves in this castle of the Dark Ages — a place now equally deserted as the streets through which we had just driven —, we had to make an effort to recollect the password, which was changed every night, and though usually typical of the military mind in the simplicity of choice it displayed, yet the later the hour, the greater the mental labour required to recall something that, hours before, had seemed so easy to memorise. I was just twenty years of age, this was January 1913, and London was in carnival throughout the following nineteen months, except for the brief festivals of the banks and churches; then theatres, ballrooms and restaurants shut, and all those who could leave London fled from it with an eagerness and speed they never showed some thirty years later, when it was bombed day and night. . . . Sometimes, therefore, after late hours, one was tired of a morning, and for that reason, of the kinds of fog already catalogued I preferred the thick yellow, when, temporarily, all parades had to be cancelled and one could rest.

Today, however, was clear, with the clearness that dwells on hill-tops and the tops of the highest towers — and this was fortunate, for we must show no fatigue. That was not permitted us. So, wearing long, dark-blue coats, with a cascade of tabs flowing down the front under our grey greatcoats, in blue trousers with a broad red stripe, and dark-blue hats peaked with gold thread, we walked sharply up and down, waiting for the clock to strike, and for the Adjutant, a just man and a very splendid figure of an officer, to come on parade. At the last stroke of eight, he would appear, accompanied by the Battalion Sergeant-Major. In his impressive stride, in the bold, severe, critical, yet tolerant, and even amused, ferocity of his glance, he appeared to sum up a tradition, to be the very embodiment of the Brigade of Guards. . . . Meanwhile, we waited for him, and to be told to fall in, at the head of the men. I rather dreaded, however, the lesson to come, for the Adjutant used to complain loudly of my personal version of the ritual voice that regimental tradition obliges the young officer to adopt for words of command — conventional sounds that none but initiates can interpret —, declaring that he could not distinguish it from the croaking of the Tower ravens.

The reader will have noticed that, since last he caught sight of me, I had, in the short space of three years, been translated as completely as any of the characters in *A Midsummer Night's Dream*. But, in the new existence in which I had, with dazed eyes, found myself, I was received with so much kindness, and had discovered so many acquaintances, and even enemies, who, in the same fashion that I had been changed from a schoolboy into an officer, had, in their turn, become transformed by the magic I described at the end of the second volume, into admirable and zealous friends, displaying the greatest solicitude to help, and to show me how to enjoy the life in which I had been plunged, and, moreover, this world contained such warmth, vitality and extravagance, and, further, was imbued with a quality so much its own, while, above all, the tenets of its faith, and the conceptions that governed it, were so new and strange to me, that I perceived myself, rather to my own surprise, to be happier than at home, happier, in short, than I had ever been hitherto. Almost for the first time in my life, at any rate for the second, I was experiencing the warm human comfort to be derived from friendship with those of one's own age. And the points in my character which must to them, with their outlook, have seemed unusual, even peculiar, were quickly accepted, laughed at with good humour, or even watched with interest.

Looking back, I suppose that the friends I made then — nearly all of them, alas, destined to be killed before two years had passed — were not those, necessarily, who would have chosen me or whom I would have chosen, had the range been unlimited. Our interests were different, — theirs, sporting; mine, mainly esthetic, — but this did not in the least mar our friendship. Their great qualities, their character and generosity of mind, completely won me over, and banished the fact from my consciousness, so that I am able to hope that, similarly, my affection for them prevented them from guessing that I was not the sort of friend, either, whom they would have selected. Alas (left hand, right hand!), I *should* have resembled them — but I did not; or my way in general would have been simpler. At least we shared one thing in common : the highest and most fantastic spirits. They possessed shrewd powers of judgement, just as did the ranks under them. The guardsmen could arrive at a fair estimate of an officer's character very quickly. And, though I must confess to being by nature a minority-partisan, I must own also that if my companions on occasion took a violent dislike to a brother-officer, it was usually justified : though not always the manner of showing it. In addition, they were supremely courageous — some of them, in a sense, fierce as young animals —, and sure of themselves with the superb assurance that belonged to those who were young at this time, and came of their class and country. These young men were splendid, and died in their full splendour, which never knew modification.

So, on the morning in question, I walked up and down the frosty square, thinking how fortunate I was to be with my companions. The curious and enclosed world into which they were inducting me — my first adult world — was full of luxury, hardship and privilege, and hedged with shibboleths, traditions and formulae. Nevertheless, within its strict boundaries of St. James's Street — a street that, from its cramped palace of brown brick, so full of the English genius for understatement, to its clubs and wine-merchants and hatters, still offers the essence of London, as the Sierpes, with its sherry-shops and cigar-stalls, presents that of Seville —, it glowed with a certain warmth of heart. Each young officer off parade, out of school, was an important unit, and treated as such; a perfect democracy reigned in the Officers' Mess, Christian names were the rule, and only the Commanding Officer was addressed as " Sir ". Much ritual existed, however, in other directions and at other times. The newly-joined ensign was instructed not only in the general and accepted code, but, if he were not already aware of it, was advised on what constituted for him the right kind of shoes, collars, shirts and suits to wear, being given pieces of precise information ; such as, for example, that when leave was granted to him, he should never spend a day of it in London, and that he must, when not in uniform — which he only wore, of course, on duty —, always, if the King was in London, wear a morning suit and top-hat.

In those days — and probably until the beginning of the 1939 war the habit continued —,[1] the Adjutant would attend the first fittings of each young officer, surveying with a practised eye the whole effect, and scrutinising minutely the cut of the tunic of scarlet Melton cloth, the smoothness of shoulders and waist. Above all, there must be no wrinkling. And this constituted, withal, an important question, both for the young man and his parents, since the uniform cost several hundreds of pounds. The review-belt alone, made of scarlet and gold, cost thirty-six pounds, I remember, and I only had occasion to wear it once ; then there was the bearskin, as well, to be fitted and tried on, and the perfection of this proved to be of so esoteric a kind that no-one new to the matter would be able to tell a good from a bad, and, myself, I never contrived to master the principles that governed the choice. The bearskin had, of course, — for it must measure some one and a half foot to one foot and ten inches high — to be sufficiently wellbalanced and well-fitting to enable the ensign to carry it on his head, and the Colour in front of him, in a gale, without mishap — and this, even with the best constructed bearskin, was not easy : because the Fore Court of Buckingham Palace gives ample space for the east wind, which the front faces, to play, while the weight of the Colour, although the butt of it is supported most of the time in a pipe-clayed belt, is considerable, and the left arm, to balance, and also for the sake of smart appearance, must swing free. In addition, however, to these necessary qualities, I may place it on record for those in the

[1] It still continues.

future of an enquiring disposition, that the good bearskin should possess an interior curl and a special gloss, at once perceptible to the expert.

The fitting of headgear and uniform and belts constituted something of an ordeal. Not only did it without exception occupy a full hour — and by nature I have always been too impatient either to deserve or to obtain perfectly fitting clothes —, but, while the young officer, prodded from time to time with questing fingers, as if he were a prize bull at a show, stood in the centre of a small closet, full of mirrors, set at different angles, so as to reflect him in his half-finished scarlet tunic, and every detail of his dress, with a kind of dull but yet varied repetition that recalled delirium, during all these minutes, a highly technical conversation was taking place between the Adjutant and the tailor. After they had debated some particularly enthralling point, the tailor would call in the cutter and ask for his view on it : but the cutter, partially blind from his work, would pretend to be deaf also. This, I think, he did as some personal form of subservience combined with defiance, that he had worked out for himself — but at any rate, every question would have to be put at least three times before he would answer. " The best cutter in London, now that the ladies have taken all the others ",[1] the tailor would say of him, adding, " But he's a very difficult man to deal with, must be given his head ". Occasionally, the tailor himself would dart at my shoulder or waist, and rip the seam open, so that the grey padding stood exposed beneath the vermilion stuff. It was true that one felt oneself to be the most important person there — as the prize bull must feel himself; the very centre of the debate. Yet, too, one felt at the same time curiously left out of things : for neither Adjutant, tailor nor cutter seemed to see the man who wore the uniform, only the uniform itself. The tunic glowed, ember-like, in the misty and pocked mirrors, and the cutter peered through spectacles that magnified his eyes to the size of a god's : he jabbed and snipped, but never spoke.

[1] When women, in the 'nineties and early 1900's, began to adopt tailor-made clothes, they lured all the best cutters away from men by offering them bigger money.

A touch of Ouida, a breath of the Boer War — even though these two influences were in contradiction —, both seemed to linger still about the life I was entering. With its ritual and formality, it was by no means the school of economy that my father seemed to consider it. One had to spend money. To this pursuit I brought the zest and sureness of touch inherited from my ancestors. The only expensive taste I did not share with my brother-officers was that for horses; I abominated them, and the brutes, with that animal instinct of theirs, knew of my loathing and returned it a thousand-fold. So I avoided hunting, steeplechasing, racing. The tastes I shared were for nearly all other kinds of pleasure. Worse still, I possessed my own individual lines of extravagance, such as large bills for books, and owing to theatre agencies for visits to ballet and opera — and never did extravagance yield a richer harvest. I could not afford it, and should not have gone — I ought no doubt to have sat in pit or gallery — but I did not. I had received little education, had grown to hate learning — associating it in my mind with authority, father, dons and schoolmasters —, and here, disguised as pleasure, was my university. The stimulus that the music of Stravinsky, for instance, afforded to my imagination.has subsequently been of inestimable benefit to my work. . . . Yet to run into debt for theatre tickets would by many be regarded as self-indulgent; whereas had I been in poor circumstances and borrowed money to send myself to college, my action would have been applauded.

No, it was extravagance — and as such, the world I am describing understood it, being tolerant in an intolerant way. Hedged though he was with countless shibboleths, in detail so minute as often to be hard to detect, yet it did not prove over difficult for a young officer, albeit his interests were not those of the average young officer, to adapt himself to the life round him. . . . To give examples from my own experience, I was never obliged to conceal my interest in the arts or to pretend to sporting proclivities foreign to my nature. Thus, when the following summer, one day while I was Ensign on King's Guard at St. James's Palace, the Captain of it — an awe-inspiring individual, with a heavy, but regular profile, and moustachios left over from the drawing-rooms of George du Maurier — enquired, after an immense effort that resembled the wheezing of an old clock about to strike, but was none the less born of a kindly intention to try to lessen the tedium of long hours spent in the red-papered guard-room, " Do you like HORSES? ", and I replied, " No, but I like giraffes — they have such a beautiful line ", he took the answer unexpectedly well, and even attempted to smile. . . . Then, on another occasion this spring, it had been my turn to take the Early Parade at 6 A.M. After breakfast, the Adjutant sent for me to the Orderly Room. I obeyed the intimidating summons. I entered, and saluted the great man. He said, looking up,

" Mr. Sitwell, it is reported to me that you were late this morning for Early Parade."

I expressed dissent.

On this, he enquired, " Were the men on parade when you arrived ? "

I replied, " I didn't notice, sir. I did not look."

I can see now that my answer, which was quite genuine and unaffected, must have been disconcerting to a mind of such excellent military punctuality and precision. In fact, for the moment it bowled him over, and I was dismissed. Later, though, I was instructed to attend Early Parade every morning for a week — but never did the Adjutant bear me any rancour for my unconventional conduct or retorts. Out of the Orderly Room, he treated me, as ever, in the friendliest possible manner. . . . As Davis, our old nurse, used to say, " I can only speak as I find ". And I write this testimonial because I have heard my regiment, and indeed the whole of the Brigade of Guards, accused of intolerance ; whereas it always seemed to me a vice from which, for an army unit, they were both singularly free. They formed, as any finely disciplined bodies must, of their very nature, a narrow and enclosed world. But the fact that these regiments were often stationed in London, and that thus the individuals composing them were able continually to keep in touch with ordinary, as opposed to regimental, life, and become liable even to the influences of European civilisation

14

in a way not possible to garrisons isolated for long periods in Aldershot, York or the Curragh, rendered existence for a new-comer much easier and more agreeable than those acquainted with other mess-rooms might have expected.

Outside this world, stretched for me one other — since as yet I had been granted little time or freedom to make friends of my own choice: that consisting of relations and family friends; though some of these, it is true, had now become estranged from my parents, a development the causes of which I hope to examine more fully in the course of the next chapter. But I must here explain shortly that my father was modifying at this time one cf his own dictums: for he felt more than formerly a certain necessity to see people. He seldom got to know, nor did he wish to know, his peers : those who possessed an ability comparable to his own, or of a similar range and depth of interest. Strange as it may seem in a man of such pronounced character, he needed now a circle of persons willing on every subject to accept as correct his views, some tediously conventional or obsolete, others fantastical and based on chimeras. To obtain applause, which had formerly meant so little to him, he was now willing to leave the shelter of the Gothic tower he had constructed for himself, and so much loved, and to sit in the sun for an hour or two. Those he met during these sorties, however, must never give vent to the slightest doubt of his essential, inevitable infallibility. But the few fringed and barbate antiquaries who survived from his earlier acquaintance showed no inclination to assume this attitude, and in consequence their visits, never very frequent, became more sparse. It was plain to him that the less you knew people, and the shorter the time you had known them, the less likely they were to contradict you. It was, in short, no longer " such a mistake to have friends ", so long as they were not really friends at all. . . . Where, then, was he to find these friends, to whom he now so often referred ?

When, in a flight of fancy, planning some trifle in which even he hardly believed — a set of dessert-plates by Lalique, with a gold medallion of my mother and himself in the centre, or some knives and forks with china handles fashioned in their image, he would now refer to a still mythical host. He would remark defiantly, as though in bravado, or perhaps because he just could not help saying it, or because he wanted to hear what I would say in reply,

"It would be cheaper no doubt to have a quantity made at the same time. Better get twelve friends to join us! . . . They'd be only too delighted!"

"Which of your friends would you suggest?" I would reply cautiously. "Let us make a list."

Brought back to reality after this fashion, his eye would go blank, and his fire would be quenched. . . . Even at the best, he must have admitted to himself, they would be acquaintances, and probably not disposed for such luxuries, even if they could afford them. But he would not allow these sentiments to escape him. Instead, he would merely toss his head and make a favourite sound of annoyance and disapproval: "Chut!", I suppose, it would be rendered in print.

Where was he to find them, this host, willing to hang on his words, to be astounded by his creations at Renishaw, and, in particular, to become in a flutter over his alterations at Scarborough, where he was proceeding with enjoyment, but at considerable cost, to turn the interior of an 1820 house of Italianate inclination into a post-Edwardian dome of pleasure? (Even in this, since he condemned pleasure, there was a basic contradiction.) . . . Would relations meet the case, and fill his necessity? . . . There were always relations. . . . But one was apt to lose touch. One ought to keep up with them more.

"You can say what you like," he would from time to time remark, allowing a note of sentiment to enter his voice, "but relations are the best friends in time of trouble." . . . It was a favourite cliché, a comforter.

"It's too high a price to pay for their kindness," I would reply; "besides, I want my friends round me when I'm in *good* spirits. When I'm depressed, I don't want to see anyone."

"Chut!" again.

In the realm of fact, he seldom saw any of his relations: so seldom that always in his mind they remained at the same age at which he had last seen them. Thus he would talk of "the Swinton girls", his cousins, when those two venerable ladies were approaching their eightieth years. . . . And this trait produced in time so curious and exaggerated a consequence that I must jump some fifteen years forward, again, to an August in the 'twenties, when my father, who had settled at Montegufoni, came to stay with me at Renishaw, which he had handed over to me. . . . One morning, I was sitting in the library. He entered, and said,

"My dear boy, I wanted to speak to you. . . . Of course, I enjoy seeing your friends. . . . But really you ought to ask more relations to stay. . . . There are all the Sitwell cousins."

"But I've never met any of them, except Bill and his family. The others never came here, that I can remember; and they're my seventh or eighth cousins. They'll think it so odd if they suddenly receive an invitation from me! . . . I don't even know whom to ask or where to write."

"Well, I'm afraid I must really *insist* on your asking them. . . . I never had time to ask them myself . . . so much to see to!"

I carried out my father's commands, and sent to the various members of the family, whose names and addresses he gave me, invitations to stay. A long silence ensued. . . . Then, after some weeks, the answers arrived, one after another — and very indignant they were, in a dignified but wounded way. All were couched in the same vein, and ran in almost identical terms. The following is a typical example.

"It was most affable of you to ask my poor old father to stay, and I'm sure he would much have appreciated it. Unfortunately, he passed away — mercifully without pain —, at the age of eighty-four, some thirty-two years ago — to be precise, on June 18, 1895, and a month after his death our old home was sold. . . . It seems strange that your father (whom I *so* well remember last seeing at Lambeth in 1884) should not have heard of these tragedies at the time."

This would have been a party of ghosts, in short, such as that other my father planned, of which I shall tell you later.

Not only, however, was one apt to lose touch with relations,

he must have admitted in his own mind, but the majority of
them were inclined to be obstinate, and not easily to fall in
with his ideas, or be interested in what he was doing for the
family. . . . Had he bought a race-horse, or even a cricket
bat, yes, they would have been willing to acclaim his action.
But they resolutely ignored his projects. Yet, above all, it was
necessary for him to find people who were willing to admire
the alterations he was in course of making at Scarborough.
Chinese papers, and others, showing exotic birds balancing on
one scaly, coralline leg among the misty, blue swamps of Indo-
China, were unrolled on bedroom walls, downstairs ceilings
sprouted into confectioners' mouldings of fruit and flowers,
and the fussy Victorian mantels turned to marble chimney-
pieces of a depressingly pure taste. A passage on the first
storey was driven through the immense conservatory, and was
supported on brick arches covered with lattice, and now, as
you walked to your bath, you looked down on the top of a
mirage of palm trees, tropical foliage, and green festoons of
creeper, sprinkled with strongly-scented white stars of blossom.
And the hall, an apartment that had formerly seemed to be
panelled throughout in chocolate biscuits, grew columns in the
night, as mango trees are said to sprout from nothing into full
growth for Indian magicians, while the floor renewed itself
with a chequered pattern of white and black marble. Exquisitely made double doors of mahogany, with silver handles,
replaced those of painted deal ; while, on the other hand, vans
of Italian furniture, of a certain beauty of design, but so badly
carpentered that it broke if you tried to open a single drawer,
arrived every noon — always as Henry was " sitting down to
his dinner ", as he phrased it — from Naples, Florence and
Rome.[1]

In the end, then, my father recruited some of the chorus to
admire these novelties from among the artistic wives of local
clergy, doctors and lawyers ; they proved adequate to the task.
He need only see them for the meal to which they were asked,
and then, after showing them the house, he could go straight

[1] See Appendix A (p. 299) for an account of Wood End in the 'seventies by my
father.

upstairs to rest, and spend the remainder of the day in his convenient retreat in the thirteenth century. It was really less trouble than having people to stay : yet visitors here and at Renishaw — and I hope to treat of them in detail in the next chapter — were more plentiful and frequent than in the years immediately preceding. Among them, though there were few persons of intelligence, was at least one man of genius, — at any rate, of genius within the Edwardian limitations imposed upon him by his epoch : Sir Edwin Lutyens. (I use the adjective *Edwardian* advisedly, because, though so much of the architect's life had been spent in the reigns of Queen Victoria, and of King George V, yet I should not hesitate to classify him, in the same way that I should classify Elgar, as essentially an Edwardian ; that decade of freedom and prosperity was most surely his home.) He often visited us, but these visits were explicable ; they were professional, he was paid for them.

One had never seen before, and will never see again, anyone who resembled this singular and delightful man. An expression of mischievous benevolence was his distinguishing mark, as it was that of his work. He would sit, with his bald, dome-like head lowered at a particular angle of reflection, as his very large, blue, reflective eyes contemplated a view, a work of art, or something peculiarly outrageous that he intended shortly to say. Meanwhile he held in his mouth, rather than smoked, a small pipe — he smoked a number of small pipes during the course of the day —, and when he spoke, his speech tumbled from him quickly, like that of an impetuous schoolboy. Though he was so far from staid in demeanour and in the things he said, yet about him there was a quality, perhaps physical, that seemed to survive in him from his Danish ancestors. His sense of irreverence, his spontaneity, his hatred of the pompous, made him a perfect foil to my father, whose admiration for him as an architect allowed a certain licence to the man and to his Jack-in-the-box forms of fun. This, together with his endless, bubbling flow of puns — and the sillier they were, the more their author enjoyed them —, *could* become tiring to those possessed of less vitality than himself. And so, though my father looked forward tremendously to his visits, and would

19

for weeks beforehand make plans for how to entertain him, yet being host did not prevent him from taking to his bed for longer and longer periods of the day when his guest arrived.

Not only did Lutyens show remarkable talent as an entertainer, but he manifested also, wherever he was, and without effort, the remarkable kindness and the insight, both genial and penetrating, of his nature. He understood at once, at any rate where I was concerned, the psychological forces at work, and the sorts of martyrdom the members of a family can inflict, one upon another. Further, the pieces of keen common sense and acute observation he threw into the bundles of nonsense with which he liked to load his conversation, gave it the spice of danger: because, sensing the difficulties of each person, but not always the manner in which to solve them, he would sometimes be injudicious in what he said, notwithstanding his knowledge of men and his ability to get on with them. The very sight of unhappiness made him unhappy: he *longed* to put things right — and then, in consequence, there was no knowing what he might not say. But in the end, with the particular ingenuity of his mind — so plainly visible in the plan of every building he made —, he could always be depended on to extricate himself and rescue his victim. One night at dinner, at about the time of which I am writing, he explained in front of me, to my father, that eldest sons always got into debt, and that it was the duty, the whole and only duty, of their fathers to pay up. . . . For an entire day thereafter my father's eyes held a strange, cold, enquiring look in them.

After architecture, the chief vehicle of Ned's personality was his humour. Not everyone enjoyed it. I did. . . . And here, for a page or two, follow some examples of it, and of the sort of incident that was apt to occur in his company. If the reader considers them to be amusing, then he would have delighted in Lutyens's visits and conversation. For instance, the brutality — for which he must have had to brace his whole being — of the question I record below, was typical of the man's kindness. . . . When in India, engaged in designing New Delhi, he stayed with the Viceroy. One night, in the middle of a large dinner-party, the architect looked round and observed that, while everyone else was enjoying the occasion, a young curate, who sat opposite, was being neglected by his neighbours, and appeared thoroughly nervous and unhappy in consequence. Lutyens, of course, at once felt sorry for him. He knew nothing of the young man, except his name, *Western*, which he remembered from their introduction before dinner : but he saw that a clinical ruthlessness was necessary, and that the only thing to do was by some means to shock so profoundly those sitting near the curate that they would take pity on him. Accordingly, when a pause occurred in the general chatter, Lutyens leant across the table and in a loud voice enquired, " Excuse me, sir : but may I ask if you are related to the Great Western ? " . . . For an instant, he saw the young man's eye pondering whether Aunt Isabel or Uncle Wilfrid could justly be claimed as the *Great* Western, and then an outraged buzz of conversation closed round him, rescuing him, carrying him off to pastures new of convivial delight. Those very neighbours who had been most resolute in neglecting the curate, subsequently, after dinner, reproached Lutyens bitterly for the superfluous cruelty of his question, and the curate himself would hardly deign to speak to him.

On another occasion, he was staying with us in Derbyshire at the time of a general election — it must have been that of 1910, when it was still requisite for a man, before he could vote, to have resided in the same place for several years. Lutyens's clerk-of-the-works, who — owing to my father's habit of delaying, changing his mind, and finding fault with everything — had already been staying at Renishaw for some months, entered the room where the architect and my father were sitting.

" Elliot ! " Lutyens asked, as soon as he saw him, " have you a vote here ? "

" No, sir."

" Well, never mind — you'll have one by the time the next election comes."

The most striking incident, however, of which I was a witness occurred later, soon after the close of the Four Years' War in 1918. . . . My father, who, during the conflict, had found himself unable to continue his building career at full pressure, was now devising new schemes. He proposed at Renishaw to throw out two wings from the north front of the house, at right angles to it, and a storey higher than the main block, so as to give to the additions the character of towers. He also intended to panel the walls of the Great Drawing-Room with mirror, and to cove the ceiling, making it also of looking-glass. These plans, like many others he made, were never destined to be realised, since, as he grew older, the very multitude of his projects defeated their execution. But they progressed so far as for him to call in Lutyens again. I was staying at home for a few days, and had intended leaving the morning after his departure, but Ned pressed me to go earlier and to travel up with him to London the same afternoon. He added, " I'll pay your fare, first-class, and charge it to your father." I accepted the offer. It was a lovely day, with that feeling in it of mounting early-summer excitement that you sometimes enjoyed in June in those distant years, and we motored as far as Nottingham, where we boarded the express, finding two seats in a compartment for six, the other four being occupied. Lutyens was in high spirits and it soon became plain that, with his sociable and enquiring disposition, he was as inveterate a train-talker as I myself. (How much I enjoy those long, anonymous conversations, in which, talking to people one may never see again, it is possible to reap experience from adopting any part one chooses ! . . . So, reader, let me warn you : that explorer, that big-game hunter, that actor, that business-man from the north, with whom you talked away the journey from Chesterfield to London the other day, may prove to be none other than the author of this book.) Soon Lutyens was plying a dark man in the opposite corner with questions.

" Where do you come from ? " I heard him ask.

" From Bradford," the stranger replied.

" I know the man who's just sold Bradford," Lutyens remarked. " He says it's the best bargain he ever made ! "

" I'm the man who bought it."

This answer brought even Ned to a standstill — but only for an instant. With his hatred of hurting people's feelings, a trait which was yet never able to overcome his impetuosity, he set himself out to erase the memory of what had occurred. He became more charming, more amusing, more entrancing company than I had ever known him to be. . . . Presently the stranger rose, opened the door, and stood for a while, looking out of the window, in the passage. After a little, when Lutyens was engaged in conversation with someone else, our new acquaintance beckoned to me to join him; which I did, rather startled and wondering what he wanted to say.

" Who is that man ? " he asked.

" He's Sir Edwin Lutyens," I replied.

" The same man who designed the Cenotaph ? "

" Yes, the same man."

The stranger returned to his seat. Ned began talking to him again, and, about an hour before we arrived in London, received from him the commission to design the War Memorial for Bradford. In the end this project never materialised, owing to Lutyens's frequent absences in India, but, so far as I remember, it was to consist of — or, at any rate, to embrace — a cruciform planting of trees.

I remember, too, that on the journey, in a rather different vein from his usual, he related to us a strange experience of his in a country-house. . . . He had been called in to plan the remodelling of a large old place that stood in a park, in remote and sombre country. It possessed no modern methods of lighting, and the atmosphere of it at night made him un-naturally nervous, though this was not in accord with his temperament. All through the dark hours he kept on waking up, imagining that he heard the flapping of enormous wings. Even by morning light, the house still had something unusual about it, he thought. . . . After breakfast, his host led him to one end of the building which was to be the first part for him to alter — the rooms were too big, too disconnected, the owner said. Fumbling with a large, old-fashioned key in a lock, he remarked, " This room is supposed to be haunted — something to do with a bird, they used to say. No one has entered it for at least fifty years ! " At last he got the door open. . . . Lutyens saw a vast room, its paper tattered, its ceiling stained. The windows were shut and bolted, but, on the thick dust — it must have been nearly an inch thick — of the uncarpeted floor, were clearly to be seen the footprints of an enormous bird, far bigger than any bird known to exist. . . .

Thinking of Ned Lutyens, however, it is his puns which his friends will most vividly remember, and the high spirits of his conversation. . . . Even today, a whole year after his death, his jokes still linger; delayed jokes, comparable to the booby-traps that the German armies were said to leave behind them. . . . Thus, the other afternoon, on sudden impulse as I was passing, I opened a drawer in a cabinet on the stairs at Renishaw. Inside, I noticed an envelope, with something written on it. I took it out, and read:

> *A lock of Marie Antoinette's hair, cut from her head ten minutes after execution.*

Carefully unfastening the envelope, I looked in it, and found within some rather coarse grey hair, tied up with a faded ribbon. . . . For a time I was puzzled, thinking how odd it was that so interesting a relic should have been left about, just anywhere, in that manner, wondering why, for example, my father had never told me of it, and how it had come here and who had shorn it — and then, about an hour later, in the way the memory sometimes acts, so that you are able to remember in detail an occurrence which only a little while before was so completely forgotten that it no longer existed, a scene came back to me. . . . It was over thirty years ago, and Ned Lutyens and I were sitting on a sofa in the library at Wood End. My father had just left the room to look for a rough drawing he had made on the back of an envelope, to illustrate a possible alteration of which he had thought whilst out walking, and which he wanted the architect to consider. . . . Suddenly, as we were talking, we heard a rending sound, and found that the cover of the sofa had split, revealing its stuffing. Ned had hurriedly seized a bit of it, pulled it out, and then screwed round it a bit of ribbon he had proceeded to tear off the edge of a curtain. Having done this, he placed the wisp of stuffing in an envelope, on the outside of which he wrote something, sealed it up and threw it into the drawer of a cabinet.

He then shut the drawer, and returned to the sofa. All this he had accomplished with remarkable speed, for fear of my father returning to catch him at it. As he sat down, he remarked to me,

" Nobody's likely to find that for a long time, and by then it will have become real."

When Wood End had been sold ten years ago, much of the furniture had been moved to Renishaw — and this was the cabinet. Had anyone but myself found this piece of horse or sheep hair — and even I had almost forgotten the incident —, it would doubtless, as the author of the joke prophesied, have passed for a genuine relic.

With the exception of the decoration of the ball-room at Renishaw, and of the design of the unfinished Pillared Room next it, even in the earlier years the many alterations that Lutyens planned for my father came to nothing. Nevertheless, year after year, my father would regularly start a new hare to be coursed by the famous architect, but in the end would inevitably employ in his place a local architect, who would more readily fall in with his patron's ideas. In fact, local architects replaced Lutyens for the same reason that new friends replaced the old. My father had discovered a distant range of relatives, too, whom he now invited to stay at Renishaw : the nearer still remained obdurate, blind to the beauties he was projecting, as to those already executed. They seldom saw him ; they did not understand him, he said. And yet . . . I wondered. In any case, in whatever direction lay their interests, whether sporting by inclination or no, these never prevented them from welcoming me, a comparative stranger, to their houses now that I was stationed in London : for kindness to young cousins was a tradition that they inherited and thoroughly approved.

Especially did my great-aunt Blanche Sitwell [1] trouble herself about me — but then, we had been friends since my earliest childhood. . . . At the age of seventy-four, though she no longer rode to hounds, her activity was amazing. She would run up and down stairs like a young woman, and the

[1] See *Left Hand, Right Hand !* pp. 170-72.

many contradictory beliefs that inspired her conversation, gave it a special quality, an earnest yet humorous vagueness. In spite of her own carelessness in matters of dress, in spite of her strong and unconventional radical views, she paid, as I have already related, great attention to the manners, outward aspect, and even clothes, of her young relatives: and letters would rain down on me on subjects extending from the way one's hair had been cut recently, and who was the best contemporary barber in London, to a discussion of tendencies on the English stage, the disestablishment of the Church, the experiences of her father's old friend and brother-in-law Sir Frederick Stovin in the Peninsular War, the sweated-labour conditions in East End tailors' shops, and the abolition of the House of Lords. All these letters, it was understood, had to be answered immediately, or a frantic note would arrive demanding the meaning of my silence. I don't know that my aunt and I shared many interests; but this in no way spoilt our friendship. At least we shared two: a universal curiosity about people, and an attitude of rather critical attention to my father's activities. Moreover, we understood each other, and she allowed me to see that in several directions she depended on me; an attitude that is always flattering, and ministers to the self-respect of the young. My father she never saw now. They had long ceased to meet; which to me was singular, for though she was an easy person with whom to quarrel, she was, equally, a difficult person with whom to remain for long on bad terms. But he used to maintain — with what justification I never found out — that she had worked against him during one of his parliamentary contests at Scarborough. And she alleged that when my father had taken a house in London, she had come one day to see my mother, and that, as she stood ringing the bell at the front door, my father, who was going out, had opened it, and finding himself face to face with her, had run away and hidden! I have already, elsewhere, referred to the wide and unusual range of her friendships, and her greatest pleasure now was to bring young relatives together, or put them in touch with other cousins, connections or friends. The last surviving member of her generation, she held all the strings of family relationships in her hands. Once, I remember, when I was asking her some questions about a cousin with whom I was not acquainted, she said, suddenly, with a kind of wistfulness, " Really, I believe soon I shall be the only person left who remembers *anything* ! "

When in London, and not on duty, I would repair every Sunday afternoon to her house in Egerton Crescent, off the Brompton Road, for tea. . . . Usually I would arrive rather early, and sometimes in the summer I would find her and her dear old friend Miss Anne Hutchinson, with hair spun of the finest white silk, both dressed in black, walking in the garden of the Crescent, which, with its trees, trim grass and green-painted tubs filled with red geraniums, still appeared to retain something of the peace of the 3330 or so Sundays of the Victorian reign. The hooting of motors, the rumble of buses, seemed far away as these two Victorian ladies paced slowly up and down in the rich, smoke-laden Sunday sunlight. Or, again, in the autumn, I would discover them already in the drawing-room, where the flickering tongues of the fire caught the shining surfaces of hundreds of small objects, all clean, polished and bright. I would sit there listening to them while I ate brandy-snaps and a special kind of plum-cake. Soon Emily, the old parlour-maid, with her hair the colour of the brandy-snaps, and that expression of caustic resignation which comes from living for many years in the house of persons of impulse and of strong will, would throw open the door and announce the name of a new arrival. Before long the room would be full of relatives, kind and unkind, amusing and boring, English relatives and Scottish relatives. And all of them would be connected in some way with the objects shining on wall and table. The old lady in the immense feathered hat who came in with her head well thrown back, as if she were a seal en-gaged in a feat of balance, was the great-granddaughter of the old man in the white wig whose portrait I knew so well at Renishaw, and to whom had belonged the Malacca cane, the convex amber handle of which, as it hung there near the door, glittered in the light from the fire ; the two china vases on the table had been given my aunt by the grandmother of the two young women who were by the window ; the silver paper-knife had belonged to the great-uncle of the sulky old man who was booming about the Matabele War : the room was full of these invisible threads of relationship between people and things, which imparted to it a very definite atmosphere.

Many incidents that occurred in my aunt's drawing-room return to my mind — one, in particular, which retains its own germ of farcical fun. My brother, my sister and I were all having tea there on Sunday afternoon. Edith was sitting in an old-fashioned arm-chair, the loose cover for which happened to be lying near by on a chair against the wall. . . . Suddenly we heard the front-door bell ring, and then the voice, well known to us, of an old friend of my parents. She was very kind, but such a great bore that my sister had already pleaded illness as an excuse for not seeing the old lady that very day at luncheon. Now here she was ! And my sister appealed to my brother and me to rescue her in some way. . . . What was to be done ? Footsteps were already on the stairs. . . . Telling my sister not to move, but to sit absolutely still, we seized the loose cover, which fortunately proved to be very loose, fitted it over her and the chair, and carried it — and her — out of the room in triumph. Only just in time ; for we passed the new arrival outside the door, and explained to her that we would be back in a moment, but that one leg of the chair was unsteady, and that my aunt had just asked us to put it away downstairs, in case she forgot and allowed someone to sit in it. . . . So we smuggled Edith downstairs, and quietly to the front door, ourselves returning to continue our tea with a distracted aunt. But she always entered into the spirit of any situation, and did not combat our prejudices. . . . No doubt she harboured a good many of her own.

A connection of ours, to whom my aunt introduced my sister and me at this time, was Lady Colvin, the wife of Sir Sidney, for many years Keeper of the Prints and Drawings at the British Museum. Sir Sidney, the author and editor of many publications, had been Robert Louis Stevenson's most faithful and intimate friend. It was to Colvin's former house, in the British Museum, that Stevenson used to go to stay when visiting London from Scotland in early years (he always re-

ferred to it as The Monument), and on innumerable occasions
Colvin had been able to help him, either with his advice,
based on a sound knowledge of the literary world in London,
or through his connections with it. Sir Sidney's opinion, at
the time I knew him, was much sought after and highly
esteemed in matters of art and literature, though some, who
may have been jealous of his influence, used to insinuate that
he was wont invariably to hedge when faced with any work
of a kind new to him, taking refuge, when he did not know
what to say, in a phrase that was certainly often on his lips:
" It stands on Its Own Feet ! " . . . Lady Colvin had, before
she married Sir Sidney, been the widow of my grandfather's
second cousin, a clergyman, and the younger son of Frank
Sitwell of Barmoor Castle. In spite of the cloth he wore, he
had proved a most unsatisfactory husband, and my Aunt
Blanche, who had remained friends with Mrs. Sitwell when
she had left him, had greatly admired her for the courage and
uncomplaining dignity with which she had behaved in days
when the position, according to English law, of a wife was still
particularly cruel, and even her own money became the in-
alienable property of the husband. Moreover, Fanny, as her
friends called her, had known adversity in other ways: for by
Albert Sitwell she had borne an only son, to whom she was
devoted, but who died, at the age of sixteen, at Davos, while
Stevenson was spending the winter there, also in an effort to
revive his health. To the memory of this youth, he wrote the
verses *In Memoriam F. A. S.*; for Mrs. Sitwell had also been
one of the earliest and warmest of Stevenson's friends and
admirers. Indeed, it was she who had in the first place introduced him to Colvin, and she could therefore in a sense have
claimed to have discovered him. And if Robert Louis Stevenson's letters to her second husband form the most sustained
collection of his correspondence, extending, as it does, over a
period of more than twenty years, yet there can be no doubt,
equally, that it was in the early years his finest letters were
written, and written to her. Consider that, dated June 1874,
which he ended with the words, " My dear friend, as I hear
the wind rise and die away in the tempestuous world of foliage,

I seem to be conscious of I know not what breath of creation.
I know what this warm, wet wind of the west betokens, I know
how already, in this morning's sunshine, we could see all the
hills touched and accentuated with delicate little golden patches
of young fern; how day by day the flowers thicken and the
leaves unfold; how already the year is a-tiptoe on the summit
of its finished youth, and I am glad and sad to the bottom of
my heart at the knowledge. If you knew how different I am
from what I was last year; how the knowledge of you has
changed and finished me, you would be glad and sad also." [1]

Now, some forty years later, the former Mrs. Sitwell — as
during Stevenson's life she had remained — had become Lady
Colvin, an old lady, with a fine aquiline profile and white
hair, who was decorative as well as beautiful. Ladies of her
generation as a rule employed no make-up, but Lady Colvin
was heavily rouged in the artificial and conventional manner
of the French eighteenth century, and this accorded well with
her appearance, which possessed sufficient distinction to allow
itself such frivolities. An almost professional diviner of literary
talent, she had been the friend of many other writers besides
Stevenson — and the enemy of several others. (Wilde, for
example, had described her as " a parrot with a tongue of
zinc "; an epigram that had gone the rounds for a whole
dreary decade, and still sounds witty and significant until you
ring it on the counter.) Lady Colvin I used to see at every
concert and first-night to which I went, and she was invariably
accompanied by the rotund and polished form of Sir Claude
Phillips.[2] During the intervals, he would remain in the stalls
to talk to her, while she continually fluttered a fan, at the
graceful manipulation of which she was a mistress. Few of her
contemporaries, versed though they were in this aid to fascination — indeed, this art —, rivalled her in it; only Lady
Brougham, and in a setting very different, excelled her.

My sister was a more frequent visitor to the Colvins than
was I, but I used also to go to their house, and they were most

[1] In a letter dated " Swanston, Sunday (June–1874) " from vol. i of *The Letters
of Robert Louis Stevenson*. Edited by Sidney Colvin. (Methuen, 1919.)
[2] See *The Scarlet Tree*, p. 58 and note.

kind to both of us. Theirs was the first salon in which I set foot, and I recall, rather mistily over the gap of thirty years, the pink glow of the drawing-room in Palace Gardens Terrace ; Sir Sidney, sitting with his back to the window, with, outlined against it, his head at the particular downward angle at which he held it, the edges of his beard blurred by the light ; Lady Colvin, armed with her fan, reclining on a sofa ; and general talk, witty and interesting, and not, as in most houses of the time, about politics — for political controversies were then beginning to rage —, but about pictures and books.

In my new life, talk of books — though I had never experienced it — was what I most felt the need of. So eager for it was I, that I became nervous and tongue-tied when visiting the Colvins. And at the Tower, the point in which my brother-officers and I showed the most divergence was in our reading matter — though, at twenty years of age, we did not realise the gulf that this constituted. . . . Edith, of course, was my chief adviser on what to read, and poetry was then, as now, her most cherished form of literature. In prose, I had already found two authors for myself : one, Strindberg, the other, Samuel Butler — traces of both of whom can be found, I suspect, by the discerning in my literary ancestry. The favourite reading, on the other hand, of my brother-officers was usually the novels of Whyte-Melville — who had himself been an officer in the Brigade of Guards —, and, at this particular moment, or just after, a current popular romance, entitled, if I remember correctly, *Poppy* — at any rate, it concerned the illicit love of a Duchess, over-eager to be co-operative in producing an heir for her husband. . . . My new friends seemed, however, neither to approve nor disapprove of the books I read ; so that I had less censorship to fear here than that which overshadowed my reading at home.

Everything that happened at the Tower possessed its own atmosphere. To catch a cold, for example, in the Officers' Quarters — an enormous, unheated Victorian formula for gothic, machicolated with a kind of prim desperation —, and subsequently to be in bed there with bronchitis, proved an unforgettable experience. I have never known a building that seemed to be so much made of stone, as though one were camping in a quarry, and the ailment itself had a special quality, as if the germs that caused it had long been confined to the Tower in the interests of public security. . . . It so happened that I was afflicted with one of these colds at a time when my father chanced to be in London.

His life now very plainly divided itself into two halves : one, fussing about the future — a state of mind much aggravated by the Lloyd George Budget of 1909 and especially the clauses it had contained about the unearned increment in Land Values ; the other, fussing about the past. (The present he did not allow to concern him, maintaining that it was a fiction, composed of the immediate past and the immediate future.) Of the first, I find still many evidences, forcibly expressed in his letters. Thus on 11th December of the previous year he writes, referring to the valuation clauses mentioned above, " The principle of the Act seems to be to value each plot separately, at the price it might fetch if none of the others were in the market, to mark future values as if they existed, to tax and rate park frontages as building land, and yet continue to rate halls as if the parks were unspoilt. . . . The fact is that the grocer who has sanded one's sugar all these years has at last got his way, and introduced the principle of petty swindles into public legislation." . . . Moreover, I recall in this connection, too, that, apt after the manner of all persons of strong individuality to surprise one by giving an unexpected twist to his own beliefs, he startled me, who knew the rigidity of his moral views, by, no doubt with a pleasing sense of his own recklessness, remarking, when I was seventeen and his alarm about the Budget and Land Values was at its height, " If the Government persists in its policy of taxing Land Values, the best thing to do will be to split up the south park and people it with illegitimate children ". To the second process, of fussing about the past, it was his wont to refer as " my literary work " — and, indeed, he worked hard at it. Called by Henry at seven, he would present himself at the British Museum Reading Room at its opening at 9 A.M. carrying a circular, deflated air-cushion, slung on his coat-sleeve like a bracelet. He would then slowly inflate the cushion and, first placing it in his accustomed place in Row L, sit down on it. Between the opening hour and twelve, he would spend his time among pedigrees, charts and records. He had a gift for such things, and they would come tumbling at him from their shelves in the same fashion that pictures pursue great experts. Returning to his hotel by taxi-cab soon after midday, he would enjoy a solitary and, because of the hour, rather unpopular luncheon. He could not bear to be kept waiting, and so, since he ate at tremendous speed — a habit which, as I have said, he always justified by alleging it to be a sign of mental energy —, the meal would occupy the smallest possible space of time. He would have Turkish coffee afterwards, chain-smoking three or four strong Turkish cigarettes. Then he would go upstairs for a short siesta in a tightly shuttered room. (In the London hotel, he ascended in the lift: but at Renishaw, since he believed that the climbing of stairs " weakened the heart's action ", chairs were sprinkled about the stairs and landings in improbable places, so that he could sit down and rest if he felt inclined.) When he came downstairs, the porter would call a taxi-cab for him, and he would go back to the Reading Room, remaining there until it closed. He thought it extravagant in others to take a taxi, but excused it in himself with the slogan — he had ready at his disposal at least one for the justification of anything which he condemned in others, but might wish to do — " With *Me*, Time *is* Money ! " . . . This routine he followed when in London until the outbreak of the war in 1939. He was then one of the few surviving holders of the " green ticket ", if not the only one, having been admitted before the age of twenty-one — when, in fact, he was eighteen — by special recommendation of Archbishop Tait, his great-uncle and guardian. . . . When my brother Sacheverell first went to the Reading Room during the 1914–18 European dispute, one of the officials asked after my father, and added, " Yes, I know *him* —, but I may say he doesn't know me yet, though I've attended him since 1878 ! "

On the occasion of which I talk, perhaps attracted by the medieval associations of my domicile to an extent sufficient to banish his fear of infection, he arrived to see me in a taxi ("Time *is* Money!"). I saw him get out of the cab, and thought how impressive and distinguished he looked, in a silk hat that made him appear taller than his six foot, and in a long coat with a wide collar of Irish beaver. He stood for a moment contemplating the Officers' Mess. I fear, however, that its architecture must have disappointed him, even though its amenities were sufficiently antiquated to allow it to rank with the oldest buildings within the Tower boundaries. . . . It was a strange two-man procession that entered my room: my father first, carrying in his hand a small primer on heredity and eugenics; and then the taxi-driver, staggering under the weight of a dozen or so darkly-bound, foxed and moth-eaten volumes: some consisting of Gregorovius's *History of the City of Rome in the Middle Ages*, others of books by Herbert Spencer and William James. But the strangest feature of the episode was that the taxi-driver appeared also to have read the Gregorovius volumes, for when, pointing to them, I asked if they were not heavy, he replied, with an air of smiling sincerity,

"Well, not to read, sir. They're a treat to read."

I longed to talk to him, but my father waved him aside.

In return for this small library, I lent my father Samuel Butler's *Way of All Flesh*. He seldom read the books one pressed on him, though he was too polite to refuse to take them. It therefore came as a surprise to find, a week later, that he had read it from cover to cover. . . . Alas, my loan had proved far from a success, for it was plain that he had immediately identified himself both with Mr. Pontifex, the rich and tyrannical publisher-grandfather, and with Theobald, his bullied son, in his turn a tyrannical father. (This second identification seemed to me peculiarly false, for Theobald was a pious clergyman, and my father was still a strict atheist.) He had read the book with great attention, and it had made him so angry that he had taken to his bed and remained there for three days, treating the effect of it as an illness. Even when he had sufficiently recovered to get about again, the book still obsessed him, and he had thought out, and was willing to propound for my benefit, a great many theories. I recall some of them to this day. He took, I remember, a particularly grave view of the likely consequences of the moral laxity he detected in Ernest Pontifex's character, remarking that it was obvious, from the end of the book, that he was " heading for syphilis ". . . . And there was the question of old Mr. Pontifex's income: upon this subject he had entered some notes in one of his notebooks, and now read them to me. He had a good mind, he said, to write a little pamphlet on the subject in order to make his views clear. It was easy for a writer like Butler, with no responsi- bilities and no experience, to state that old Mr. Pontifex enjoyed an income of ten thousand a year: but *did he?* That was the point. People were dreadfully careless, and exaggerated in these matters beyond endurance. Only the other day, Lutyens had said to him, " People say you have an income of forty thousand a year; have you ? " People would say any- thing ! Probably poor old Mr. Pontifex had only three thousand a year at the outside — and that, with income-tax at two shillings in the pound, and Lloyd George's new super-tax and threat to Land Values, was very little for a man with a family. . . . In short, the same arguments I had often heard him advance on the subject of Meredith's baronets, Sir Willoughby and Sir Austin. . . . And here let me add that his talk opened my eyes to a quality that this delightful book, *The Way of All Flesh*, possesses in a particular degree. It is the perfect book to lend to the right person. In future, I always carried a copy with me, in my bag, wherever I went, and I recall that some years later, in January 1919, when ill in Queen Alexandra's Military Hospital at Millbank, I lent it, in return for a good book in another sense, and with the same satis- factory and even dramatic results, to a young army chaplain who came to afflict us poor helpless patients with his presence and fanatical views.

Samuel Butler, my father considered, encouraged self- indulgence; and of all forms of this sin, extravagance was the worst. . . . My bills were mounting, but not so much as my father made out, for he possessed his own methods of calcu- lating, his own mathematical processes. I did not much care; my father had placed me here; it had been no wish of mine, and I had better enjoy myself in the ways in which I saw my companions enjoy themselves. Perhaps the self-indulgence against which my father thundered with the inspired eloquence of a preacher was wrong : but, looking round me, I came to the conclusion that it seemed to make people easy and amiable and kind. . . . I looked at my new friends again — how fine and tolerant they were —, and tolerance was a quality which, after recent experiences, I had come especially to appreciate. . . . Yes, self-indulgence and extravagance seemed to make people tolerant and generous; they showed the virtues of Oliver Twist's attitude, the courage that says " I *will* have more ", the moral beauty of Nietzsche's " yea-saying " as opposed to " nay-saying ". Let me sing here the praises of the extravagant, and laud extravagance itself.

Avarice and even carefulness have always to me seemed to be vices. I avoid the skinflint as though he were a source of contagion, stricken with some plague that consumes his vitals. I even turn from the words that describe this mortal sin, such nouns as parsimony, niggard, screw, scrimp, lickpenny, such verbs as stint, scrimp, pinch and gripe. I have even created the complimentary adjective *penny-foolish* as counter to the odious penny-wise.

It has always seemed to me that there should be no poor, and that people should not have to trouble about money (though often have I had to trouble about it myself) : for money was made by man, for man, and not ordained by God. If it does not suit us, we should alter it. Extravagance has done more for the world than ever has thrift, but a private person is a more likable spendthrift than is the state. (Private persons spend money, at the worst, for their own gratification : states spend it to crush their neighbours. On extravagance the arts have flourished continually, that of building in particular.) The mind of the thrifty is a sad, miserly and miserable mind, without imagination, cutting the coat to the cloth : and it manifests an extraordinary hatred towards the lazy. The rage of the successful little man against the indolent is a moral indignation of the vilest kind, for the gifts of the lazy man to his more industrious brothers have been numberless — and I speak without prejudice, for, as to myself, I cannot bear to be idle for a moment and am, congenitally, a fusser, a plodder, one who takes trouble. All the short-cuts, all the labour-saving devices have been the fruit of ingenuity born of sloth. The lazy man stops to think, and the extravagant is obliged — if he is to survive — to make money. It was this vice which chained me to my desk, and fashioned me into a writer. The urge to spend more than I possessed, to buy pictures and books and works of art, to travel, was the spur to ambition; though always I was vain, and glory is my element. Had I been content, as the prudent advise, to live within my pay and my allowance, I should have learnt to pare and prune and scrape, it may be, but I should never have won renown. I should have remained a mute, inglorious Osbert Sitwell. But my blood did not lean in that direction. I heard from far off, in many directions, the drumming and singing of the exuberant in life and art. I was of their race, and their faults are mine. And my lack of thrift, my squandering, which was part of my inheritance, not only acted on me as if I had been obliged to earn my own living, but without them the range of feelings I could express would have been more limited : my extravagance taught me to fear poverty, and the depths to which it could bring a man. Driven to my pen, the one instrument I could wield, I found a new happiness in the exercise of it. Moreover, my very lack of practical understanding led me in the end to some slight comprehension of practical affairs. I began to supervise and take an interest in the financial results of my labour. But, best of all — except the new happiness that in time my art brought me — was the sense of independence.

If, when I was a young officer, I had been told that one day I would be able to earn my living honestly — for I do not call being so indifferent an officer as I was, earning my living honestly —, or, far more unlikely, to make a name for myself, I would not have believed it. I was singularly incompetent. Though able with ease to understand the most obscure poetry and the most difficult prose, I could never comprehend a single fact or tenet in the Drill Book — was it called Manual ? —, a brisk, clever lay-out of the more simple military exercises, simply expressed. I could read it over and over again, as formerly I had been able to read a Latin or Greek Grammar, and nothing of it would stay in my mind, which became a stone, rolling, gathering no moss, a dry, empty stone. . . . What *could* I do? I wondered.

If in the two previous volumes I have talked little of my ambitions, it is because I entertained none then — except to leave school and to get away from home. That was enough. Indeed, my ideas in general were at this time of rather a negative order. I knew what I did not want to do — most of all I had dreaded entering the army, because I hated discipline and heartily disliked communal life as I had known it at school. Further, I had not enough self-confidence to allow me to cherish ambitions. I was always being told my faults, and it seemed to me that the catalogue of them was just and by no means exaggerated. I agreed with my father in thinking that I was ill-qualified for any profession. . . . And it was precisely this sense of weakness that led me into captivity for a while : since, before being translated into an ensign in the Grenadiers, I had travelled in a strange land, among savage tribes — let us see how it happened. . . . Eight o'clock was striking.

M𝚈 accomplishments as a boy, and my lack of them, have been duly charted in a chapter of an earlier volume. Already, for example, I have confessed that at school, and for long after leaving, I knew no French — yet only yesterday I met an old companion from Bloodsworth, who, falling to tell me of his son's school-days, and then reverting to our own, remarked, " We didn't think much of you, I remember — you were too good at French ! "

This summing-up shows once more how difficult is the path of objective truth, even when the writer is most sure of the accuracy of his statements. Nevertheless, this much I can say for certain : the phrase that seemed to sound like a theme through the miserable composition of my school-days, and subsequently through my career in the army, and occurred in every report, public or confidential, was the truncated but haunting sentence,

"MIGHT DO BETTER IF HE CHOSE ".

Such, however, was not my belief, for I was most diffident, though full, as well, of senseless pride.

By disposition I was fond of Nature, but preferred to it, as I prefer today, the study of art and the enjoyment to be obtained therefrom. And in Nature itself I was more interested by those things that approached nearest to art, — flowers and shells and trees and falling water. Outwardly, my character had altered : for when I had gone to school I had been intensely sociable, but now I had grown shy as well : and, by another contradiction born of my schooling, had become both melancholy and gay, being as silent with those I disliked as talkative with those I liked. I loved the solitude as much as I enjoyed, too, the life of cities. Extremely high-spirited, my greatest advantage was that my constitution did not allow me to be depressed, even by the most severe occurrences, for more

than forty-eight hours at a stretch. That I must have inherited ;
its origin was no doubt physical, and connected with my large
frame — I am over six foot, and even then was by no means
meagre — and with my whole physical set-up ; for the fair
and florid are perhaps less prone to melancholy than the
dark of hair and skin. Perhaps it was this same quality which
enabled my ancestors to plunge without fear of consequences
into the battles of medieval times, and, later, into their great
flights of extravagance : yet this advantage was singular, for
many members of my family were given to nervous fussing and
fretting, qualities that in the end exercise upon the character
an erosive effect. I possessed, further, that disregard for money
which I have described, and which brought so formative an
influence to bear upon my career. In addition, I suffered to an
extraordinary degree — and, looking back, this seems strange
in a young man of seventeen or eighteen — from boredom : a
fact that deeply shocked my father. People, he said, were
never bored in medieval times. It was a modern and degener-
ate emotion. And I recall that once, forgetting his attitude in
this matter, I complained of feeling bored, and he reproved me
with the words, " I never *allow* myself to feel bored ". He
became very angry when I unwisely retorted, " That's just the
difference between us — I never allow *myself* to bore other
people ! "

This boredom, perhaps, was symptomatic of the artist,
constituting a premonition of the feeling he experiences in
those terrible moments of repose when he finds himself unable
to create. . . . At any rate, works of art, to go to a picture-
gallery or concert, or to read great poetry, were the only
things that lifted it from me. . . . And here, too, a curious
fact emerges, for though I had been conversant since childhood
with many of the masterpieces of Italian art and architecture,
and though, when my sister was in the house, I lived with
music and poetry, yet my overwhelming and, as it were,
creative love of the arts came to me through my introduction
to modern works, and so in this manner my approach was a
little different from the ordinary. Indeed, I had always preferred modern to renaissance, and renaissance to antique art,

except in very young days when I had been somewhat of a history-snob : I had consistently appreciated better the works of human genius nearest to my own days : but soon I grew to understand the Primitives, through my love of the Post-Impressionists, and to adore Bach and Mozart, as I have said, through the avenues opened to me by my favourite modern masters, Debussy and Stravinsky. About works of art, as about people, I had always possessed a great and consuming curiosity. I would be happy for hours, talking to someone I had not met before, and reading the strange book of his or her character. There were other qualities, too, that I knew in my heart to be derived from my heredity ; among them, the more than ordinary share of pride and vanity that in those days I possessed.

These were humbled every day by my father's continual snubbings and condemnation of all my ways ; they were to be further mortified by events. . . . During this whole time, the shadow that moved with us, wherever we went, was growing and darkening : some agency was at work, both in the family and outside it, loosening the fibres, darkening the colours. Something was going wrong in the world, and could surely be felt by the sensitive, through the intense sweetness of being alive at that time ; something, too, had gone wrong in the house. The airy vistas and green pleasaunces of the garden were delusive in their grandeur, and behind them lay the mean streets, the pawnshops, the prisons — the prison. But these things could not be seen. As the world looked, in contrast to how one felt it to be, it was at last flowering. This was the moment of Europe's fullest bloom. In spite of the fact that it occupies so small a part of the surface of the globe, for a continent, it was the West End of the world. All the trade, all the benefits of exploitation, flowed in to enrich it. Luxury goods streamed out from its capitals. Even the usual drink of the crowds, of the poor — tea or coffee —, was cultivated by under-paid labour in dark continents where Nature was still fierce — and as for cocoa, the soothing bed-time drink of the middle classes, it was proved to be grown under conditions almost of slavery. Nevertheless, Europe flourished ; the rose-leaves had not yet begun to fall, nor the fruit ostensibly to become corrupt ; but already the decay of the political state, the structure, was immanent, though few recognised it. Everyone throughout Europe and America, everyone, of all nations and classes, except a few who, disagreeing with the verdict of the majority, were termed " cranks ", was convinced of the reality of material progress, and therefore of the coming of the kingdom of heaven upon earth. Only material things existed, and we believed as blindly in material building-up as, in wars, we believe in material destruction. You could see the improvement — and touch it — in every country ; and so, since material improvement alone was of consequence, the world at large was enjoying one of its happiest moments for centuries.

Yet for me, the time between leaving Eton and finding — or rather being thrown into — a profession, was only lit by the flame of my animal high spirits, and perhaps by a certain power of imagination. 1910 and '11 were, I think, the peak years, both of my father's irritability and of my own misery. . . . In part, my fatr 'r's condition was caused by the very width of his range, by the superabundance of his plans and projects ; in part, by my mother's utter lack of interest in them, and inability to pretend, by her rages, too, so inexplicably easy to rouse; while, on his side, his perpetual gloomy prognostications about the state to which even the simplest and most natural courses of conduct would reduce one, combined with a lack, as it were, of warmth and spontaneity to render him a very far from ideal companion for her. She had, the reader of the former volumes will recall, been married when she was seventeen, and I find a letter from his former tutor — not the most tactful of men — to my father, which contains the following sentences.

" After all your theorising we shall look for something peerless in your bride elect. . . . To be married in less than a month takes the breath away. . . . It is too late to enter into a discussion of the advantages of ' marrying out of the school-room ', so I am afraid I must submit with a good grace to seeing my theories disproved by practical demonstration. . . ."

My father had thought that it would be easy for him to

mould the character of any young girl, and took no account, except in his own case, of the influences of heredity. Throughout his life, it was his ill fortune to misread and misunderstand the character of those around him, and, in consequence, to cast them wrongly for their parts. To them he assigned precisely the merits, no less than the faults, which they did not possess. This was perhaps chief of the qualities that in the end nullified his great strength of character and remarkable gifts, just as his irritability cancelled out his natural kindness. The inevitable discovery of the fact — and his eventual recognition of it — that he could not influence in the least the development of my mother's disposition, led him to feel embittered against her *family*. And it was for this reason, chief among others, that when we were alone together he would so frequently regard me, for minutes at a time, with a cautious, sidelong look of distaste, and then exclaim suddenly, in a tone of marked disapprobation, " You smiled just like your uncle ", or " You said that just like your grandfather ". (When, in this connection, he used to me the word " your ", thereby, as it were, seeking to fix upon me the responsibility, it always, of course, signified a relation of my mother's.) He remained on the watch. Thus, though it was easy already, when in a hurry, to hire a motor to reach your destination, he successfully persuaded himself that it was my practice to charter a special train : a sin I had never committed. He used, therefore, to say to me, from time to time, in a broken-hearted voice, with a sob never far from its sound, " I do hope you won't take a special train. It's your grandfather and uncle coming out all over again ! " In addition, he indicated faults that were more my own : but even the good points, that from time to time — and how infrequently — he saw in me, were the product, equally, of his imagination. For example, he used, towards the end of his life, to say to people, when I was coming to see him in Italy, " The advantage of seeing Osbert is that it keeps me in touch with modern slang ". . . . Such misconceptions — even this one, as will later be seen — led often to amusing sequels : but they prepared the way, too, for disaster. They led him in particular to place trust in the untrustworthy, no less than to quarrel with, and perpetually denigrate, those in his employment upon whom he could rely. So it was that he came to be frustrated continually, on occasion to be swindled in small ways, and, at the end of his life, to be defrauded on the grand and tragic scale.

Thus, too, he began to make the most singular plans for his children when they grew up — or so, at least, it always appeared to me. Often he used to deplore the strange chance by which, having taken so much trouble to get intelligent children, his whole early life having been modelled, apparently, on a sort of Nietzschean-Darwinian uplift scheme towards that goal, we three had been sent down — or up — to him. Just as Dr. Arnold had prayed before the procreating of his children, with what beneficial results we all know, so my father, representative of a less pious and seemingly more scientific generation, had entered upon periods of the most rigorous training, both physical and mental — and look what he had received for his trouble ! It was really very unfair, most disappointing. . . . And that the Life Force should have shovelled my sister on to him was even more patently unjust than that It should have allocated to him my brother or myself. Birth, no less than marriage, was, plainly, a lottery : but whereas he had gone in for it to obtain for the next generation a straight nose and charm, he had drawn a booby-prize, an aquiline nose and a body inhabited by an alien and fiery spirit. . . . It was difficult to know, really, where to begin the list of just complaints.

The girl was grown-up now, and seemed to have developed a most objectionable sense of pity, which made her an uneasy companion for one. You never knew what she might say or do. Once, though her whole allowance was only fifty pounds a year, he had caught her giving five shillings to a beggar. " Such a mistake ! " And, after all, it was really his money. He should have been consulted. She seemed unable to pass a tramp or a beggar without giving him something, whereas the correct thing to do was not to *see* a person of that kind. She could not play games, and the extent to which she loved music was un-ladylike. She possessed no small talk, and could not, even now, recite Austin Dobson — and was it not even worse : was it not *would* not, rather than *could* not ? Because her memory for poetry, he had found out from the governess, was remarkably good, and when travelling by train abroad she could find peace during long and bumpy nights by repeating to herself the whole of *St. Agnes' Eve*, and various entire passages from Shakespeare. . . . There had also been that unfortunate episode at Bournemouth, which had caused a great deal of pain and worry to older people.

I asked what the " unfortunate episode " was. . . . It had occurred thus. . . . My sister had been paying a lengthy visit to my grandmother Sitwell, to whom she was much attached, at Bournemouth ; in which camping-ground of godly invalids, everywhere breathing heavily in red-tiled shelters, pitched *à la japonaise* under pine trees, or reclining on beds and sofas under turrets and pepper-pots of red brick and rough-cast, behind luxuriant hedges of arbutus and fuchsia, over which they can distinguish the spires, rain-grey, of many churches, my grandmother had taken a house. The prevailing atmosphere of religion and old age may at times have been a little uncongenial : but the life to which my sister was exposed at home made her eager to pay as many visits to my grandmother as possible ; at least she was always treated with kindness and consideration, and allowed that dignity which is so precious to a young human being. At first, therefore, my sister was very happy, for she was away from home, and the tormenting which in her case the word spelt. But the circles of visiting clergy that, wherever my grandmother might be, at once sprang up round the old lady like a circle of plainly inedible fungi, took soon to wrestling daily with my sister over the poems of Algernon Charles Swinburne, with whose works she was at the time intoxicated. They were immoral, the toadstools pronounced, and she should not be permitted to read them. Canon Groucher urged on my grandmother that they should be impounded and burnt. Any reasonable girl should be content, so far as poetry was concerned, with the works of T. E. Brown and Elizabeth Barrett Browning. In the course of time, my sister became so much enraged by the continual attacks made upon her favourite poet that she determined to show her feeling for him in a manner that could not be mistaken.

Very early, then, one lovely September morning, she had flitted, having given no previous notice to my grandmother of her going, and, accompanied by her maid, had boarded the small boat that plied from Bournemouth to Ventnor, Isle of Wight. There, a few hours later, under the bright pennons of the summer weather, with its fleecy white clouds and high-flung seas, a singular spectacle must have greeted the curious eyes of any passers-by. A tall, fair, rather thin young lady, paler than usual after her rough journey, yet with colour coming and going from the love and defiance in her heart, disembarked, bearing a large sheaf of red roses : after her, the second figure in this frieze of two, came with faltering steps a woman of about thirty, with all her lady's-maid trimmings dishevelled by the crossing, her face a sour green, and wearing this morning an expression of the plainest condemnation of the whole enterprise in which she found herself engaged, and of dislike (if the spectator could discern that much) both for poetry and the sea ; she carried a jug of milk, a honeycomb, a wreath of bay-leaves, and the young lady's coat. After a few moments my sister found an open cab, drawn by a horse so old that Swinburne himself as a boy might have ridden behind it, and drove, with her maid still disapproving, through lanes just tinged with autumn's first fine gold, to Bonchurch : where, alighting, the procession entered the churchyard. After a furious battle with a sexton, who objected to such foreign ways, Edith triumphed and, bending low under an enormous fuchsia, its tasselled flowers of scarlet and purple trailing over a head-stone, in the Grecian mode poured the milk, and placed the wreath of bay-leaves, the honeycomb and the red roses, upon the grave of Swinburne. . . . This safely accomplished, she drove back with her maid to Ventnor, and returned to Bourne-mouth and my grandmother. An appalling storm broke and long raged round her head, alternating with calm patches of religious resignation.

My father, when news of this exploit reached him, was most displeased : it was plain that the girl would never make a success of anything. He began to lay his plans. Later on, in a year or two, she had better enter the shop, near Piccadilly, of a once fashionable photographer, whose bankrupt business he had been obliged to take over in cancellation of a bad debt. He could afford to pay her a salary of a pound a week, and she could find out of it her own money for dress and all the pleasures to which in these days the young considered they possessed a perfect right! I was his eldest son — well, that entailed its own place, *ex officio*, in the Universe. For the rest, he would reserve judgement on what it would be best for me to do, until it became clearer for what precise profession I showed least aptitude and liking. But for Sacheverell's future he had already arranged : he could either become a lawyer in Sheffield or mineral agent to the Sitwell Estate; which in either case could offer him a considerable amount of work, which he must, of course, for his part, undertake to execute at special rates. (" In late medieval times, younger sons often did such things, went in for trade, and lived in provincial cities, Sheffield or Birmingham. . . . Charmin' life in many ways." " Certainly not ! Why should provincial cities be different from what they were now, in medieval times ? . . . Such a mistake to quibble.") . . . To return to plans for my own future, it was not so important to make his own, as to prevent mine.

During these years, I could do little that was right. Golf had succeeded puff-ball, as puff-ball ping-pong, for the test of a man's ability as leader. (My father liked the game particularly, for he had been able to lay out two golf-courses, and proposed soon to build club-houses — one was to be planned by Lutyens, with a fan-shaped dining-room, crystal chandeliers and fleur-de-pêche chimney-pieces, so that Sheffield business men could feel at home : whereas you could not really build a ping-pong or puff-ball pavilion.) Everywhere in England and America, statesmen were already preparing their triumphs of 1914 and '39 by spending long days on the golf-course and long nights at the bridge-table. One would be lost in an uncharted world without some understanding of these games. But I showed no capacity for golf — and so, every day in the summer holidays of 1909, of which I am talking, this singular

47

man would send for me, and storm at me about my failures in this respect, as in many others. He made no attempt — and all this genuinely with my welfare taking the first conscious place in his heart — to perceive in what directions my interests lay, to make use of them, or draw more out of me. Instead, he most assiduously and effectively sapped my self-esteem: and when I was just at the age — sixteen and seventeen — to need every grain of it I could summon up.

There seemed no-one to help me. Sacheverell was too young, though he always fought valiantly on my behalf. Edith was still away a good deal, in Paris and Berlin and staying with friends — and, had she been at home, her own state of sub-jugation would only have been worse than mine, and she could have done nothing to aid me. Nor did my mother, even if she had been able to understand the position, seem now to possess any inclination to come to my rescue. Her own affairs, though she did not in the least comprehend the extent of the catastrophe which was beginning to loom in front of her, were now starting to worry her. She complained, too, of feeling middle-aged. She attended to nothing in the house, chose no wall-paper or cover, undertook no household duties — nor, indeed, would she have been allowed to do so by my father, had she attempted it. She contented herself with sitting in her room, among bunches of tuberose and sweet geranium, reading innumerable newspapers. Occasionally, she would give vent to a favourite maxim. One I remember well, because in subsequent years it seemed strange to hear it coming from the lips of the mother of three authors: " *Never put pen to paper* ". . . . In reality, however, this was said in allusion to the growing number of quarrels — mostly on matters of business, for he did not write letters to friends — in which, owing to his habit of letting his pen indulge in comments and strictures that were far more disagreeable than those he was accustomed to pass verbally, my father involved himself.

This tendency was, for its part, the result largely of a growing refusal to see things as they were; a characteristic I must again stress, because of its subsequent most calamitous results. Thus, one day, some years later, he suddenly demanded, " Where is that cabinet full of beautiful old Leeds china that I arranged in the ball-room last year ? " Plainly he believed in it, and thought I had sold it secretly. Yet it had, so far as any of us were aware, never existed. As an early instance of what I seek to indicate, and one amusing in itself, I produce as Appendix B on page 301 the long extract from the Estate Correspondence which is entitled " A ' Fatal Gift of Shrubs ' and some Roses " : [1] for in this, the statement of the elder Hollingworth, in 1896, that my father had begun to find fault with everyone, and in this fault-finding to border, when it suited him, on deliberate untruth, perhaps indicates that particular point in his life at which he ceased to be able to tell those things that he created by his fantasy, things that he feared or loved, or just imagined, from those that possessed an objective existence. Never did my father permit anyone to argue with him, or to state views that were contrary to his own. That there could be such, he would not allow himself to perceive. Nobody had argued with him, nobody had contradicted him now for several decades, perhaps for nearly half a century. If anyone ventured to dispute any opinion he held — as sometimes we children did — or to combat any particularly extravagant statement about, for example, some friend one knew much better than he did, he would omnisciently reply, with an air of final and absolute authority, and without deeming it necessary to offer proof or divulge the source of such, no doubt, mystical awareness, " *We happen to know* ".

Even when still a boy, he had been very certain in his opinions, though he had begun to inhabit his isolated ivory tower, heavily fortified against personal intrusions, at an early age. A renewed glimpse of him as he was when a very young man, this time through the eyes of a stranger, may help the reader to understand his subsequent development. On December 15, 1880, Mrs. Ewing, who was staying with her brother, Sir Alfred Scott-Gatty, near Sheffield, writes to her husband :

". . . Doctor (Sir Alfred Scott-Gatty) and Dot have been very busy on Sir George Sitwell's pedigree. It has proved in some respects a very fine piece of work to enthusiasts in that line.

[1] To this, I have added, as Appendix C, a later correspondence, "A Demonstration".

There was really one marvellous linking of a chain accomplished by the finding of a will full of the pious prayers and vows and family allusions that old wills contain, which linked a certain old Knight who went to the Holyland with a branch where the scallop shells appear in the coat.

" The Sitwells live close to the Estcourts, and I've been there in the old days, but never met this youth unless as a child. A curious specimen of highly bred and *educated* young England, twenty, and full of Galton's books on heredity, physiological and psychological questions, old prints, the German school of etchings, etc., desperately envying Dot for being able to sit *inside* the British Museum Library, when he (as a minor), has to sit in an outer court of the Gentiles ! ! He told me what he should like *best* would be to live in Nuremberg and collect old books. Quite sure he could get me to Malta under the influence of narcotics. He said very gravely (intensely fair and otherwise exactly like Prince Arthur as we remember him at Government House, Fredericton) ' I often suffer from nerve exhaustion myself, but with me it takes the form of rheumatism in the deltoid muscle, and yields at once to Galvanism '." [1] That had been long ago : but as a snail into its shell, so he fitted into his ivory tower today. If, formerly, he had made the sorties we noticed, though they had become more and more infrequent, now that he carried it about with him, he was scarcely able to fight his way out. His natural aloofness had hardened, and encased him. If middle age had softened him, it was in the wrong places. He began to seek human sympathy ; but unable to see his path in the modern world, he sought this relief from people who could not supply it, who could only give flattery. And now, moreover, he was adopting, or trying to adopt — for he was never really able to succeed in it —, the common ideas of those with whom, for the sake of their sycophancy, he surrounded himself. (Of these I shall write in the space of a page or two.) His desire to interpret what they supplied as what he required, rendered him still less able to recognise the truth when he approached it. Together with sad attempts to escape into what he believed to be the

[1] Supplied by Mrs. C. Maxwell, by kind permission of Colonel Mackenzie Smith.

contemporary world, there came a general decay of his Gothic
mould and personality ; which had, for its style, to be strict and
limited. . . . Nevertheless, if he showed himself agreeable, now,
from time to time, to those whose duty and responsibility it was
to return praise, it made him even less inclined to take a favour-
able view of those whom Nature had placed round him. In
further compensation, it caused his letters to be couched in
more and more offensive terms. So courteous in ordinary
conversation with strangers, and in many directions both kind
and imaginative, it yet seemed as if when my father took up a
pen, he just could not put things in an agreeable way. On the
contrary, he went to the greatest trouble to render his letters
sufficiently unpleasant, writing them over and over again in
quest of perfection. So well did he succeed in this respect that
one near relative, and a trustee of his marriage settlement,
came so greatly to dread the sight of my father's handwriting
on an envelope that he taught his valet to distinguish it, pick
it out and burn it, without informing his master. Let me give
an instance of how he wrote to me when I was eighteen.
". . . Thanks for the accounts. I am always struck by how
much better off you are than I am. You give a footman ten
shillings when five shillings at the outside is the proper thing,
and porters a shilling, when I give sixpence. It is very generous,
but reminds me of Jack Brale, who, when he travelled with me,
bought franc cigars when he could put them down in my
hotel bill, and half-penny ones when he had to pay for himself." Yet, since I was inexperienced, and my fault was venial,
all that was necessary was for him to tell me quietly, without
flourish, that in his opinion I was inclined to give too much.
Asceticism had begun to constitute for others a duty ; but the
standard no longer applied to himself. The chief and most
noticeable point in his private relationships was a system of
fault-finding, as with a divining-rod, that continually grew and
strengthened. This, in its effect, militated against his ever
getting the best out of the people round him : in fact, to sum up
in the words my agent has frequently used to me in the past,
" The worst of Sir George is, he's so damned discouraging ! "

To the disagreeable letters he wrote — and in the next

few years I was to receive my fair share of them — my father would refer in the phrase " a rap over the knuckles ". . . . " I had to give Major Viburne a rap over the knuckles." . . . And here let me proceed to offer an example, more subtle than some. As the reader has gathered, for the past twenty years my father had been writing books, chiefly of local, genealogical or antiquarian interest. Since his serious illness of a few years before, he had written with more regularity, and in 1909 John Murray had published his remarkable volume of essays [1] on the principles governing garden architecture, from which I made a long quotation in the previous volume. A year or two later, at the period with which I am now beginning to deal, he produced a small volume entitled *The Pilgrim*.[2] These few pages, bound in brown paper, were to have formed a chapter in the family history — at which, his *magnum opus*, he worked for so many years, though it unfortunately remained un-completed at the time of his death in 1943 — and concerned an ancestor, called *Walter de Boys* or *del Bosco*, father to Simon Cytewel, first of our name, who died on a pilgrimage to the Holy Land in the year 1250 or 1251.

This little book abounds in Gothic ingle-nooks, and contains a great deal about the wild flowers that grew then — or at any rate subsequently, in the author's imagination — round the gloomy windings of the Rother, the waters of which river are today dark and desolate as those of Lethe. As in many books written by gifted amateurs, and dedicated to the pre-sentation of an idealised past, all the flowers of the year are out at the same season : nor, in spite of the rigid standards prevalent in other directions, do garden varieties hesitate to mingle with their poor and uncultivated relations. Moreover, a tendency to instruct the less informed in the matter of medieval homes and habits occasionally breaks, somewhat breathlessly, through the congealed surface of the prose. And so here I give, as a truthful summary of such books, though by no means pretend-ing that it is a literal quotation, the passage that follows.

---

[1] *On the Making of Gardens.*
[2] Printed for the Author, for private circulation, by W. H. Smith & Sons, Scarborough.

" *The smiling valley of the Rother lay spread beneath the Pilgrim's eyes, as he stood under the old oak tree, now decked in leaves of palest gold, gazing toward those pleasant waters, from which, every now and then, a young troutlet leapt into the air from very joy. Never had the fair month of May seemed to him more beautiful. The banks of the stream, deeply indented, were gay with snowdrop and meadow-sweet, with aconite and eglantine and buttercup, with coltsfoot and cranesbill, with sweet gillyflower and the starry blossom of the wild garlic, with toad-flax, willowherb, mignonette and stinking pigsbane, with convolvulus, catmint, old man's beard, primrose, peony and the gentle lousewort. And Walter's eyes filled with tears, as he remembered that in an hour or two he would be leaving his warm old half-timbered hall — with its cruck beams and open hearth in the centre, and with the hole in the roof through which the smoke might escape — for the wide world and its dangers. It might be that he would not see the dear old place again.*"

A letter from my father to Turnbull shows that the author had sent his land agent the proof or MS. of *The Pilgrim*, and had asked for — and, in fact, received — his advice. The phrasing, I think, indicates that, after the manner of most authors who forward their work accompanied by a request for " honest criticism ", that which he really sought, indeed craved, was by no means the reader's frank opinion, of which he would be resentful, but in its place, applause, congratulation and fulsome flattery. In this letter of his, one of my favourites among all of them, to me the sound of his voice underlines every word — and that I believe to be one of the main though least recognised ingredients of literary style. The sudden breaks, the snubs, the bland assumptions — that concerning garlic is particularly delightful —, the mixture of pretending to agree, and, even, to admit error, and then the sudden masterly bounce out from ambush to administer a sharp " rap over the knuckles ", all these are familiar to me.

THE CURZON HOTEL, MAYFAIR, W.1
March 26th, 1911

DEAR PEVERIL TURNBULL,

So many thanks for your note on *The Pilgrim*. I think you were a very sound critic, and some of your suggestions I have adopted, though not all. You were quite right as to the sentence with "wares of cloth and bronze and amber" in it, but the only thing really necessary was to replace the comma after "amber" with a semi-colon. The punctuation was wrong as it stood. *No!* — hollies *were* cut for feeding sheep in the winter before roots were invented. Gorse *is* very black when the buds first open. And I think the smell of garlic charming at a distance — though not too near. Nor can I agree with you when you say that one must remember weeds are weeds. I do not think there are any such things. You should not look at them from the utilitarian point-of-view.

I have written by this post to Messrs Coutts & Co. to pay in £200 from my estate account to the Sheffield Bank.—Yours very sincerely, GEORGE R. SITWELL.

Nor was the letter to which he refers the only criticism he received. Well do I remember the time of *The Pilgrim* coming out, because, while we were at Renishaw, my sister took up a copy which my father had left lying on a table in the ball-room, and, as she read it, becoming a little fatigued by the Wardour-Street panoply of it, seized a pen, inserted in one place an omission-mark after the recurrent name *Walter de Boys*, and wrote above it the two words, *né Hopkins*; a simple joke, but one received by the author of the book with particular displeasure.

That summer, while at home, I was in such continual disgrace that I hid myself as often, and for as long, as possible, and, if I heard my name called by my father, kept out of the way, since I knew it must portend something of an unpleasant nature, another explanation or rebuke, either in private, with a formal air of solemnity, or — this in order to satisfy a sense of power — in front of people for whom I did not care. What my character needed to regenerate it, my father told me constantly, was for me to have to do something unpleasant every — and, if possible, all — day: a doctrine born of the puritanical sense of sin which I have already noticed as so strange a trait in a man of his origin and outlook in other directions. . . . What was there? . . . What tasks offered themselves, that were sufficiently odious and oppressive? . . . Then an idea came to him. I had said that the idea of the army as a profession did not appeal to me. The very thing! A fine, healthy time in the open air; and knocking about with a sword provided excellent exercise, and proved splendid training for after-life. (This, as I have said, constituted always a favourite phrase of his, but I was never clear in my mind whether it referred to some later incorporeal state of existence — in which in any case himself did not believe — or to a subsequent period of this earthly life. . . . At any rate, if anyone made some such remark to him as, let us say, " Poor old Miss Catesby! Have you heard? at the age of seventy-eight, she's lost all her money, and been obliged to take a post in an office ", he would always reply comfortably, " Such a good training for after-life ! ") What branch, then, of the service, should it be? Well, I particularly hated horses, so it had better be the Cavalry. . . . A wonderful life in the open air, which gave one a good appetite — one felt fit for anything. And what an opportunity to use your brains — you could always play polo. He proceeded to recall to my memory what he had told me before; that, some five or ten years previously, when he had been in command of the local Volunteers, a General who had come down to inspect the regiment had said to him, " When politics took you away from us, the British army lost a Napoleon ". (At this time, he was peculiarly conscious of his all-round universal ability, and used sometimes to say to me, as if to emphasise the gulf that separated me, inheriting, as I did, my mother's blood as well as his own, " Of course, *I* could have made a success at anything to which I turned my hand ".) Then, again, he would go on to sketch life in the army; of which he knew a good deal, for he had read Froissart and other Chronicles, had been as a young man in the Yeomanry, as well as later the Volunteers, and had talked to Major Viburne about it. One never felt so well as under canvas! And if it was bad weather, one could always go and sleep at home.

Instead, then, of being sent to Oxford, where — who knows? — I might really have learned something at last, I was packed off, very suddenly, to an army crammer's; an institution now defunct, rendered happily obsolete by the reformed system of obtaining commissions. Of life in this establishment I have already been accused of giving an account.[1] So I will say nothing on this occasion except that I rather enjoyed it. I had, indeed, dreaded going there, and when I first arrived, had been ill at ease. Every moment I could spare, I spent in reading Shakespeare — to my surprise, nobody seemed to object. There was no attempt, as there would have been at Eton, to " rag " my room, or burn the books. For the assembled " young gentlemen " — in the terms which Fagin applied to his rather similar select band —, though most of them, refractory by nature, and uncompetitive in spirit at examinations, had been sent here by dissatisfied, and often enraged, parents, as to a more genteel Borstal, showed themselves to be unusually tolerant; perhaps because they were treated as grown-up persons. Of course, there were exceptions to the Borstal trend, and among this section I soon found friends: notably two, who remained among my most intimate until they were killed five years later in the First Holocaust. These were James Glass, a young man of intelligence, feeling and the highest spirits, and Rafe Barclay, a great-nephew of Trelawny, who seemed to bring into a duller world something of his uncle's vehemence of living. And here, moreover, at this crammer's, I found myself, for the first time, rather popular with my comrades. In consequence, the months passed quickly. I did not do much work: but for French had as tutor a genuine Frenchman, and I learnt at last to speak it after a fashion, and even to write rather formal letters in the language. Moreover, I was encouraged by the teacher of English to write essays, at which he thought I showed some ability. He was a Scot, and I have always remembered his looking up from an essay of mine he was reading, and saying, in his Doric voice, with an expression of delight, " Hist! It's an epigrum!" He then read aloud to my fellow internees some rather feeble but snappy sentence that I had written. It was almost the only word of commendation that I had earned throughout the lengthy days of my education.

In the world outside, the usual calm prevailed, and only

[1] In a story called " Happy Endings ", published in *Dumb Animal*. (Duckworth & Co., 1930.)

artificial clouds or smoke-screens seemed to darken the horizon.
The papers supported or denounced the proposed curbing of
the power of the House of Lords. Political excitement, they
told us, " ran high ", but against the more genuine tension of
later periods, it seems like a switchback, a *montagne russe*
compared with Mount Everest. Little seemed to happen.
King Edward still reigned. Everything was calm — yet people
began to talk of war, and one of Pélissier's Follies, dressed, if I
remember rightly, as a charwoman, sang a popular chorus
which ran,

> There'll be no wo'ar
> As long as there's a king like good King Edward,
> There'll be no wo'ar,
> For 'e 'ates that sort of thing !
> Mothers needn't worry
> As long as we've a king like good King Edward.
> Peace with 'Onner
> Is his Motter,
> So God Sive the King.

It seemed unlikely that the great historic calm would
break ; why should it ? If Germany went to war — and no
other foe was to be seen — she would gain nothing. And the
world now recognised that it was governed solely by the wish
for economic welfare. . . . The notion of an army career
seemed pointless.

I saw little of such friends as I had possessed before this
time, for, perhaps owing to the punitive nature of the establishment, holidays were as rare as must be those from Borstal, and
never seemed to coincide with holidays at other places, such as
Eton ; to which my brother had now passed. But I contrived
to see a certain amount of him, motoring over to Windsor
from time to time, to meet him. When I did so, if possible I
avoided passing through Eton itself, so much did it depress
my spirit. Moreover, I had, to my surprise, succeeded in
making a new friend outside my savage surroundings, though
in a most barbarous locality ; for among the relations with
whom, a year or two before, my great-aunt Blanche Sitwell
had put me in touch, was Lady Chetwode — the granddaughter
of her eldest sister, Lady Combermere. And in the months of

which I write, Star Chetwode had, by her kindness and charm
and gaiety, done much to alleviate the dullness and misery of
my existence, for she was living in Aldershot near-by, where
her husband, Sir Philip Chetwode — afterwards Field-Marshal
Lord Chetwode, O.M. — was commanding his regiment, the
19th Hussars. She had a most unusual zest for life, a quality
which found its expression in the laughing quickness of her
words, and she seemed able even to civilise a house in
barracks in Aldershot, joining it to the contemporary world
outside. She quickly became — and has always remained —
a favourite cousin, and with her I used to meet her graceful
and enchanting sister Primrose, whose death at an early age,
in 1919, is still lamented by many devoted friends. . . . I
must mention, too, another relative who entered the lives of
my sister, my brother and myself at this time: our young
Virginian cousin Evelyn Sitwell, who now paid her first visit
to England. Her rather sleepy charm, for even her voice
seemed to have in it the genial indolence of southern climes,
at once endeared her to us. She lived for some two years or
so as a member of the family, and, under the circumstances,
it exhibited real tact, no less than genuine feeling, to be able
to do this and yet never make mischief. On the contrary, she
seemed to make life easier for all those with whom she came in
contact.

During my first term at the crammer's, I was allowed, too,
to go away for a few days to pay a short visit to Bath to my
Sitwell grandmother, who had taken a house in Royal Crescent.
Now eighty, she had not begun to fail yet, and was able to
drive round the town and show me some of it. Herself had
not seen it since the days when, as a child, she had stayed
there with her parents; at which distant period there had
been old people still residing there who remembered Bath in
the eighteenth century. I was amazed at the beauty of the
city, so much more complete, even today, when it has suffered
bombing at the hands of the Germans and devastation by one
of the most Philistine Councils in England, than was any city
in Italy, more beautiful than Vicenza was, because more solid,
more anchored to the earth than that papier-mâché dream of

an antique world as it should be. It was November, and hills and fields, and the sun itself, had, it seemed, clothed themselves in the brightest pheasant feathers, and the grey city, disposed with such grace upon the various slopes, appeared to exist within a globe of opal. I felt at once, as any stranger must, the ancient life and order of the place, and for the first time comprehended an important fact: that all European cities for their fullest flowering need a Roman foundation.

The summer before I went to my crammer's, I was, as I have said, in continual disgrace at home. I suppose all this time I must have been very much attached to my father, or I could not have been so wretched. My self-respect had entirely perished; for of what use was I, if my father so little esteemed me? After all, he was the most intelligent and learned person of his generation who was within my range, the most intellectually developed and nervously equipped. But my feeling for him must, within the space of a year or two, have very much altered, until, resembling in truth for once my relative whom I have mentioned, I would feel ill for an entire day at the sight of his handwriting on an envelope. The state of mind to which I was reduced already, persuaded me almost to dislike my home, where every tree and vista seemed to re-echo my father's voice. Sometimes I would, nevertheless, hide in the garden with Sacheverell; but he, albeit he invariably took my side, seemed at this period more popular than I was with the family . . . so for the most part I remained in my bedroom. It was high up, and no-one would climb all those stairs to look for me — and, another advantage, I could see for myself through the open window what was happening.

The garden was in gala this year. Over the rounded top of an ancient holly, which grew against one of the angles of the house, where it jutted forward, the lawns lay spread in their richest, fullest beauty. The hedges had grown and were by now substantial, and the whole design, the counterpoint of bright mown grass and deep shade, of water and of trees, had settled down, and looked as if it had existed always. This year, within the mysterious fullness of their setting, this year, in the ultimate Edwardian summer, the flowers had attained a

peculiar richness typical of the epoch, for Lutyens's old friend
and mentor, Miss Jekyll, had been sent the plan of the garden
beds by my father and had issued her decrees for them : in one
part they were to be filled only with blossoms of blue and
orange and lemon-yellow, in another with French eighteenth-
century blues and pinks. The heads of dahlias and zinnias and
carnations and roses were heavier and more velvety than in
the previous decade, and the scent of the box hedges and of the
various flowers was wafted up to the window, while at dusk the
fragrance of the tobacco plants and the stocks became overwhelming, seemed almost as strong as that of the tuberoses in
their tall vases in the drawing-room, or of the bowls of stephan-
otis and gardenia. But now, in the day, the eye followed the
gleam of water from fountain and pool to the lake below, on
the surface of which the weed showed here and there in wide,
moon-gold patches, the weed supplying a backing to the glint
of the water as quicksilver does to a mirror, and beyond, rising
through layers of sun and mist, which exaggerated the height
of the hills, could be perceived the distant bulk of Bolsover,
seeming more a cliff or a precipice than a castle, and of Hard-
wick with its triple towers. Set, tumbling at curious angles, on
these heights, villages, no doubt hideous in themselves, showed
from this distance the miniature blue perspective of Italian
hill towns. . . . But I heard people talking. . . . Peering out
cautiously, I observed my father peacocking about on the
lawn, among an imported bevy of sycophantic females. He
was wearing a grey wide-awake hat, a grey suit, and had, slung
round him, a pair of binoculars. He was pointing with a stick
towards the horizon, stabbing it, as it were. His voice, very
clear and decisive, but rather thin, floated up to the window.
" All that belongs to *me* ! " he was saying, in answer to a
question, and, with a final stab, " What we want there is just
a cascade between the distant trees. Nothing looks so well or
points a view so aptly as falling water ! Not everyone can
manage it — but it's quite easy for me." And he added
confidentially, with a little smile of self-congratulation, " Between ourselves, I have over two miles of lead-piping up my
sleeve ! " The Bevy looked impressed, I thought, by this

clever but unexpected piece of legerdemain.

The Bevy had succeeded to, and replaced, the Fun Brigade, and was much more heterogeneous in its composition. All the members of the Fun Brigade had come of the same race, class and creed, and, in a large sense, of the same family. Their interests, if limited in scope, had been identical. No-one belonging to it had been capable of understanding or admiring my father's imaginative creations. Further, though so pliable in other ways, yet the whole body was resolute in that not one member of it was willing to try to find favour with the master of the house by applauding him in this direction. *Esprit de corps* frowned on so great an outlay of money on things one could neither kill, eat, wear nor ride. Thus, when my father with pride showed to these people the lake he had made, the dam which was now being dug out in the Eckington woods, or propounded some new, still more grandiose scheme, they merely smiled wistfully, unconvincingly, while quickly calculating how much it had — or would — cost, and how many pheasants could have been reared, how many foxes torn to pieces, for that sum of money. . . . What waste ! . . . So they would only comment " How neat ! ", " How weird ! ", or " Isn't it *killing* ? " in the token phraseology of the day. (Indeed, he seemed to be able to obtain no response from anyone; for when he had lately observed a superannuated collier watching the digging in the woods, and had asked him " Are you thinking of the fishing there will be ? ", the old man had replied gloomily, " No, Sir George — I was thinking what a wunnerful lot o' suicides there'll be in that blinking pool.")

My father needed more than this. Just as I have confessed that I require flattery in order to work at my best, so did he, for the most perfect evocation of vista or torrent. For this reason, for this purpose, the Bevy had supplanted the Fun Brigade, and now reigned at Renishaw in the summer months. . . . There had been, however, an awkward interregnum, when the old guests, piqued by my father's neglect of them, had refused to return, and the new band had not been formed. My mother, bored without visitors in the house, used to send perpetual telegrams to people imploring them to stay. Henry, handing one of the wires to the Postmaster, was heard to ask,

" Mr. Wilks, don't you know of anyone who would like a fortnight at Renishaw Hall? "

All the same, he was amazed with the former habituals for being refractory, and when someone had enquired of him about a member of the Fun Brigade, a certain Gerald Dancaster, whom Henry considered a mollycoddle, " Isn't Mr. Dancaster coming here again this year? " had replied,

" Well, I rather expected the gale would have blown him in last night."

The new applausive body, the Bevy, possessed three or four main props, such as Madame Amboise, Miss Camber-Crawshaw and Miss Fingelstone, who could be relied on to lead the whole company in admiration of what he was doing — and for the rest, there were, as we have seen, the wives of former supporters in Scarborough, people for whom, for one reason or another, he used to say he felt sorry, adding with a somewhat gracious air, and the particular gesture of his hand, descending in stages and with a slight flutter that always accompanied it, " We ought to show them a little kindness ". But, as I have said, immured in his tower, he now felt really a great need for feminine sympathy, as well as for flattery, and he could rely on the Bevy to produce it, so much of it, as it were, for so many days' visit, in the same way that prostitutes provide love by the hour.

Madame Amboise, plump summary of her race and epoch, was in quite a different category from the chorus, whose names, even, she affected never to be able to learn. She was much more cultivated and intelligent, and at the same time much more absurd. An enormous Russian, of middle age, with thick white hair piled up like meringues, and a complexion of palest lilac, in the manner of many of her fellow-countrymen before the Revolution, she suffered from a dilated soul and was always eager to tell you of its symptoms. But her interests were by no means confined to these, for she was faintly tainted, too, with European culture of *l'Art Nouveau* period, and further, she seemed to be particularly at home in a world, imperceptible to others, that lay precariously unbalanced midway between politics and the psychic. She carried about with her, moreover, an atmosphere of political scare, bringing with her into this calm Edwardian scene a premonitory breath of the coming great disasters that were already being prepared on the golf-courses. In consequence, the comfortable did not enjoy talking to her : it was as though a tramp in rags had entered the drawing-room and sat down. They were obliged to ask themselves " Can there be anything in what she says ? " — but only for the moment. Fortunately for their peace of mind, she was so patently ludicrous in other directions — as are so many other prophets once they stray from their precise dominion — that it was soon possible for the inhabitants of the drawing-room to reassure themselves, dismissing doom with a light titter. She was ridiculous, they said : and this was true. But she could not, of course, be expected to recognise it ; or that the creaking machinery of her charm, the golden net of her recollections, made her still more absurd. She aimed at creating an effect, and she succeeded. More than on her beauty, she relied on her charm, her voice, and, above all, her sympathy, which she was always ready to dispense, and which was so thick that, as though she were a medium producing ectoplasm, one could almost see it. She liked, too, to darken the background against which she displayed herself with talk of her hard life, and she would insinuate the existence of some great political mystery which had imbued even her childhood with dark tones. When other children had ridden donkeys on the sands, she had sleighed behind a reindeer over the drear Siberian snows — or so she gave one to understand.

Born into intellectual circles in Moscow, she had, in fact, spent her youth in the best tea-merchant and international *milieu* in that city. As soon as she had grown up, her family had taken her to Paris, where she had met and finally married the son of Amboise, the painter, and friend of Ary Scheffer. But the mists of the past had swallowed this rather nebulous figure. (Later I found out in what fashion.) Now was the time of *Il Fuoco*, D' Annunzio's famous novel, and I think Madame Amboise, in spite of her northern origin, saw the whole of life through his eyes, rather than through those of a Russian novelist.[1] Be that as it may, in the course of a few decades her life had opened up in the directions natural to her. She had specialised as the confidante and friend of all minor royalties of artistic leanings and unorthodox views, and used to sit in the loggia of the palace at Sinaia listening to Carmen Sylva reading her own poems. She had also drifted into the position of becoming mistress of a rich Englishman, a friend of King Edward's. He was one of those strangely prominent figures, half politician, half journalist, whose semi-inspired and pompous bungling, and easily-disavowed statements of policy, marred the diplomacy of the opening years of the century, and whose continual interference in foreign affairs constituted one of the chief factors that promoted the First World War. This great love of hers, though on her side permanent, had after a year or two degenerated into a chronic state of guerrilla warfare : but this in no way caused her to feel any sense of humiliation, and she would talk freely, and as though they were matters of romance, of the various ruses and stratagems she had employed, and of the cunning devices by which she had secreted herself in his house, and the promptness with which his wife had discovered and flung her out of it. These stories combined with her friendships, and her position as the discarded mistress of one of these mysterious beings, lama-like in the diplomatic sphere, and an architect of the recently established but still rickety *Entente Cordiale* — which showed all the well-known signs of Sir Titus Tittlebyte's workmanship, in that it was neither an alliance nor not one — to afford her still an occasional place at a luncheon, though never at a dinner-table, in Paris. There she had for many years led an existence full of incident, both psychic and material — though the material incidents had of latter years been of a rather negative kind, confined to these snubs or booby-traps, and to being ejected from her most ingenious hiding-places. She came to us to find peace, as she said — or, perhaps, merely because for the

[1] At that time, stories of D' Annunzio's amatory exploits circulated throughout the cultured drawing-rooms of Europe, as, a hundred years previously, had the tales of Byron's adventures. In this respect, as in others, no-one has replaced the great Italian writer.

moment she had nowhere else to go. For hours, if she could find one of us to listen to her, she would talk in her smooth, slow, rather deep and evenly accentuated voice. Sometimes she would be very confiding. " ' Madame Amboise, Hélène, may I call you ? ', D'Annunzio said to me, when last I saw him, ' It is not for your beauty that I love you, though that too is unusual, but for the so-velvety bloom of your voice : call me by my name, call me *Gabriele*, for I love to hear you weave the sound of it upon your lips : yours is the *Voix d'Argent*, the *Voix d'Or*, the *Voix entre Chien et Loup* ! ' " Still with the dagger turning in her heart — for she dearly loved Sir Titus (but then so, unfortunately, did his wife) —, she would talk to my father of Rodin and of Lalique, until he began to entertain a new project — which never, of course, materialised — of having fountains of glass designed for him. " It would amuse the members of the golf club, if we erected one on the Course," he remarked to me.

The first time I had seen Madame Amboise was about a year before, when my mother took my sister, my brother and myself — aged respectively twenty, ten and fifteen — to see her in a hotel in London. We waited for her in a room which was called the *Reading Room*, though plainly no-one had ever read a line in it, and there was nothing to read except a dusty trade-journal and thin pamphlets on New Spelling and Judge Rutherford's Religion. For the rest, there were a few dry but clotted ink-wells, a few rusty, sticky nibs that seemed to have been dipped in liquid hair, a few closed blotters, with neither writing-paper nor blotting-paper, and some visitors sitting in green and creaking wicker chairs. At last a heavy footfall sounded, and Madame Amboise advanced through the open door, clothed like a matador in a trailing cloak of scarlet velvet. She glided towards us as though in a trance, as though not seeing the faces round her, but only ours. From a distance away, still sounded that memorable and mellifluous voice.

" Ah ! my friend, my friend, I, Hélène Amboise, have had my love betrayed for a young girl of seventeen ! *Écoute!* He has introduced her to his wife and family ! "

She would have liked often to talk to my mother about

her soul, but on the only occasion she had attempted it my mother had listened most patiently, and at the end had counselled the taking of a strong liver-pill, a remedy that she prescribed for every ill, moral, physical or mental, and this advice had discouraged Madame Amboise. With my father, she had soon realised, too, that it was equally impossible to talk on such matters, because, as though he were a character in a Tchekhov play, he would, if the subject were not to his taste, carry on a conversation, apparently in answer to what was said, albeit in reality bearing no relation to it and existing on a totally different subject and level. Thus, while the poor Russian lady would be diagnosing the mysterious symptoms of her soul, he would reply with tender details concerning garden furniture in Byzantine times, or explanations of some pedigree of the twelfth century. Therefore, her feelings pent up in this fashion, Madame Amboise would wait and if she found my sister alone would discuss for hours the state of the interesting invalid prisoned within her large hyperborean body. She would have liked to consult Sacheverell on the matter — he was now twelve —, but he gave her no encouragement, being intent only on asking her a million questions about her native Russia. Besides, he did not like her, for, notwithstanding her pining, her soul, and the snubs and humiliations she had suffered, she was inclined " to be bossy ", as Henry said. She liked to manage everybody and everything. But when one day she said smoothly to Sacheverell, " If I were you, I should change my suit before tea ", she received the uncompromising reply, " I daresay you would — but *I wouldn't*! " To me she talked not only about her soul, but about her past life, of which I learnt now in much detail. One day, for example, she told me, in slow, low, hollow tones, of her husband and his fate. " Monsieur Amboise was thirty years older than I, a young girl, and when after two years he retired permanently to the Asylum, his delusion being that everywhere he went he was haunted by the sound of my so-beautiful voice, I mourned him as a father, rather than as a husband." . . . At other times she discussed the future of the world. Very clearly, through her clouds of psycho-idealism, she saw looming the coming war.

Indeed, she was one of the few persons I know who perceived it — but then she had been privileged for years to watch her friend Sir Titus Tittlebyte at work, preparing it.

Though she was prone to interfere, Madame Amboise was also very kind and friendly, willing to enter into the spirit of anything, and I remember an old friend of my family, Eve Fairfax, and my brother and myself, inducing her to roll down a steep grass slope; it was as though a mountain were descending. Her rendering of English, too, was a great joy, and often supplied a welcome touch of low comedy. Thus, as I write, an effective, if — to make use of a former Bloomsbury colloquialism — " rather music-hall " sentence of hers comes back to me. After the fashion of many cultivated foreigners, she deliberately made a point of being frightened by domestic animals : and on the occasion to which I refer she had been for a walk in the park at Renishaw, when a frolicsome young heifer had crossed her path. Accordingly, she returned to the house at once, and, looking very large and plainly out of breath, entered the drawing-room where my sister, my brother and I were sitting, and remarked in that velvet voice, the sound of which had earned the famous encomium from D'Annunzio, but which was now punctuated at frequent intervals by a sound like an engine letting off steam,

" My friends, I have met a bull-child in the park — and he has put me into pants. Since then, I am in them always ! "

She liked to sit for hours in the garden, holding over her head a parasol with a coloured lining that, under the sun's play, caused hot, Renoir-like tints and tones to pass over her countenance. But she still saw herself as an enchantress, still felt youthful under the mountains of fat which the years had deposited upon her form. She did not, even though she liked to emphasise how graceful and sprightly she had been as a girl, really believe, I think, that she had much altered.

" When I was eighteen," she used to say, " and my mother took me to walk in the Tuileries Gardens, people would turn round and stare, and I would hear them say ' Look ! See her ! What a lark, what a *lark* ! ' "

Though Madame Amboise spent as much of the day as she

could sitting out, and talking, or going round the garden with my father, listening to him unrolling his schemes, and was never to be seen writing a letter, yet she invariably received a large post — thick envelopes, heavy, and with several foreign stamps on them.

"It's a rum go," Henry would remark to me. "Every day the old Russian grampus gets those letters — and always the same number, seventeen. And it's my belief the handwriting on all of them is the same, though it looks different and the envelopes are different shapes. . . . No one could ever *write* on the number of pages that's in 'em. It's too much, altogether. Nobody'd have the time — let alone the wish. It's overdoing it, and them foreigners are a lazy lot, too. . . . No, you heed my words, sir : *there's a mystery somewhere* ! . . . But she's one of the best of them. I'm sure I don't know where the Great White Chief finds most of the people he asks here now. I've got a good mind to fasten up a notice on the front door ' *Rubbish may be deposited here* ' ! "

I did not pay much attention to what he said. Besides, Madame Amboise would take her letters up to her room when they arrived, and after reading them in seclusion for an hour — which seemed, considering their length, a very reasonable time to take over it —, would descend again, with a visible aura of glory, of international news, round her, and proceed to distribute scraps of information as if feeding the birds.

"Natasha de Roquefort — she was a Keschinsky — writes from her château near Tours ; the harvest has been wonderful, and if war comes, will prove a great support."

"Marguérite de Sedan tells me in her letters that a German spy, wearing a *pickelhaube*, has been found hiding in a *Pavillon d'Amour* at the end of the garden, on their estate in Burgundy. He had a semaphore with him, and had cut off the little fingers of all the children in the neighbourhood."

"Melincourt writes that war has been postponed until after the winter."

"Sir Titus Tittlebyte says that Madame Caillaux has warned him that war is near."

So the tape unrolled itself upon the news-machine.

It was a year or two before the truth came out and Henry was proved to be right. . . . One summer, when Madame Amboise was leaving us to pay a series of visits to friends in France, she asked a fellow-guest in the house, whom she had known previously, whether she would mind addressing and posting every day seventeen envelopes — already stamped — to the various addresses. It did not matter, Madame Amboise said, what was put inside, so long as it was bulky enough — anything would do, book-catalogues, old newspapers, anything !

" But why seventeen ? "

" Because, child, it is my lucky number. Besides, to live in the world, it is necessary, absolutely necessary, to receive every day a large post. Then I can give my hosts the news from England."

" But surely not addressed in the same handwriting ? " her intended accomplice persisted.

" That does not matter in the least," Madame Amboise replied, " though there is nothing, my friend, to prevent you from using a different nib for each envelope, if so you wish. It will not be a great charge, and I, Hélène, will pay."

Alas, in the end, poor Madame Amboise reached a place where she could neither give nor receive news. The war, which she had so long foreseen, nevertheless caught her un-awares. In August 1914, she was taking a cure at an Austrian watering-place, and had been swept off to an internment camp, — the same in which her countryman, Nijinsky, found himself. And in my mind's eye I see her, still intent on her soul and on her love, following the great dancer about, and telling him in her " so-velvety " voice of her experiences. . . . Moreover, she could never bear to be left out of things — " I, too, I, Hélène, am a dancer," she will have said: " D' Annunzio said to me one day ' Hélène, your words are like a ballet, you dance with the sound of your lips ' ". . . . Nijinsky's mind in any case was beginning, like Monsieur Amboise's, to fail, and Madame Amboise died in the camp in 1915.

These sad days, however, were still in the future, and at the moment, as I looked out of my window, she was bumping and flapping about the lawn with my father. . . . On his right came Miss Camber-Crawshaw, leader of another contingent of the Bevy. One of several sisters, she belonged to the super-annuated dairy-maid type, and possessed a voice that, like a mill, ground silence into its component parts. She had joined up in the first place as a friend of my mother's, but half-way through her career had changed sides, and become a Yorkshire intellectual and esthete, eager to support my father's every plan. . . . Beyond Madame Amboise walked, in a flutter or scurry of sweet-pea or pastel-coloured scarves and chiffons, the wife of a doctor from Scarborough, kind, innocent, really nice; while beyond Miss Camber-Crawshaw followed Miss Fingelstone, who made a very different impression.

Little in stature, but plump, Miss Fingelstone belonged plainly, by shape of eye, nose and chin, to the lesser birds of prey; was most like, perhaps, to a small, well-nourished sparrow-hawk. Her brown hands, too, resembled claws, but were hidden by grey suède gloves. Just as such a bird for its own purposes has developed its own ingenious form of camou-flage, so this little old lady, when she walked in the garden, always wore a black mantilla, to soften the lines of her musty face, flecked with feather-like markings, the colour of liver. And when, as occurred some years later, I occupied a room next hers, and was obliged to listen all night to her most individual snoring, that seemed to follow its own hideous rules of climax and susurrant diminuendo, I used to lie awake wondering whether this music, too, might not be contrived of her volition and design, calculated solely, like the stertorous breathing of the owl, in order to deceive the mice, on whom she, in reality unsleeping, intended suddenly to pounce. Similarly, she could pour over her watchful eyes, as hard as olives, a film of oil that, as it were, magnified their apparent limpid plausibility, and drew mice toward them, as a lamp attracts mosquitoes. (I have never seen such oily eyes.) For the same reason, perhaps, she liked to encourage among those acquainted with her the belief that she resembled, physically, Queen Victoria, because this erroneously provided for her the perfect moral background against which to work her schemes, and to carry on her profession : which was to live in Venice on a basis of commissions extorted from any tradesman who sold an article to a foreigner. From the local antiquaries, she reaped a particularly rich harvest : but no object, on a stall, or sold on the pavement, was too small in price to pay her toll. Palaces, flats, statues, furniture, hideous glass figures, provisions, boxes of matches, tortoise-shell combs, shawls, foreign newspapers, picture-post-cards of pigeons, all yielded their proper percentage. For this, she was immensely respected, if not liked, by the Italians, and, in addition, she knew every foreigner who resided in the city, and soon became acquainted with all those who came to visit it. In order to accomplish this more easily, she had made her-self into an expert — and she was by no means without brains — on various aspects of Venetian life in former times, likely to interest strangers, and wrote books on these subjects — a quantity of small, plump volumes. The books greatly attracted the mice. And if in a Venetian drawing-room a young girl were to ask a question about ancient customs in the city, or an undergraduate to propound a theory connected with them, someone there was certain to remark, " You must ask Miss Fingelstone : she's sure to know all that there is to be known about it. . . . What ! You haven't met her ? Oh, you'd *love* her ! Very strict and old-fashioned in her ideas — a real Victorian lady : but she knows everything about Venice." The subjects of her books possessed just that flat flavour of boredom stalely spiced with local sentiment, the titles just that alliterative ease upon the tongue, with every now and then, perhaps, a faint suggestion of innuendo — nobody would ever be certain whether conscious or unconscious, — that appeals to English and American visitors. Among the better-known titles were — and still are :

> *Tears from the Bridge of Sighs*
> *Titian and Trifles, A Causerie*
> *Nights with the Doges*
> *Glass-blowing in Murano*
> *With Ruskin on the Rialto*
> *Amblings with Aretino*
> *A Treasury of Tintoretto*

MARS VICTORYALL

Routs and Ridottos
Tidings from Torcello
Gleanings from Goldoni
Venetian Courts and Courtesans,
and
Byron — or Love on the Lido !

As Miss Fingelstone's fame had increased, she proceeded
to turn a further penny — and at the same time to attract yet
more mice — by giving public lectures on the same subjects.
In fact, she was a clever and business-like old woman — and
when I tell the reader that my father's bargains in furniture,
decorative pictures, glass and china, wrangled over with their
owners for days before he acquired them, in the end inevitably
contributed their quota to her upkeep, it will be realised that
she was dauntless and persevering as well. . . . She was,
when I first met her, already an old woman, and lived to be
very ancient. Possessing a certain degree of real intellect and
ability, as she grew older she became desperately eager " to
keep up ". And it was because of this that, after the First
World War, when my father was past sixty, and when either
the sparrow-hawk had grown decrepit or the mice more wary,
and she had come to stay with us in Tuscany for a rest, I heard
between her and my father a fragment of conversation which
has always remained with me. . . . She sat next to him at
dinner the first night of her stay, and not having seen him since
1914, enquired,

" I meant to ask you, Sir George, what do you think of
Freud and his theories ? "

" Nothing, Miss Fingelstone, nothing whatsoever."

" And of Einstein, Sir George ? "

" Nothing — nothing at all."

With such ease can great territories of the human spirit be
abolished.

Even at that age, Miss Fingelstone was still active, and
now, below me in the garden, she was advancing at great speed
behind my father and his rout of ardent-eyed admirers. . . .
As I watched, I could not help seeing that the members of the
Bevy did not really understand their job. My father liked still

to be alone, except at moments. They haunted him overmuch. Though at times he developed this craving for sympathy, by now it had been satisfied. He was so eager to be back in his study again, in his familiar world of knights and men-at-arms, of oubliettes and other gothic, antique gaieties, of raps-over-the-knuckles to those whose ways he did not approve, and hints on practical matters to the practical, of mazy climbing in genealogical trees, and hours spent in medieval Aleppo, that he was now walking towards the house almost at a run. (He always walked fast, taking rather short steps, with a hardly perceptible inward action of the left foot.) But the Bevy did not know how to take the cue, or how to give it. They merely doubled their own pace. Now they were sweeping across the lawn in echelon, towards home, my father still leading by a long head. Suddenly he stopped, seized his field-glasses, swung round and surveyed through them the horizon. Only Madame Amboise appeared glad of the rest, for he had forced the pace, and she was plainly "in pants" again. The rest of the Bevy waited and stirred uneasily. . . . Had he forgotten they were there, they wondered. It might be awkward: for sometimes, in moods of abstraction, he seemed hardly to recognise them or know who they were. They examined one another's dresses, scrutinising them with a minute, sidelong attention, bit by bit. Then, at last, he turned and spoke, his words floating, clear and distinct, up to my window.

"The colliery over there has ceased working: you see the great square building at the side. Now that the lease has lapsed, I propose to turn it into a Triumphal Arch — just break through the middle, knock it out, and stucco the remainder! One would have double twisted pillars, each side, as they would in Italy, and a *stemma* above." Then, after a moment's pause to receive the Bevy's astonished acclamations, he added, "I only hope that Osbert will appreciate all that I'm doing for him — I moved that mound three yards further to the west last year, Miss Fingelstone, and pulled and dragged the two old yew trees —; but he seems to show no aptitude for anything!"

It was after these holidays, during my first term at the

crammer's, that my father bought the castle — or rather half of it — in which in later years he was to live, thereby substituting for farce, with moments of tragedy, the purest *Commedia dell' Arte*.

He had been motoring with Miss Fingelstone, an Italian, a rival bird of prey, who was called Barone Pavolino, and another friend, an Englishman, all of whom were accompanying him from Florence to Siena, where they were to be his guests. The driver took the wrong road, and the motor then broke down beneath the walls of an immense old castle. (Sometimes, since, I have wondered whether it might not have been a diplomatic breakdown, organised by Miss Fingelstone or the Baron.) On the terrace above, the cellar doors were open, and the peasants could be seen treading the grapes, for it was the season of the vintage. While the driver was trying to mend his machine, my father walked round, outside the walls, through vineyards, to the other side, where stood the garden entrance. Upon the high rusticated piers that rose, one on each side of a seventeenth-century gate of wrought iron, stood, not the usual beautiful Italian garden statues of stone or lead, but two figures rather small for their position, and made, he perceived under the blotches of golden lichen and stains of time — or perhaps of fire —, of white marble. Both represented men in togas; one had a beard, the other figure had lost its head. Yet, dry in execution and formal as they were, these two statues proved to be infinitely romantic in their history, symbols and remnants of a forgotten episode in history, that catalogue of aggressions to which the passage of time adds beauty and poetic justice.

The family which had settled here, round the central tower, in the eleventh century, was called Acciaiuoli, and from here its members had set out, in the thirteenth century, to conquer, first Malta, and then Corinth and Athens; in which two cities they had reigned for a century and more. Their chief residence was the castle they had built of antique fragments upon the Acropolis at Athens, and the ruins of which continued to stand there until the beginning of the last century. They, doubtless, were the Dukes of Athens in whose realm

Shakespeare laid the scene of *A Midsummer Night's Dream*. They possessed, too, a castle upon the Acropolis at Corinth, and the skeleton of this crumbling rock fortress still rose above the cliff when last I saw Corinth, in 1935. . . . Eventually, some eighty years before the taking of Constantinople, the Turks suddenly made an onslaught upon Athens and captured it, alleging as the reason for the attack the notorious cruelty of the Acciaiuoli Sovereigns to their subjects. Then the deposed Dukes of Athens went back to their Tuscan home, bringing with them these two classical statues, of a rather bad epoch, all that was left to them of their famous realms. And three centuries later, when Cardinal Acciaiuoli had added to the castle and modernised it, making the ramparts into garden terraces, and building a theatre where his plays could be performed, he had erected the two statues at the entrance. . . . Now the vast house had already belonged to strangers for some fifty years, the great rooms had been subdivided, and the place had become a village of nearly three hundred people, with whole families of peasants, and its own shops, bakers, shoemakers, tailors. . . . Yet it had suffered curiously little damage; the terra-cotta figures in the grotto had been broken by children throwing stones at them, it was true; but even the missing head of the Greek statue — which turned out to be that of Aesculapius — was found a year or two later, buried some three feet in the ground, just underneath its stone pillar.

My father announced to me his purchase in the letter that follows, written about a month before my seventeenth birthday.

MY DEAREST OSBERT,

You will be interested to hear that I am buying in your name the Castle of Acciaiuoli (pronounced Accheeyawly) between Florence and Siena. The Acciaiuoli were a reigning family in Greece in the thirteenth century, and afterwards great Italian nobles. The castle is split up between many poor families, and has an air of forlorn grandeur. It would probably cost £100,000 to build today. There is a great tower, a picture-gallery with frescoed portraits of the owners, from a very early period, and a chapel full of relics of the Saints. There are the remains of a charming old terraced garden, not very large, with two or three statues, a pebblework grotto and rows of flower-pots with the family arms upon them. The great saloon, now divided into several rooms, opens into an interior court where one can take one's meals in hot weather, and here, over two doorways, are inscriptions giving the history of the house, most of which was rebuilt late in the seventeenth century as a " house of pleasure ". The owners brought together there some kind of literary academy of writers and artists. All the rooms in the Castle have names, it seems, as the Sala of the *Gonfalonieri*, the Sala of the *Priori* — twelve of the Acciaiuoli were *Gonfalonieri* and twelve, I think, *Priori*, — the Chamber of Donna Beatrice, the Cardinal's Chamber, the library, the Museum. There seem to have been bathrooms, and every luxury. We shall be able to grow our own fruit, wine, oil — even champagne ! I have actually bought half the Castle for £2,200 : the other half belongs to the village usurer, whom we are endeavouring to get out. The ultimatum expires today, but I do not yet know the result. The purchase, apart from the romantic interest, is a good one, as it returns five per cent. The roof is in splendid order, and the drains can't be wrong, as there aren't any. I shall have to find the money in your name, and I do hope, my dear Osbert, that you will prove worthy of what I am trying to do for you, and will not pursue that miserable career of extravagance and selfishness which has already once ruined the family.—Ever your loving father, GEORGE R. SITWELL.

This letter puzzled me : for I was not conscious of having been extravagant. *I* had not bought a castle big enough for three hundred people — not even half of one. *I* was not proposing to make my own champagne.

Chapter Three
INTERLUDES AND DIVERSIONS

Directly my father had concluded the purchase
of the whole of Montegufoni, war broke out between Miss
Fingelstone and the Baron on the important matter of the commission; to which in its entirety each of them laid claim. This,
indeed, was to prove a fight to a finish; but of the bitterness of
the ensuing protracted operations, no murmur ever reached
my father's ears, nor the faintest breath of their underlying
cause. In the end Miss Fingelstone, after many a summer, lost
the battle, but then she started at an initial disadvantage, since
this was not her own Venetian country, but a Tuscan terrain,
over and in which the Baron knew precisely, after a lifetime's
experience of similar warfare, how to dispose his troops.
Moreover, his mind was bold and in no way limited, and
though engaging himself whole-heartedly in the struggle, he
prepared, too, grandiose schemes for gaining after-the-war
trade. With this object in view, he now started in Florence a
small factory — and not so small at that! — where he designed,
and in his spare time supervised, the manufacture of hundreds
of oblongs of the most objectionable machine-made tapestry;
highly-coloured, painfully realistic scenes, of which the favourite
depicted Beatrice, in type a German prima donna, meeting
an offensively austere Dante on the Lung' Arno, against the
inevitable background of the Ponte Vecchio. These panels,
first tattered judiciously, and then sprinkled by special process
with a chemical dust that aped Time's fretting, he sold for
large sums to wide-eyed pork-packers and innocent armament-
kings, explaining that they had been discovered hanging
behind a more modern wall in the ancient *castello* recently
acquired by an Englishman, Barone Sitvell: or, alternatively,
to millionaires of more criminal instinct and origin, he insinu-

ated, with the tip of his right index-finger pressed in an intimate and knowing manner against his right nostril, that he had found them — without my father's coming to hear of it — rolled up in a cupboard in the great tower, and had said to himself at once, " Mebbee, these I should not tak : but Provvidenza intended them for Signor Pozenheimer's Medieval Centre in California ! " After this manner, in this one direction alone, he made a fortune within the space of a few years.

As well, he allowed his imagination to roam along other paths. Florence, I fear, bored him : perhaps he tired of his Italian Baroness, whose shrill voice echoed under the dingy composite vaulting and along the corridors of his flat, so bare and yet befringed, so modern in its squalor, and medieval in its conveniences, so cold to the touch as to fill the human body with a premonition of the tomb ; while, as if to emphasise this feeling, in the narrow hall an enormous clock, shaped like a coffin, gave out the very sound of Death scything away the minutes. . . . At any rate, before long, he succeeded in persuading my father that an excellent trade in wine — for our new property was situated in the Val di Pesa, the best Chianti district in Italy — could be established with South America. With this delusive aim in view, my father was induced to pay him annually a handsome sum, with which to spend each winter in Rio de Janeiro ; where he soon became respected — a good deal more respected than in Florence —, and where he maintained a quite sumptuous second establishment, fitted with every modern convenience, including a flashing-eyed Latin-American wife. In the hall here, too, stood a clock : but this time, appropriate to the place and household, a cuckoo-clock, immensely admired by his Brazilian friends, mocked the hours. Every evening, too, he occupied a box at the Opera — which made him very happy, for he possessed a real Florentine love of this kind of music, but at home could not afford to indulge it. . . . The result was that, though the Baron enjoyed himself, the wine business, which in its small way had been a flourishing local concern when bought, now trailed off and disappeared altogether.

It will be recognised, therefore, that, contrasted with such ingenuities, poor Miss Fingelstone's schemes — a penny here on a dozen postcards, a lira there on a china plate, the fraction of a twenty-centesimi piece on a glass of cyprus, or half a lira on a gondola-fare, seemed trivial and without sacred or diabolic fire. Thus, taking into consideration the size of Montegufoni, in which a number of people could live unnoticed, the Baron had prudently decided to provide himself with, and furnish, a flat there, from which he could properly direct his feudal extortions : whereas Miss Fingelstone could only afford to pay, very meagrely, one of the peasants dwelling in the Castle to inform her by telegram when the Baron proposed to be away for a week or two, or planned to leave for South America for the winter. On the receipt of this intelligence, she would, even though it interrupted her in the middle of writing a new work for the mice, entitled *Round the Convents with Casanova*, at once take the night-train for Florence, wheezing and snoring through the blue night of the mountains in a third-class compartment, on arrival catch an omnibus to the nearest village, and thence walk to Montegufoni : where she would wring from the wretched peasants her tribute, and return to Florence, like a Fertility Goddess, loaded with wine, oil, corn and lemons. . . . But alas, she was a foreigner, and patriotic sentiment did not support her, as it did the Baron. The peasants grumbled.

Even when all this has been said, the Baron would have been ill-advised to underrate his adversary, especially in the matter of the main battle, which she conducted most ably. Fortunately for himself, he made no such mistake. Further, both antagonists punctiliously observed the rules ; for, just as in the most bitter and stupid international outbreak certain laws obtain, governing, for example, Red Cross procedure, so the rules of this warfare decreed that neither the Baron nor Miss Fingelstone should denounce the other to my father ; they were allowed to invent and repeat to him lies about each other, but they must not tell the truth — worse than any lie that either could invent — : that would have lost them the good opinion of the onlookers. The Baron, therefore, had to be content with giving my father hastily improvised imaginary details of Miss Fingelstone's impassioned love affairs — details

so plainly in the Italian idiom as to declare themselves false at
once —, while, for her part, Miss Fingelstone was obliged to
confine herself to insinuating that the Baron was not an
Italian nobleman at all, but a pawnbroker's bastard from the
poorest quarter of Florence : equally, this allegation was
denied by every feature he possessed. . . . But, again, just as
even in the most savage conflict both sides call off hostilities
for an hour or so to enable Red Cross ships to reach the ports
of the adversary, so both Miss Fingelstone and the Baron were
obliged to conspire for one purpose alone : to keep my father
away from the Castle.

In a letter to Turnbull, written about the same time as,
but a little later than, that I quoted at the end of the last
chapter, my father gives more details about his new acquisition,
and mentions once more the prospect of champagne.

My dear Peveril Turnbull,
    You will be amused and alarmed to hear that I am buying a
castle in Italy, formerly belonging to the Acciaiuoli, Dukes of Athens.
. . . It is rather larger than Renishaw, and twice as broad, cost
£250,000 when largely rebuilt in 1160, and shelters now several
dozen families besides the two owners. . . . I propose to put some
rooms to rights, and perhaps to go there for a few weeks in the vintage
time, to see my own champagne made. . . . The air of forlorn
grandeur is very attractive, and this I hope to keep.—Yours very
sincerely, George R. Sitwell.

Already, I think, in this letter one detects the results of the
propaganda put forward by Miss Fingelstone and the Baron.
He no longer proposes to use the whole of the house, nor even
part of it for a long visit : yet assuredly his heart had never
previously failed him before any scheme of building or restora-
tion. Another difference to be noticed between the two letters
is that in spite of his emphasis upon it to me in the first, there is
in the second no mention of the fact that he had bought the
house in my name — or, indeed, of my name at all. . . . As for
the champagne, the phrase, and its recurrence, are indicative :
they tell us that, tempted by the beauty of the place, and by his
own sense of its beauty, to yield, by buying it, to an admirable
but, from a worldly point of view, unwise impulse, he was now

trying to brazen it out by adopting a man-of-the-world rôle completely alien to his nature: a man-of-the-world would never excuse him for buying a white elephant because of its beauty; but champagne — that was another matter! Besides, to him champagne was a symbol; when drinking it, he felt dashing. In reality, however, mead would have interested him more: but when he had ordered Henry to ask for it, at the Piccadilly public-house that, when in London, he frequented, he had omitted to do so. Or so he had said. The truth was that the Great Man was becoming shockingly forgetful. . . . And that reminded him he had entered a note, under the heading, *Mead, the Right Way to Make it*, in one of his notebooks — but which of them could it be in? It must be in one of the two or three dozen, either in the library or in his study. Quite easy to find, but for the moment he couldn't lay his hand on it: which was a pity, but he could tell me shortly what it contained. Shut the door! He had come to the conclusion that probably in making mead people did not use the right kind of honey. " Such a mistake," he added, " not to consult me ! "

Meanwhile, year after year, the Baron and Miss Fingelstone, furiously at battle in all else, still continued to unite in their efforts to frighten him away from his Italian estate: otherwise they might lose their share of its products. Having previously combined, when the purchase of it was in question, to sing its practical advantages, for they knew he could see its beauty for himself —, having lauded the purity of its water-supply, the ease with which a mountain torrent could be converted into electricity for him, the healthiness of the air, and the sheer joy of living in the Tuscan countryside, they now alarmed him by pointing out continually the difficulties of lighting and heating, the dangers of the night air and the harshness of the mountain climate, and terrified him, both for his own health and that of his family, with stories of some of its present inhabitants having become afflicted with typhoid and phthisis: they even, it was said, borrowed a chlorotic young girl from an institution, and paraded her here for him in a shawl and wheel-chair. . . . These arguments and object-lessons for a time produced a considerable effect, and it took him a decade to acquire immunity from them. As another result of their propaganda and nerve-war, I was not allowed to see Montegufoni until three years later, for he became diffident about his purchase of it.

Pleasures during those years were few. I was not encouraged to join my family in their travels abroad, except on the occasion to which I will revert in a moment. . . . I had gone up to London in February for an Army Entrance Examination. . . . What do I remember of that visit ? . . . The lines of hopeless questions, weakly gelatyped, which as your eyes became more used to the almost invisible ink employed, still further overwhelmed you with their arid impossibility ; the faces round, listless and despondent as my own, or brisk and satisfied with a kind of fox-terrier alertness ; and *The Dollar Princess*, successor and rival to *The Merry Widow* at Daly's Theatre. . . . Looking back, I seem to have visited this piece with various of my companions from the crammer's several times during the ten-days period of the examination. Gay, inane, these trivial voices, struggling so complacently, so happily, with the tunes allotted to them, yet reach me across the footlights, and beyond them across the litter of two dead worlds that separates me from that stage. The melodies still flutter like moths in the mind's darkness, and for a moment the faces, light and gay, imbued with a kind of innocent, because brainless, sophistication, and with an artificial freshness, precisely equivalent in its relation to the genuine thing it counterfeits as are the artificial and equivocal cardboard blossoms that surround them to the roses and lilies of a garden, prosper again under the slides, out of the dust of the wreckage. . . . The melodies still flutter : and, indeed, the popular tunes of each epoch have a particular value in translating and crystallising the dreams of the time, to their appropriate rhythm. . . . But more strongly than all these things, I recall Madame Amboise ; for I had been placed by my parents in the very hotel in South Kensington in which she was staying.

There, after the examination was over, I fell ill, developing a high temperature, and she most kindly nursed me, sitting by my bed for many hours, it seemed day and night, and telling me all this while of her soul and of the affairs of her heart. I was feverish, and, in consequence, cannot remember all she said : but I recollect the first time she entered my room, she began, "You are ill. . . . I, too, have suffered." Then she paused, and brought out very slowly the word "*Hark!*", and after another interval, proceeded, "You notice? . . . There is a temporary change in my voice. D'Annunzio observed it at once! 'What has happened, Hélène,' he said to me, 'where is the so-velvety texture of your voice, which always reminded me of the odour of red roses?' 'My friend,' I replied, 'it has been destroyed by the whooping-cough : but the doctor says it will return with the summer flowers.'" Through the mists engendered by illness, I can still see, too, her form looming, white, elephantine, romantic, subtle, melancholy and absurd, as she related to me instances of Sir Titus Tittlebyte's cruelty, of how, when she had hidden one day in a china-cupboard in his house in Paris, she had fallen and smashed a piece of Sèvres, and of how Lady Tittlebyte, attentive but malign, attracted by the sound, had opened the door and dragged her out, bleeding as Boadicea, and covered with a fine layer of bits of china ; powdered porcelain such as cottagers use as an extra food and inducement for hens. Even Sir Titus had not taken her part, but after regarding her with extreme severity, had said, "This is no suitable place to find you! The friendship that exists between us does not authorise you to break my wife's china!" . . . I recovered quickly ; I think a little owing to these stories, which took me to a new land, and thus afforded me a change complete in itself ; I lived for many days in a world compounded of Tchekhov and of low comedy, that was yet raised again by the genuine sadness that ran through it. During this time, I grew really to like and know Madame Amboise, though she would talk to me about my own soul, as well as hers, for many hours. And I was grateful to her, too, for recommending my father to send for me to join him and my mother and Edith in Sicily, where they were staying. . . . She liked to see people doing the things that they liked doing.

Accordingly, at the end of March, I went to Naples, where

Henry met me and conducted me to Sicily. It was certainly
a short journey, a night and a morning: but it was my first
sea-crossing, except for the Channel, and Henry's nautical
interests, his ability and, indeed, inclination to explain every
detail of the voyage, why a rope was lowered here or a sailor
shouted there, or some sound of humming issued intermittently
from the engine-room, served to make him an ideal companion.
In the tender light of the earliest morning, the sky being green
at its edges as the sound of an Arcadian pipe, we sailed through
plains of unbroken rolling blue, only varying in their trans-
lucence. Here, for the first time, between Scylla and Charybdis,
I saw a flying fish leap from one sea hedge to another. Soon we
approached Messina, which had only recently been destroyed
by the great earthquake that seems now — and, indeed, seemed
then —, like the sinking of the *Titanic*, to have been a portent to
Europe of its coming disasters. We passed near enough to the
city to see its painted façades, lime-green, pink and golden, in
this light of the Homeric world, and still intact, though through
the gaping windows showed the dark-green groves of the
mountainous background. In those days, ruins on such a scale,
and the result of destruction in modern times, constituted, it is
singular to recall, something of a curiosity, a sight which drew
travellers to see them; whereas now they encumber the whole
world, and the stench of the dead, crushed and torn beneath
them, rises up to insult the anthropomorphic god of mankind.
But the seas around were smooth as lawns, and even the beggars
who lined the quays at Sicilian ports, and collected round the
porches of churches and entrances to cloisters, seemed to have
none of the sense of ominous horror aroused by Lousy Peter,
or by the scarecrow whose voice had first taught me the meaning of words. . . . We landed somewhere near Taormina,
then only lately invented as a resort, and we proceeded thither
to join my family. . . . With what distinctness I can recollect
my first glimpse of the snowy cone of Etna, floating, unim-
aginably high in its isolation, far above the clouds, as I drove
from the coast, up hills cracked by the sun, and out of the fissures
of which grew huge bushes of red geranium, as tall, almost, as
trees, and the shapes, ragged-edged saws and cylinders, of

cactus and agave, strange to my eyes as would be plants from Mars, to the little city above. . . . This was to be my first experience of such a place as Norman Douglas describes in *South Wind*.

On this ledge of rock, baked by the sun, and surrounded by asphodel, iris, and the numberless flowers of the Sicilian spring, every ordinary judgement was reversed, and other standards prevailed. Worries and fears, either personal or national, could not for long exist in such surroundings. Local scandals, local gossip : this was all that mattered or was serious in a world given up to madness. The streets, with their delicate miniature palaces of tufa, in sepia, gold and black, with the pointed arches of their doorways, through which one obtained a vista of a *cortile* or cloister full of drifts of soft, profuse, light-coloured flowers, translucent-petalled flowers that were new to me, as well as of roses and carnations in March, with their fountains and wells and shrines, and their small shops, displaying for sale objects in wool and silk and olive-wood, the making of which had been imposed upon the inhabitants of the place by kindly but strong-willed English ladies, were crowded with characters native and foreign, noble and the reverse. There was, for example, old Major Frazer, a fine Highland Scot, good and generous, who had resided here for many years and was much respected by the Sicilians. A retired soldier, he had been attracted to the place, perhaps by the cheapness of it, and lived in two rooms, in one of which hung a fine water-colour by Turner, the first I had seen in private possession. He was now a handsome old man, and, when he walked in the streets, always wore, by an adaptation of the local fashion, a rug of the Frazer tartan, thereby imparting a suggestion of Raeburn's portraits to the almost tropical scene. In his gifts to the poor — for he could never pass a beggar by —, he showed an almost Spanish generosity.

Of a very different nature was the Baron von Gloeden, the photographer, and forerunner and archetype of many subsequent followers of his profession ; at which in some respects he excelled. He specialised in neo-Greek studies and, by a kind of transposition of musical-comedy ideals, he was adept in the recording, for example, of young Sicilian shepherd youths, equipped with a pipe to play, cut from reeds, a crook and a lamb, and reclining naked and at ease under the dappling shadow of gauze-like clouds of almond-blossom. The Baron himself, a tall, thickly-clad German, with a beard and heavy spectacles, resided in the chief hotel with his sister, but received visitors in a large studio in the town. He did not speak English very well, but possessed a favourite sentence, explanatory of his sister's preference for domestic life, which he proffered to all strangers the first time he met them, and which, since it possessed a fascinating syntax and rhythm of its own, I remember to this day and here append : " My sister, the Baroness von Gloeden — or, as you would call her, Miss —, she has not the artistic-spirit, Sicily-loving, got, but in her rooms cakes-and-the-most-delicious-coffee-making, she stays " !

At seventeen, one enjoys every moment of life that circumstances, or more usually parents, permit one to enjoy. My father, always at his best when abroad and removed from worries, was during this visit unusually kind, and one instance of it, and of my own young clumsiness, remains in my mind. . . . He was forming a collection of Sicilian amber. This substance consists, like all amber, of fossilised gum or resin, and displays the usual range of amber tones, from pale or dull yellow to deep brown or tortoise-shell ; but its rarity resides in the fact that, having been baked for centuries or millenniums under the lava rolling from Etna, it has by this process acquired opalescent fires and reflections in hay-colour and light-blue and dark-blue and green and crimson. Large examples are scarcely ever found, and it is only to be obtained at all in Catania, the neighbouring seaport, where pieces of it are washed down the great slopes of the volcano by streams that carry them to the shore. . . . A few days before my arrival, then, my father had purchased the finest bit of Sicilian amber he had ever seen, and one afternoon he led me on to the terrace of the hotel in which we were staying to show it me, unwrapping it from layers of cotton-wool — for it is fragile —, and told me to take hold of it myself and place it in the sunlight, so that I could see the full subtlety of its colours. After the manner of the hero of

Dostoievsky's novel, *The Idiot*, when he took up the vase, I knew, I felt, that I was destined to drop it, and tried in consequence to evade my father's instructions: but no, with the kindness that instilled his present mood, he insisted — and, sure enough, it fell from my hand and was dashed to fragments on the paving of the terrace. . . . Not a word of irritation escaped him: but the memory of his forbearance reproached me for many a day.

Both my sister and I enjoyed our stay at Taormina, and the incidents that accompanied it; most of all, perhaps, visits to the theatre — a large, disused church, which had been taken for the season by Grasso, a great actor, and a cousin of the better-known and older actor of the same name who used, before the First World War, to give seasons with his company in London. The Grassos, indeed, were a famous theatrical family, and this bulky young Sicilian, with something of the physique of Charles Laughton, seems to me to have been, with the single exception of Chaliapin, the greatest actor I have ever seen. From a seat in the front row of the stalls I used to watch him nearly every night. The place was always crowded, packed with men. No Sicilian woman ever appeared in the stalls, and when my sister accompanied me it was necessary to take her to a box, rather hurriedly put together. The audience was mostly composed of peasants and, from the actor's point of view, the keenness, the naïve but quick perceptions of the Sicilian mind, the immediate response evoked by any drama, or any actor, containing the quality of fire, from skin, heart and blood, must have rendered it the most perfect instrument upon which to work. For hour after hour these simple people sat there, while Grasso led them to a world where existed almost every emotion.

First, at six o'clock, there would be a curtain-raiser, then came the drama or tragedy, which opened at 7.30 and continued until eleven, followed by a farce, which ended about one. At that hour the more serious of the audience withdrew, and a music-hall performance began, and went on until three. Grasso himself only appeared in the second and chief item of the evening, but the accomplished members of his not very

large company provided the entire entertainment. Throughout the whole of this varied programme, the audience remained
intent on every gesture, every word from the platform that
served as stage. They sighed, moaned, shouted, sometimes with
rage, sometimes with laughter, sometimes with approbation,
while the plaster angels, blowing their trumpets up into the
air from the walls, decomposed, under the heat of the hastily
improvised lighting system, into showers of white powder
which fell on the heads and shoulders of the men below. . . .
The scenes of the plays — alas, I do not know who wrote them,
but some may have been, perhaps, by the hand of Pirandello,
then an unrecognised Sicilian playwright — were all laid in
Sicily, and the action took place in farms, or in the homes of
peasants, of workers in the sulphur mines, or on the stony,
terraced vineyards on the slopes of Mongibello — as the
peasants call Etna. Love and jealousy formed, as a rule, the
chief themes, and death by violence the culmination. Grasso
possessed no physical advantages except a large frame, taller
than that of most Sicilians, and a lumpy but mobile face. He
indulged in no ranting, but was quiet, with a suave and terrible
quietness, menacing, sullen, sometimes flaring up into an acrid
and appalling gaiety that only made more clear the underlying
solemnity and power of the whole being he was representing.
By means of his tenseness and his silences, no less than through
his outbursts, he could cause a feeling of foreboding to inhabit
every cardboard tree, every painted backcloth, which thus his
passion made real. He was, in fact, a great actor, though one
never destined to earn, as he would have done, a world-wide
fame : for he was drowned a year or two later, with all his
Sicilian company, while crossing to South America ; I take
this occasion, over the chasm of more than thirty years, to
salute him and proclaim his genius.

While Edith and I were at the theatre, my mother and
father would be playing bridge in the long hotel drawing-
room, its walls covered with red brocade in a large pattern,
and containing huge console tables with tops of gaudy Sicilian
marble, supported, I recollect, by camels' heads in a very
burnished gold. Usually they played with a Polish Count —

who for some reason was living in a hotel in Sicily and not on his estates in Poland — and his charming Danish wife; for both of whom they had formed a great liking. Indeed, they were a fascinating couple. Count Stanislaus Taratoffsky was dandiacal, well dressed in the Slavonic male way, just tinged with Teutonism. There was a touch of the Kaiser in his pose, both in the position in which he stood and in the upward sweep of his moustachios; a cross, as it were, between the Kaiser and a debonair chef, for he also wore a well-trimmed, pointed beard. On the Teuton side, it was to be noticed that one of those hunting shaving-brushes that Austrian and German magnates liked to wear in their hats, seemed, even when absent, never to be spiritually far from the ribbon of his Homburg. The Countess, a Scandinavian ash-blonde, was exquisitely pretty, with finely cut features, and a curious and becoming pallor, like that of a white-skinned peach. She was very quietly dressed, and wore her clothes with distinction; the only surprise being the tattooed blue rose that one saw, poised under her left shoulder, when she wore a low gown in the evening.

Soon the Count and Countess were installed as valued friends, spending much time with us at Renishaw and at Wood End. Moreover, my mother and father launched them, with success, on many of our relatives. . . . You could not say that the Count was learned, but he appeared to be extremely well versed in the great traditions of his home and country — he was descended from the Polish Kings —, and the accounts he gave of the feudal customs still extant in his domain were deeply interesting to my father. They seemed so original, so like and yet unlike those that had obtained in any other part of the globe. Though he was worldly, it was impossible to disapprove of him. And she showed excellent taste in every direction, and manifested profound interest in all my father's schemes. . . . Moreover, they were both so kind, and eager to take my sister out in Warsaw, in return, no doubt, for the kindness they were receiving.

These new friends came to stay with us then frequently — but I saw little of my other friends. My time was limited, my pleasures were circumscribed — chief among them in these years being the visits I paid to Renishaw in October and November, in order to learn to shoot. Sometimes I went there by myself, sometimes accompanied by my father. Then, with so few people in the house, we lived for the most part in the Carolean core of it, and everything as a result looked as strange to us as if we inhabited a different mansion in a different world. But, even though we used only the Little Parlour and the Great Parlour, abandoning the large eighteenth-century apartments, nevertheless you could feel the vastness of the stretch of rooms that lay there beyond, on each side, empty. . . . But were they empty, for at moments during the evenings as we sat by the fire, so many creakings and rustlings made themselves heard, so many of those inexplicable sounds of an ancient dwelling-place, that it appeared as though there were more ghosts than human beings in rooms and corridors ? One would say to oneself, it must be the wind : but I still do not believe that it was. Phantoms, when one is young, no more prevent sleep than do the hooting of engines or other modern noise — but those we heard were ancient, issued from some cave in time where they had hidden and to which they returned, or so it seemed to me. After being out all day, however, I usually slept through the night, as one does at that age, and only remember a single occasion when I was woken at about two o'clock. I was occupying a bedroom next my father. A small, sinister chuckle from beyond the wall roused me, and then my straining ears caught the words, spoken in his still, clear tones,

" *They may think I shall — but I shan't* ",

the first part of this antithesis being spoken slowly, the second, snapped out more briskly, with a crackle, as it were, and followed again by such a laugh as I had heard first. I never found out the subject of this rather ominous consultation with himself, nor did I like to enquire. It had too much alarmed me.

Not only was the house different at this season, the garden, too, offered a different world. Here, because of the smoke in the air, the fall of the leaf comes early, the masts of the elms and the limes in the avenue were already visible, and a Dutch light, clear and crisp, entered through the bare branches, and this in its turn gave a lightness to the house in the mornings which it lacked in more umbrageous months. Moreover, while the approaching winter made the garden naked in some respects, as it did the trees, in others it brought clothing. The yew hedges had not long been clipped, and stood plumb and regular as walls, but the statues — for neither Roman nor Istrian stone will endure the frosts, even of their own country — had been voluminously covered. (Only St. George, our patron saint, and fashioned of English stone, stood, with his lance tilted, as in summer.) And, indeed, the shrouding of the statues became here a sort of ritual marking of the change of season, as is the vintage in more fortunate climes. The first to go were Neptune and Diana; they were wrapped thickly in bracken, already damp and brown, and then draped in canvas, so that they lost for the ensuing months the graceful air of epochal allurement which rightly belonged to them, and turned to large, primitive, figures, more fit for winter on these heights; forms that seemed roughly hacked out of chaos, though still compact of it, by neolithic axes. Next, the Warrior and his Amazon, at the entrance to the Wilderness, were padded against the cold, and then it was the turn of the two Giants, holding their clubs. Finally, the fountains of red Verona marble were enclosed in wooden cases, the shape of pyramids and painted a dull green. And all these objects, in their winter coats, shaggy as those of the horses in the park (and here the winter coats of beasts are noticeably thicker than in the south), sank into the sad, streaked background of winter tree-trunks, branches and sky. The very landscape closed in on us, removing Bolsover and other great buildings on the distant hills, by interposing barriers of cloud. . . . But this time, too, had its own beauties, and one early morning in November, when the young light, just born, was green as the first leaves, and exhibited all the delicacy of something that would soon perish, I saw, as I looked from my window, five swans sweep down from above the house towards the lake below, circle it, and then descend upon the waters.

In the October visits, I would start out very early. Coming downstairs, I would find, even at that hour, huge fires of our native coal, age-old product of these very valleys and hills among which I was to spend the day, their actual substance, blazing already in the large grates; vast logs of coal, used in this countryside as wood elsewhere, were flickering and intertwining their blue and green and red flames, and giving life to the sombre, misty rooms. As I opened the door to go out, I could see that on the plateau facing the north front, the great beech trees, which retain their leaves longer than other kinds, were now fully invested in their brief autumn fire, and stood like pillars of flame, freeing themselves in the sunlight from the night's vapours. I got into the dog-cart and was driven down the hill, observing how the sun made the dew on whole stretches of grass glitter as if it moved, and turned peaceful meadows into quivering lawns of fire. . . . When, after some twenty minutes, we reached the beginning of the Eckington woods, there I would find Maynard Hollingworth, Mark Kirkby and Dick Humphries waiting for me. Then for another twenty minutes we would walk through these forest-like hills and valleys, which today exhaled their autumn smell, composed of bracken and fungus and foxes and fallen leaves and the red berries of the rowan which littered the paths after a recent gale. And here and there, too, a birch tree, recently felled, added an aromatic freshness to the air. In the very centre of the woods, the beaters were grouped, talking together and chaffing in their broad tongue.

In this atmosphere I spent an enchanting but eminently unsuccessful day, since my shooting of pheasants was no more competent than my shooting of partridges a month earlier. I think, though, that I felt more shame in missing this larger and more glorious bird. I was a profoundly, almost an inspired, bad shot; I never, I am thankful to say now, approached so near my mark as to wound a bird, or a beater, even. It must have been, I can see from this distance, a disheartening job for Hollingworth and Kirkby to try to teach me — but that I thoroughly enjoyed the open span of each day was proved, at the end of all these autumns, by my eventual bag, which was to be of a different, and I hope more permanent, kind.

And October

October was Luke Kembley's month,
When the golden castles of the corn
Had been slighted by the roundhead autumn.
Then, red as the berries that grow
On the hawthorn hedges — oh!
He could walk after pheasants with a gun.

Day and night,
Spring and summer long,
He would lurk in the woods,
Eating bread and cheese
And never resting,
Preparing for October.
He would guard the sacred birds,
He would give them to drink,
He would offer up grain at their wooden altars:
He would even secure
Their effigies of straw
Within low branches
So that,
    In the dark,
A panicked poacher
Could fire for ever at a sitting pheasant,
And no bird would fall.

In the night he would stalk the running sounds,
Pursue the flickering lights:
Then the blue tapestries
Would rustle sullenly, swaying
Puffed out upon the breath
Of the lank,
The dank, green ghosts
Of dead forests.

But

October was the month,
When the northern air is crystal
And the berries grow all red upon the hedges — oh!
When the tall trees grow antlers,
And the three-prong'd leaves of the bracken
Undulate on the pure air
Just as the triple tails of imperial goldfish
Wave through their transparent element;
When even the Sun,

Magnificent Inca,
Wraps himself each evening
For his ceremonial farewell
In gigantic pheasant-feathers.
Then Luke Kembley's breath
Lingered behind him on the air,
As he walked back through the dusk
To find the sharp fingers of the fire
Gilding Mrs. Kembley
In the cottage on the hill.

But now through the cold and the long Octobers
The frost-flowers grow on the stiff stone borders,
And the dark winds blow
Through the lepers' window
And the Parson blows his nose
As he passes in,
And the sky above
Is as dull as sin —
And the poachers trample down the dying woods,
And the pheasants are few,
    The pheasants are few.[1]

October, indeed, has a beauty of its own in this country of
misty valleys and bold hills; the whole landscape seemed to
have been fashioned for this one month, this particular purpose.
Men, dogs, pheasants, and the creatures that scuttled away
under the fallen leaves, or through the filigree tunnels of the
bracken, seemed to share this autumnal, early-morning brisk-
ness. Rather late in the afternoons, when the autumn sun had
already been a little obscured by the net of the mist, night's
vanguard, we would go to luncheon with Mark Kirkby, in his
cabin, on the spur of a hill in the middle of the woods, a citadel
from which, day and night, he could keep watch on the comings
and goings of pheasants, foxes and men. . . . We would sit
on benches and eat cold pheasant and cheese, and apples and
small pears, plucked that very morning from the golden billows
of the trees in the stone-walled orchards, trees that from their
age gave a special taste to the fruit, to the pears, a certain
taste of wood for all their sweetness. The keen air of the dying
year would blow in at the door. Above us, over the cabin roof,
the rowans, huge trees for their species, stretched in apparently

[1] From *England Reclaimed*, by Osbert Sitwell (Duckworth & Co., 1927).

tropical splendour, with clusters of glittering berries, orange and scarlet, each small globe offering a miniature planet to catch warmth and colour from the now almost lateral rays of the sun, which, notwithstanding its coat of mist, still retained autumnal power. Nevertheless, the patterns of the bracken, with its intricate moth-coloured lace, were already beginning to be smudged with the evening's damp, and soon the flowing mountain grass would be wet as river weed, and all this imparted a feeling of coldness, as well as of scented freshness, to the air.

Just as in previous years, during the summer holidays from Eton, in the month of September, I had learnt to know, through walking over them, every inch of stubble in the fields, so now, in the months of October and November in these years, I grew to know every tree in the hanging and dipping woods. The various parts possessed their own character, and many of them had names in harmony with it (though perhaps none were so appropriately styled as the prehistoric site owned by my family at Whiston over the county border, and called Blue Man's Bower) : there was the great sweep of bracken under stout old oak trees in High Bramley Wood, the deep lane of the Drug Road, as it is called, so straight and narrow, the oppressive, sighing darkness of Hangman's Wood, the enclosed green world of Seldomseen or of Low Park Lathe, and the open valley of Neverfear. And this last, with its long, narrow fields, in the summer full of ragged-robin, and with the trout stream, the Moss, flowing through it at one side, and the whole strip flanked by high banks of trees, has a strange history attaching to its designation. . . . One summer night, so short a time ago for the birth of a myth as the sixties of the last century, three men, sickle-makers from Ridgeway,[1] at the far end of the valley, were walking along the footpath which leads through it to Eckington. As they proceeded towards the woods through these rather isolated meadows running between the two cliffs of wood, they saw a ghost — undeniably a

[1] As I have explained elsewhere, Ridgeway is one of the last surviving places where hand-made sickles are turned out, and have been turned out ever since the reign of Elizabeth. They are chiefly exported to Chile and Peru. A local proverb says, " There is only one fool bigger than the man who uses a sickle — and that is the man who makes it ! "

ghost, because of his blanched and almost luminous transparency, and because of the stirring at the roots of the hair which the very first glimpse of him aroused — approaching them in the full moonlight. Greatly terrified though they were, they stood their ground, even though they did not advance towards this stranger from another world, but the spectre continued on his way undeterred, and as he drew nearer he spoke, saying, " *Never Fear!* " and dissolved into the pearly light. And this valley has ever since borne for its name the words the phantom pronounced.

Sitting now in the sunshine that flowed through the door of the cabin, I listened to Mark, " the Dook o' Ploomley ", or watched him, because often he fell asleep directly he sat down, his dog — the Clumber spaniel Plumbley Friar, successor to Pan — falling asleep by his side at the same time, for they both lost many hours of the night in guarding the woods. (Though he was much attached to Plumbley Friar, many of his worries concerned dogs ; and his talk was full of them, " poaching dogs ", " dogs on the loose and prowl ", " self-hunting dogs".) But even when awake, on these occasions at luncheon, he did not eat much, reserving his appetite until he reached home : since on food, as on other matters, he possessed his own ideas. Thus, he would never eat an orange unless he could devour twelve, and his favourite dish was the local Wickersley Pie, a recipe from just across the Yorkshire border, which included in its ingredients, as was fitting for a product of the sturdiest and largest of English counties, at least two couple of rabbits, beefsteak, ham, oxtails, kidneys, wood-pigeons and any game that was available : [1] while a sweet that he liked for supper during the autumn and winter months was frumety, made of creed wheat [2] eaten with milk and treacle. . . . Mark had altered very little since the reader met him some dozen years before,[3] except that he looked stockier than of old, his

[1] To give some idea of the scale of this dish, I may say that a nephew of Mark's informed me that he made an estimate of what the ingredients would cost, if you could obtain them in the war years : it amounted to £7 !

[2] *Frumety* is a local variation of *frumenty*. *Creed* wheat is wheat which has been cooked slowly. Creed, chiefly a dialect word, is derived from the French *crever*.

[3] See *Left Hand, Right Hand!* pp. 176-7.

complexion was a little redder, and he seemed to have acquired still more blue protuberances where the shot — as I thought it, though in reality it was the atoms of black powder from an alarm-gun which he had been setting one Sunday morning in the woods and which had exploded full in his face — lay embedded just under the surface of the skin. He had grown stiffer, too, especially about the shoulders: for, since he kept such late hours, he was apt, while actually driving, to fall asleep suddenly, and to wake up in some ditch into which he had pitched on his shoulder. (He had no sons or daughters of his own, but he liked particularly to drive about the country with his builder's cart full of children: usually his wife's nephews, to whom he was devoted.) For the rest, he was, if anything, more sure of himself, more ducal.

In the age in which he existed, and which he just survived, English life still retained its ancient gift of continuity, the threads composing its web had not yet been severed by the gashes inflicted by two wars. Classes were more distinctively separate, while at the same time exercising a greater influence one on another within narrowly defined but acknowledged orbits: certainly among those between whom such a relationship existed, clerk and master, gamekeeper and squire, there was less of social awareness, less watchfulness and incomprehension. And so it is that, though I possessed no liking for sport, only an understanding of its primitive appeal, and though, too, my subconscious mind may all the time have been engaged, not with the incidence of pheasant, hare or partridge, but with the capture of this rustic deity, personification in appearance, manner and speech of the rough colours of the landscape, and his transference into another kind of life, Mark Kirkby became a friend, as well as one of my favourite models, and that I can rightly claim a place for a summary of his life within the frame of such an autobiography as that which I attempt to create: the picture of an artist, depicted at work against the background of his epoch. It is time now for the sketch of Mark as he was in the first volume of this book, when I was five, to grow, as my knowledge of him and appreciation of his character had developed in the interval, and to expand into a portrait of a sportsman in his native woodland, as he was when my companion in my eighteenth year. So, then, let us stir the embers again, or, to vary the metaphor, disinter for an instant and examine the image of this country god, now, as the decades pass, buried deeper and deeper in the memories of a handful of people, destined year by year to dwindle.

At the time when I was learning — or trying to learn — to shoot, Mark was about sixty years of age; a sturdy, dynamic, rotund sixty. He had been born on the hill opposite Renishaw, at Mosborough, and was the son, so his marriage lines state in the antique phrase, of a cordwainer. He went to the old village school, Camm's, in Eckington, founded in the seventeenth century, and his parents, he said, paid a fee of 2d. a week for his education. Before he had reached the age of ten, he had started work, taking the roughly-shaped hand-made sickles from the forge on Mosborough Moor in which they were made, to be ground at a wheel in the woods; the implements were first piled in panniers, and then carried by donkeys, whom he guided and accompanied. It was these solitary journeys with his beasts in all weathers, at all hours, through the woods, which inspired him originally with his interest in them, an interest that later developed into a whole-hearted devotion. After this fashion he had, while still a boy, grown to comprehend the secret life of these green solitudes : he had traversed these paths when they were deep with snow, and the bare trees, now loaded, turned to the shapes of monsters ; he had traversed them when the hills were hidden by drifting curtains of rain, when they blazed in summer splendour and the vanity of full leaf, or lay breathless and brooding under the volatile thunder-mountains that grew every moment, only to be, in spite of their apparent magnitude, dispersed within an hour into the merest transience of light, sound and water. It must have been, though, — and no doubt it was — the autumn that he most loved, even then. But, at whatever season, this was his territory. And he grew to know more about its moods and secrets than any man since the Doomsday mill had been built at the brook's edge, under the cliff beneath the Norman church. The tide of its poetry passed over him, to leave a residue unsuspected by himself; for he would have believed all his interests to be practical, and his ears were by no means intent for overtones or echoes, only for the Chinese cries of the pheasant, or the stealthy, cracking footfall of a poacher. . . . Before he became monarch here, he had seen other trades, being employed for a time in a footrill colliery in the woods, and after that as a journeyman stone-mason, until, finally, he went into business on his own, and was made a partner in a local firm of builders. Then he had married, moved to Plumbley Cottage, perched on a hill covered with clumps of gorse and harebells, above the valley over which, now being engaged by my father as part-time gamekeeper, he reigned. Henceforth, horses, dogs, guns, poachers, wild creatures of all kinds, constituted, together with singing — for he had a deep, rich, bass voice —, his chief interests.

It is difficult for someone not acquainted with such a mode of life to imagine how busy Mark was throughout the year, how much there was for him to organise, besides the actual shooting-parties and the strategic disposition of shots and beaters. Each month brought its own activities. The game in the woods was wild, without hand-rearing or importation, so the year began for him at nesting-time. Then there were footpaths to watch, and trespassers to follow: while, to discourage other kinds of raiders, dogs or foxes who might disturb sitting birds, he would, in order to kill the scent, daub a wide ring of gas-tar round the nests. Soon summer would be drawing on, with the ceaseless fight it entailed against vermin; there were stoats and weasels to be trapped, and magpies' nests to locate and destroy. With August came the time for bushing: that is to say, thorns must be cut down and placed in the open pastures between the woods, so as to prevent the netting of partridges. Then, after the harvest had been reaped, and on hill-top and in valley stood in its gold turreted castles, transient yet recurrent, and thus more abiding than the greatest buildings of Nineveh, Tyre or London, there were the rakings to be gathered and their transport to the various feeds to be arranged. Mark excelled, too, in the fashioning of sham pheasants to which I alluded in *Left Hand, Right Hand!* — birds made of sticks and bracken fastened together with wire, that had then to be tied on the branches of trees as a lure for poachers. Even the veterans were sometimes taken in, and Mark was always a proud and glad man when he heard of some antagonist of many years' standing having fired at one of these dummies. As October drew near, the hedgerows that divided the park-like land of the meadows adjoining the woods had to be searched in the golden-veined mornings for what he termed " snickles ", the local word for snares (so that the wags of the countryside say of a young man going to marry a woman older than himself, " 'e's been fair snickled "). Usually a few of these wire circles would be discovered towards the climax of the pheasant season. There was night-watching to be done, especially during the moonlit nights before Christmas, when every sound in the valley seemed to lie on the air of this white silence for an instant longer than at other times, and every crepitation and murmur could be noted. The alarm guns had to be set and moved at frequent intervals, and some time during the winter the rakings would give out, and then Mark would insist on the birds being fed with threshed corn, and, in consequence, boxes — the wooden altars to which my poem alludes — were installed, and he would have a shack at each feed, so that he could count the birds and sum up the stock. In snowy weather was the time to read the hieroglyphs that only snow provides for those cunning enough to decipher them, and thus to learn the paths and ways of the vermin, and the entrance to their homes, or whether there has been any un-usual visitor or disturbance. At this time, too, if young trees had been planted, there were rabbits to be kept down. And, all through the year, there were dogs to be trained. His day dogs, — Clumber spaniels, as a rule —, must, above all, be hard-working and possess powers of endurance, and unite the qualities of setter and retriever, while for night work he chose dogs of the bull-mastiff breed. For the use of these, a dummy was placed on a hillock behind his cottage. Training began at dusk, when only the outline of the figure was visible, and the first step was to teach the dog to land with front paws straight on the dummy's shoulders. Later, a real man, protected by leather clothing, mask and gloves, would be substituted — though not seldom it was difficult to find a man willing to take on the job —, and he would adopt the local poacher's many tricks of dodging, sparring and running away. All this was necessary : for poachers, it must be remembered, in such an isolated and lonely tract of country, set in a very thickly populated industrial district, constituted a real and constant menace ; moreover, they were a dangerous set of men, and Mark's life had several times been threatened. On one occasion, three of them, who owed him a grudge, launched an attack on Plumbley Cottage on a dark night at 2 A.M. Mark at once got up, and fired his gun, before dressing, through the open window. And he and Mrs. Kirkby — an ideal companion for him and a woman of great courage — put the culprits to flight, collared one and followed for a considerable distance the other two, who were by then crawling on hands and knees to avoid identification.

As for his animals, horses and dogs, like himself they must be high-spirited, though at the same time his imperious disposition demanded from them implicit obedience. . . . Once he obtained it, however, he became a kind and careful master. One of his dogs, Venture, a boarhound cross dog, was so well trained that his owner had only to point to an object for him to bring it ; a habit of which one of Mark's nephews, a schoolboy who came from Sheffield to spend every holidays at the Cottage, learned to make good use. The boys of the neighbouring village of Mosborough were very quarrelsome and liked to gather in great numbers and attack any stranger — or foreigner as they judged him — of their own age : but this lad would take Venture out with him, and when his opponents set on him, he would point at the cap of the ringleader, which Venture would then faithfully retrieve. This was most effective in stopping the onslaught, but unfortunately in several instances the dog brought back large portions of human hair with the cap, and the parents complained and raged together. . . . But Plumbley Friar, who was by Mark's side now, in the cabin, was the most famous of his sporting dogs, known everywhere in the countryside, and one of the few sporting dogs who would retrieve water-hens or coots. Mark could work him with a single look or gesture. Everything his master said, Friar understood. For instance, on one occasion, when rabbiting in Foxton Wood — annexe to his chief domain —, a ferret got stuck, and when, intending to draw the creature with the scent, Mark shouted " Bring a rabbit ! ", nobody took any notice of his command except Friar, who immediately went up to a mound of rabbits that had been shot, and selecting a body, brought it to his master.

Then there was Gyp, a bull-mastiff, who shared with my ancestor, Dr. Wallis, of whom I have written in *Left Hand, Right Hand!*, the distinction of having taught the dumb to speak; for the dog leapt one night on a poacher fishing for trout in the Moss, knocked him over, and held him down by the shoulders, and had altogether frightened him so much that when in due course Mark arrived on the scene, the wretched intruder cast a look of entreaty at him and with an effort brought out the word " Mes-ter ! " This was the only time he had ever been heard to frame a syllable, for he was a mute, known to Mark as Dummy ; the same whom some years before, as I have told, he had caught shooting pheasants. The next day, Dummy must still have been labouring under his fear of Gyp, for a note reached Mark, on which was written, laconically and piteously, " Me fish no more ; me fish elsewhere ! " And, indeed, Gyp was formidable enough, and had, not long before, thrown three men on the ground in succession. . . . At his best, Mark must have been an unusually good shot, and he used to declare with pride that once, harvesting at a farm belonging to his wife's uncle, he had killed forty-six rabbits before he had a miss. It will, then, be understood that his natural prowess made my natural lack of it the more disappointing.

Of Mark's diverse, indeed numberless, activities, the shed in which we were sitting was the very nerve-centre ; and as we ate, if he were not too sleepy, he would talk of many things. He did not, I think, often tell us of his young days, except sometimes to touch on the superstitions of the sickle-makers of fifty years before. The grinders, for example, he told us, were most credulous, and, among other beliefs, held that to allow a donkey to put its head into the wheelhouse was to challenge bad luck. Any boy who permitted it would earn a cuff or a kick, accompanied by the words " Does tha' want him to larn t' traird ? " (Evidently this superstition had its origin in the necessity in former times to preserve the secrets of Sheffield steel.) And sometimes, too, he would tell us stories he had heard in his youth of my great-great-grandfather, Sir Sitwell Sitwell, and how, coming back from hunting his pack in the woods, he had smelt a delicious scent of cooking, and had stopped to see what the grinders were cooking. They were frying scallops, as they were called locally, slices of potatoes, and they invited him to join them, and he ate with relish until, at the end, he saw with dismay the three-legged iron pot in which the potato slices were cooked ; for, when the cooking was finished and the fat had cooled sufficiently to set again, the pot was just overturned and left as it was until next wanted. . . . But, as a rule, if Mark did not fall asleep, he would talk of more recent events and people, or relate his various adventures in the woods. He used to allege, though, that he had never felt afraid during his vigils there, which not seldom lasted all night — never, except once, and that had been on a Saturday night. He had been in the middle of the large valley, standing at the bottom of the path known as the Drug Road, which led direct from his house on the heights to the stream below. It was nearly midnight, and the whole region seemed desolate, for it was heavy with the fogs of the district, there was no wind, no sound, nothing stirred, except occasionally an owl could be distinguished hooting somewhere in the damp darkness and desolation. Suddenly he heard a voice crying " Lost ! Lost ! " It did not seem far off, and he turned and followed the sound. In the adjoining field, a large park-like meadow which contains two thickets bounded by circular iron fences, he found a man walking round and round the outside of one of them. The stranger explained that he had missed the path to Marsh Lane, a neighbouring village on a hill-top. Mark offered to put him on his way, taking him as far as the stone bridge over the stream, for after crossing that he could not mistake his direction. . . . They walked for a good time in silence.

Then, as they neared the bridge, the man suddenly wheeled round, pulled a revolver out of his pocket, pointed it at Mark and shouted, "Are you the beggar who's been following me?" . . . Somehow or other, Mark quieted the man, got him over the bridge, and then left him : but Mark was convinced that on that night he had met a madman, and one who was probably homicidal.

Usually, though, the happenings were of a more rustic and peaceable order. There would be, perhaps, unaccountable sounds in the night, voices coming from far off, or the cries of unseen water-birds, coot or geese, that fly at so great a height as to be invisible. For this sound there was in the locality a special name, which must go far back into medieval times. "What's that noise?" someone would ask, to receive the answer, "It's the Gabriel-hounds overhead!": for the packs that the Archangel lets loose at night are held to carry a burden of omen for those who hear them. . . . And Mark, indeed, was superstitious himself and he would relate how, one night in his cottage, a grandfather clock which had not worked for years struck suddenly the hour, and a little later a messenger arrived from a village near-by to say that his wife's aunt had died at precisely the instant it had struck. . . . But to return to the woods : on one occasion he had fallen into the dam in the valley ; an enterprise of my father's, newly constructed. (Of this I shall have more to say later.) How he got out he never knew, for he was a feeble swimmer. It only emphasised his distrust of my father's activities in the architectural field ; especially he disapproved of dams and pools and lakes and fountains, and the cost they entailed, remarking in his builder's lingo, " I dorn't horld with all this lading and teeming ". . . . Often the night would pass without event. Long hours of watchfulness, he said, and often nothing to report, no result; but of one thing he could be sure, he would remark in his idiomatic speech : that in the morning, there would " always be a frizzle waiting for me at 'orme, at six ", or sometimes he varied it with " a crackle " ; by both of which he signified a rasher of bacon frying in the pan at Plumbley Cottage. I remember, too, his describing a neighbouring squire, of whom he entertained no very high opinion, as " a can o' sops ". And when he saw a Rolls-Royce or some other super-expensive motor drive by him on the road, he would pensively observe, " You wouldn't get many o' them for a shilling ! " And if someone smashed an object he would say, " Tha's made Mulligan's Mother on it ".

A character himself, he possessed an understanding of character in others which rendered him a doubly diverting companion. He would regale us, for instance, with stories of Mallender, who came from Mosborough, about a mile from where Mark lived, and was of so irascible a nature that on one occasion, when rain was pouring down and the weather-glass still marked fair, he seized the instrument and, taking it out of the house, shook it vigorously, and at the same time addressed it angrily with the words, " Now see for thysen if it in't raining ! " Or he would talk of Harvey, the gamekeeper of the neighbouring estate of Oakes at Norton. A Norfolk man, and a typical product of his native county, he was tall, lithe, spare, alert, of a rather ruddy complexion, secretive, taciturn. He wore mutton-chop whiskers, but under them had cultivated for use a smile, benign, captivating, innocent. He possessed an unusual ability to forgo sleep, compensating himself for it by taking short naps at intervals, and this, no doubt, was one of the natural attributes that helped to make him a master of his trade. So, too, did the marvellously effective intelligence system he had evolved, suited to the locality and based on a technique of visits to public-houses. Thus Mark would relate, as we sat there on the bench in the cabin under the sighing autumn trees, how one night Harvey had been in the bar of the Old Harrow at Gleadless, near Oakes, and to every appearance incapably drunk. He had spilt all his beer down his thick gamekeeper's waistcoat, and had eventually fallen head-long in the passage outside. Among the group of poachers present there, however, had been one who was acquainted with Harvey and his ways, and remained unconvinced and suspicious. Accordingly, he decided to follow the game-keeper, and eventually came back to report that when he had last seen Harvey, he was " running down t'lairn like a greyhound ". . . . Of his abruptness and taciturnity, Mark would give several instances. For example, when old Dr. Bagshawe, a cousin of the owner of Oakes, was a member of the shooting-party, Harvey had instructed Mark, " tak the Doctor down t' drive and post him ".

" How far mun I go ? " Mark had enquired.

" Till you're just right," had come the reply.

And again one night at the Bagshawe Arms, there had been the following conversation.

" Mister Harvey, where do you get your boots made ? "

" I make 'em myself."

" And what dubbin do you use ? "

" Devil's Dung ! "

(Indeed, Harvey's boots were, as will be seen in a moment, a matter of some consequence to others.) And Mark would also repeat with relish old Harvey's slogan, " Hard hats, leather leggings, and umbrellas, damn them ! "

Mark had learnt much of the craft of gamekeeping from Harvey, and entertained a great regard for him. Sometimes Harvey would come to Plumbley Cottage to spend two or three nights, but these visits were rather dreaded by Mrs. Kirkby, who never knew, when Harvey entered the house, whether it was just to pay a call or whether he had come for a visit — never, that is to say, until, without a word, he took his boots off; an act which constituted a formal announcement of his intention to stay. Similarly, he would never say when he meant to leave.

Mark would tell us, too, of deaf old Sam Shaw, Harvey's great antagonist. Shaw lived across the valley, at Ridgeway, and, thus situated between the Sitwell and Bagshawe estates, occupied a fine strategic position for poaching. He possessed an extraordinary, unaccountable sense of the presence of game, and would suddenly announce in the high-pitched, oracular voice of the deaf, " Sure as there's a pheasant in t'woods, it's in yon tree ". And he always proved to be right. . . . For many years he alternated between poaching and gamekeeping, never, until towards the end of his life, remaining for more than a season or two at either. Once, when he applied for the post of gamekeeper at Renishaw, the agent, noticing his deafness, had objected that it would render him useless since he would not be able to hear a shot at night, nor a pheasant go up. Sam's reply was, " I can either catch 'em or keep 'em, Mester ". He obtained the job. . . . Of his most famous encounter, when he was a poacher, with Harvey, this was his tale, as repeated by Mark. " Me and young Ardles was setting snares in Sicklebrook, when someone all at once jumped on me back. I thought it was Ardles having a joke, and carried him at a run for a few yards. Then I looked down, saw t'breeches and leggings, and then I knew it were t'Mester. It weren't long before I unloarded him. We had boarth put t'guns down. I picked his'n up, and he picked mine, and we boarth started to run. I tripped oarver a briar, and he went oarver t'top of me. Before he could get up, I dodged back and got away with his gun." . . . In the end Mark had taken Sam as henchman, and very reliable he became. . . . He died some few years after the time of which I am writing, and his last words to the doctor — also a keen shot — were typical of him : " You've got t'old cock bird down, Doctor, but I don't know whether you're going to bag him now or not ".

Mark would tell us all these things admirably and with gusto, if he were not too sleepy : for by this time he would be at his best. When one met him in the morning and asked how he was, he would usually reply, " Better in 'ealth than temper ". And, indeed, he could grow very heated in the process of protecting the interests of others, as the letter that follows — of this very time — from a gardener to the agent, testifies, as well, perhaps, as carrying across to us something of the sturdy quality of the quarrels upon which he would enter with zest on a good day.

At RENISHAW HALL
Dec. 31, 1909

HONRD SIR

The way I was insulted while at my work this morning, I can do no other than report it, asking you to put a stop to same.

It harose this way, out of me having the dog loose. I was working on the lawn at the time, not knowing but what the dog

was with me, as she seldom leaves me. In the meantime Mr. Kirkby
was advancing through the stable yard, and the dog, having left
me, made a dash at his dog, however not happily biting. I heard
someone shout, and went at once, Mr. Kirkby meeting me after
the fashion of a bull in a rage. I might have been a child, and him
someone in authority to hear him tackle me in front of two of the
Estate Men and some Rough-Looking men he had with him, telling
me I had no right to have the dog loose and was exceeding my
duty and had done so in more cases than one, and he had told
me before I was not to have her loose when he was about and a
Lot More. He insulted me to such an extent that I felt a fool as
one of Sir George's servants.

It is also circulated in the Distric that I have all But lost my
situation which is casting a reflection on my character. This is
no doubt owing to so many strange men coming on the place, and
Mr. Kirkby pointing me out to them as The Man Who Killed the
Rabbits.—I am your most humble servant, HUMPHRY STUBB.[1]

So, of a late afternoon in the cabin in the woods, we listened
to Mark giving his version of such high acts, and the days
passed, both elongated and telescoped by the pleasure I found
in them. As, previously, in the month of September, I had
mooned about, with my eye on everything except a possible
covey, to the dismay of all those who had my true interests
at heart, while the partridges glided past my very nose and
shirred their wings in my ear, so now, similarly, careless, I
trudged through the damp and fragrant woods, where sometimes the bracken grew as high as my shoulder. A sort of
intoxication of happiness, that had no connection with shooting,
but a great deal with poetry, and with that first childish experience of rapture upon the cliffs at Scarborough which I
have described in the first volume of this work, enveloped my
whole being. At times it has seemed to me curious that out of
those long days spent in the open while engaged in a sport for
which I did not care, and at which I proved so great a failure,
was born, a full fifteen years later, a set of poems [2] that belonged so essentially to this particular countryside. Neither
my companions nor myself could have then divined that the
essence of these mornings would be found thus recorded —

[1] Spelling as in the original.   [2] *England Reclaimed.*

and I mention these facts only in order to show what diverse experiences may constitute the raw material of a work of art; it is impossible to tell what ingredients are needed to set up the required fermentation, or how long the essence will take to distil and to mature.

Plumbley Friar was rousing his master. It was time to go; for me to return to the house with its candles flickering through the windows of the dark façade, each flame as small and pure and bright as a bird-song in a wood, and with Henry, in the hall, on the look-out (even here, on the grassy heights, he carried with him, somehow, the suggestion of a sailor on evening watch); time for Mark to return to his cottage at Plumbley, hanging above the woods.

Evening

Of an evening, Mrs. Kembley
Would wait for Mr. Kembley on the hill —
Waiting a little frightened,
For the woods under were so still,
                        So still,
For the mist crept up the nearer valleys,
Whispering white and chill;
Down in them something murmured
            (Was it the distant rill?),
More dusky grew the long green alleys,
And the voices of the woods stabbed, sharp and shrill,
Then the nearest light winked yonder,
            Miles down, by the mill,
And the Roman road ran straight and silent,
Empty and waiting, it seemed, along the hill.
She knew there was no reason to be frightened,
There was nothing for her to fear.
The valleys thus were always whitened
By the mist; the cruel wood voices sounded shrill
Always when all else was still —
But darkness was sidling near,
                        And nearer,
And Mrs. Kembley waited on the hill. . . .

These, then, were among the interludes, brief and few, from the crammer's; at which establishment I passed two years that saw the death of King Edward VII and the Coronation of King George V. I was given by Peter Lycett Green a seat outside the Abbey from which to view the procession. It was a wet June day in England — and can any kind of day be wetter ? — : glory outside the Abbey was a little dimmed : but the arrival of the Abyssinian envoys lit with an African splendour even this darkness. Their lion-skins and cloaks of gilded feathers impressed me more than anything I saw that morning. And it was almost the first time that, thus watching its living representatives drive by and dismount, I realised the continued existence of Ethiopia into the modern world; but before King George's reign was over, we were, even the laziest-minded of us, obliged to take it into account.

In the autumn of the Coronation Year, my grandmother Sitwell died. She had been growing weaker for the past twelve months, and it was sad for those who loved her to see one on whom so many had depended, now dependent on others. Her firm will and able brain had not failed her, but an immense fatigue assailed her. Though her hair was white now, she did not look older, but the passage of the last few years had made her finer, had given a sense of transparency and had deepened her expression of resignation and sweetness. At her death, with the breaking of so many links — for most of her household had been in her service for a lifetime —, Ernest de Taeye and his wife came to live at Renishaw, and, in consequence, the garden began to show a floral splendour and ingenuity it had never before known.

No doubt Ernest missed my grandmother, for though she had not the artist's sense of levels and proportion that my father always exhibited in the continual plans he would put forward for a lay-out, she possessed a much greater love and knowledge of flowers, and was thus able to appreciate immensely all Ernest's cleverness and care. Moreover, she could express her feelings, and tell him of the pleasure she found in the results of his work : whereas this my father could not do. Nevertheless, my father, also, cherished a great regard for Ernest, and showed it in his own way, by erecting three new hot-houses, a practical tribute, and by building for him in an unused kitchen-garden — that had in the eighteenth century been a paddock for the Sitwell race-horses — a mansion.

Assuredly one could not call it, as my father did, a " Gardener's Cottage ". It was too substantial, too stately, for that, and in order to build it the old quarry in the park, from which the stone for Renishaw had been cut, was reopened.

Her new house, with its L-shaped sitting-room, and the beamed oak ceilings in each room, was at once a source of pride, pleasure and dismay to Mrs. de Taeye. Soon from every window issued a scent of new bread, cakes, jam, cordials ; or one saw her hurrying — though this when applied to her is an insufficiently dignified and amplitudinous word — in and out with washing. In one window of the sitting-room, the large pot of Scarborough Lilies which she had brought with her, and which had flowered every year for several decades, seemed to bloom more often for her than once a year, and showed behind leaded panes its smooth vermilion trumpets. This was the only flower she allowed herself in the house. Even when I had been a small child, she had been a bulky Noah's Ark figure : and now she had grown more massive still, which made it yet more difficult for her to uphold the passionate standard of cleanliness that as a Yorkshire freehold-farmer's daughter she had inherited. The spiders, on the other hand, appeared to have grown more nimble, and " Derbyshire spiders " seemed to her a more wily, foreign race than those to which she had been accustomed. And " them naked beams of Sir George's ", as she called them, might have been put up there, out of reach, solely to torture her. . . . Each time she heard a crack from one of them, she looked up, and thought she could detect a new fissure, and a sly face peeping down sideways at her out of it. And the ceiling was so high, difficult to get at, even with a broom. Moreover, directly she looked in, first thing of the morning, she could see all the spiders swarming, like sailors, up their ropes. . . . Oh, they were a crafty lot, she told me. . . . But her nieces would soon be coming to stay with her, and they would help her ; for I think Mrs. de Taeye had a feeling that, in matters concerning her lifelong war against spiders, she could only, in reality, depend upon members of her own family. *They* would understand. Even Ernest she found dull on this one subject.

Certainly Ernest was more interested in the garden than in his own house. During the next twenty years, he came, I think, to love Renishaw more than he had loved Hay Brow. He was an artist and, after the manner of artists, was always at work. When himself not planting or overseeing, yet things growing, or the prospect of their growing, were always in his mind, in the same way that situations, characters and psychologies abide with a novelist. All fruits and flowers were to him obviously the symbols of a divine order and providence, a fresh source of marvel to him every day; and of this trait there were many outward signs. Thus, I loved to watch him, slightly stooping now, with a forward tilt of his large body, and crowned with his Flemish straw-hat with its enormous brim sloping downward all round, crossing from behind the stables to the back of the house, carrying a basket with a bunch of grapes in it, or some peaches plainly almost too delicate to be touched. Somehow, as he almost stumbled along, thrown forward by his weight and height, he conveyed, by the very manner in which he handled the basket, an idea of the beauty and precious inviolability of the fruit. And the way he pointed out to one, too, the monstrous ingenuity of some recently acclimatised arrival from Africa or China, saying, with his slight Flemish accent, in his serious, solemn voice, " Them's a lovely new thing ! ", this emphasised the same quality. He worked without ceasing. Only on Sunday afternoons would he nominally take a little time off, and even then I would see his huge figure, standing still, absolutely motionless, at a distance in the park, and, as I approached nearer and could see his face, would perceive that he was contemplating some tree with an indescribable expression of loving regard, as though in mute praise of all creation.

About the same time that Ernest's house was finished, a break occurred between the Stanislaus Taratoffskys, on the one hand, and my mother and father, on the other. . . . There had been misunderstandings on both sides. The Count and Countess had thought my father a much richer man than he was, a millionaire; an opinion in which they had been confirmed by their visits to Renishaw, for, with its fat flocks and herds, the English landscape, so green and lush, even in August, looked incredibly opulent after the sandy pastures — like those of Aldershot, alternately baked and frozen — afforded by Polish plains, where a few pinched-looking goats scrabbled among the stones : and my mother and father, for their part, had been under the impression that the Count and Countess were — a Count and Countess; whereas now they stood revealed as two of the most able and celebrated card-sharpers in Europe. He was the son of a Latvian chef; while the captivating Countess, though she did not belong to an ancient Danish family as we had believed, had been most certainly recruited from the ranks of an ancient profession. . . . Still, when they had visited us, it must have been *en vacances*, off duty, for my father seldom played cards, and never for money, and my mother only played for the lowest stakes. Besides, they allowed their host and hostess to win, so that their friendship — and I hold that they were genuinely attached to my father and mother — can be seen to have possessed a pure and disinterested nature. Even my father's hypothetical riches served, perhaps, as an ideal, a thing of which to boast, rather than constituting a practical aim. Indeed, the innocent gaiety of this couple when staying with us, during their holidays, reminds me now of the similar high spirits shown by Madame Tellier's girls on their country outing, as described by Maupassant.

My own opinion on the matter was — and is — that the Count and Countess were the most interesting and amiable of my parents' new friends. I found myself unable to censure any particular person for the friendship formed, or for its inevitable rupture. . . . Not so my father. He knew precisely where to lay the blame.

" I must tell you about Lutyens' visit to Renishaw," [1] he wrote to me. " He will plan the Whiston Golf Club with a square terrace between projecting wings. In the centre a square well or court, with a staircase down into it, opposite the entrance. The members can have luncheon or tea on the

[1] For an objective account of Renishaw, and my father at this time, see Mr. Hamilton Temple Smith's letter, which he has kindly allowed me to publish as Appendix D, on page 308.

terrace. The material is to be rubble faced with plaster, and we have saved half the cost of carting.

"Lutyens was very nice about Ernest's cottage, and I think he really liked it. He told me again that he is working at my idea of glass garden statues, making a Venus four feet high for the centre of a fountain. It is to be cast and chiselled, and being a new experiment is sure to be horribly expensive, perhaps nearly a thousand pounds.

"How dreadful all these disclosures are about poor Countess Taratoffsky! What a pity your mother ever took her up!"

B<small>Y</small> the middle of December 1911, it was recognised that I was a failure, too, at the Establishment for Young Gentlemen in which I had spent a little over two years. Indeed, I had contrived that autumn not to pass the Entrance Examination into Sandhurst — in those days no easy matter, especially for one who, like myself, suffers from a race-horse-like eagerness to win, even if engaged against his will in the contest: a nervous craving that shows itself, too, by a curious physical as well as mental intentness, causing pains to run along the arms, the hands, to the extremities of the fingers. After the result of this examination had been announced, a pause of a month or more ensued; during which period I seemed to be in a No-Man's-Land, a vacuum, a spiritual Coventry in Pont Street, London, where my parents had taken a large, hideous and rather haunted house. Every person living in it seemed to be affected by the prevailing atmosphere. Even Henry had lost his tumultuous humour; for he was engaged at this period in the smouldering dispute with his employer which ended, a year later, in his most prolonged temporary disappearance from the scene. The pantry was desolate, void of personality. Even his foil, Pare, appeared unable to rouse him, accustomed though he was by a judicious course of questioning to draw him out. But perhaps this was merely due to Pare's own growing depression; he was suffering more. The light he could see was dwindling; with increasing difficulty he groped his way, and his wife, who during the last twenty years had suffered from long periods of insanity, had grown worse again, so that the restraint put upon her had become more stringent, and he was hardly allowed to visit her. His face was developing a tragic, staring seriousness of its own, broken ever more seldom by the smiles that formerly Henry's tales had brought to it. . . . But Henry's and Pare's new melancholy was scarcely greater in degree — even though they possessed more obvious reason for it — than Sacheverell's and mine. Many matters were going wrong in the household.

No leaf moved. One waited for the storm, and wondered what manœuvres, if any, were taking place behind the screen of silence. . . . Sacheverell was on holiday, and we spent much time together. I was now just turned nineteen, and was promoted to have a shilling a day as pocket-money; it did not go very far. However, we would contrive somehow or other to visit the current exhibitions, or to go roller-skating at Olympia, where the idle of all ages bumped and rolled and clanked and danced along the vast wooden floor to music: for it was the moment of one of the periodic crazes for this form of exercise. In the annexe, I recall, was a colony of midgets on show, the first I had seen: little people three-feet high, who seemed to share among themselves the same features, pudgy, pale and blurred, as though their forms had never quite been crystallised; and one of them, a woman, told fortunes and claimed to be able, from studying you, and holding your hand — which she could hardly reach — to divine your Christian name. And certainly she produced and wrote down on paper *Osbert* and *Sacheverell*, and often, since, I have wondered how the little creature succeeded, for the words can have been by no means easy for her to guess, and, that I know of, we had afforded her no clue to them. . . . Of the exhibitions, the most notable was that of Futurist paintings, organised, at the Sackville Gallery, by Marinetti and his English followers. Prefacing the catalogue to it was a fiery manifesto by the Futurist Boss, calling on the Italians to destroy their ancient monuments; an ideal since realised in another way. There was, however, about both preface and the work shown, combined with a certain lack of sensitiveness, a genuine, if somewhat literary, dynamism, and a breath of prophecy pervaded the whole gallery. The twentieth century, with its unparalleled disasters and catastrophes, had at last smashed and bungled its way into the realms of art. The very titles of the paintings — such as *The Street Entering a House* — exercised, nevertheless, an invigorating effect upon the imagination. But the canvas I best recall from the show is the *Café Pan-Pan* by Gino Severini — the first time I had heard the name of this artist, who was destined to become a great friend of both my brother and myself, and to do much work for us. The picture to which I allude presented, in an admirable convention, the movements of people dancing at a café.

At Olympia, the noise and rhythm lulled the heart-aching sense of expectancy that living with my father and mother in these years promoted. Thus, always waiting for some volcanic disturbance to be sprung on one, it was yet impossible beforehand to tell from which direction the storm would come. . . . Nevertheless, as we clanked round the rink at tremendous speed, to the popular tunes that were now for the first time becoming tinged with ragtime, Sacheverell and I could not help wondering why the next few months, and my place in them, were never discussed. It was difficult, with my inexperience, to foresee in what manner I could be lassooed. The sinister hush continued to prevail, and I was still involved in no plans for my future; which now, suddenly, was never mentioned. I was not even found fault with : nor did my father any longer even invite me to join him in his simple Sunday expeditions, to see the furniture, china and silver on view at the Victoria and Albert, round the marble halls of which he would walk with an air of irritable concentration.

He seldom now visited a picture-gallery, for he sought only for decorative themes, and would say, after contemplating, for example, some great picture by Botticelli or Titian, or a carving by Michelangelo, " I am afraid it gives *me* nothing ", as if to help *him* design a spoon, or the leg of a chair, had been the whole aim of the particular genius at whose work he was looking. . . . But these halls, though he disapproved of their architecture, " far too fussy and unquiet ", constituted a fore-taste of his heaven. For hours he could roam, examining the details of cabinet or table, fountain or fork, as it pleased him : (but what a pity, he reflected, he had not been there at the time these objects were made, to offer his advice !). Sometimes he was accompanied on these tours of inspection by his only friend — though even at that, the friendship was all on one side —, a quivering shadow, with a wide mouth and palsied jaw, and a top-hat quaking on his head, known among us as the Silver Bore. This naïf, middle-aged bachelor, the personification of burgess respectability, had been animated in infancy with a false equivocal energy by some cousin to St. Vitus, so that he often intimidated other equally innocent people by the winks he gave them and the faces he made. He had been at Eton with my father, and had remained attached to him. My father asked him to stay with us for a week every seven years, but when my family were in London, this loyal friend would call and talk to us about Queen Anne Silver — nothing later than Queen Anne was to be regarded, and foreign silver was, to say the best of it, un-English. My father never listened to what he said, and seldom seemed to see him, so that sometimes, as children, we wondered if the lively wobble with which his old friend faced life had not been designed in the first place to catch my father's attention. . . . Nevertheless, my father always referred to him as a sort of God of Good Taste, a bearer of standards. I think they both enjoyed their mute Sunday rambles round the show-cases, my father, still and attentive, looking with swift glances from one object to another; his friend, the lights in his top-hat quivering, grimacing away at staid Queen Anne coffee-pots. The convex polished sides, the curves of urn and cream-jug, so static in themselves, reflected in miniature the caricatured doll of this mouthing figure with his stuttering movements. When faced with the ostentatious work of some, as he considered him, decadent craftsman, such as Lamerie, he would be positively convulsed by emotion. In ten years' time the Silver Bore, whom I here introduce, was destined by fate and the pressure of his own incurable stupidity, which alone in him was solid and stationary, to gibber and wince me out of making a fortune. . . . This the reader will learn in a later volume. . . . But now I could no longer watch his antics; I was not asked. I began to feel, indeed, as if I was not there at all; inaudible, invisible, I waited. The days passed.

Then a portent occurred: a General Sitwell, a cousin of

whom I had never heard previously, or who had only been glimpsed hazily through the mazes of Indian jungles or African scrub that had imperially concealed him, now sprang, fully accoutred, from the pavement of Pont Street. He was a singularly simple, high-principled, courageous and delightful man, and I grew later to appreciate his character — but at the time I did not regard him with much favour. All that I could find out about him was that he came from a stone castle in Northumberland, which had been left to Sir Sitwell Sitwell's younger brother, Frank, the gambler — the boy in the green coat, sitting on the ground and holding up the cards in his hand, in the group by Copley — from whom he was descended. He was, therefore, my third or fourth cousin. . . . He and my father were much closeted together ; the silence that surrounded me became greater. Something, at last, was in the air : what could it be? Even Henry, who usually appeared to possess a special insight into the workings of my father's mind, could not help me. . . . Then, one morning, I found out : for I read, suddenly turning a page of the newspaper that had just arrived, that a 2nd Lieut. F. O. S. Sitwell had been granted a commission in the Yeomanry, and was, from the Yeomanry, attached to a famous regiment of Hussars. . . . For a moment, I wondered who this stranger, bearing my name and the initials that I associated with school-life and had grown to hate so bitterly, could be. . . . Then I understood. . . . I was now under Military Law. For me to refuse to fall in with these plans, which would culminate in my transference, after a few months, from Yeomanry to Hussars, would have rendered me guilty of mutiny. . . . It seemed better to go quietly.

Thus press-ganged or shanghai'd, as it were, from London to Aldershot one snowy afternoon, there followed a brief stretch of my life which I shall never forget. . . . In Aldershot, a polar cold prevailed, and the air was thick with fog of the texture of a polar bear's pelt. Out of these unfathomable, and therefore vast, spaces of frozen fur, of white and yellow, there showed occasionally a horse's teeth or glaring eyes, or a frost-bitten or port-nipped military face, conjured up out of the gloom and darkness, like a materialisation at a séance. It was

a reiteration, I realised at once, in starker and more uncompromising, less interesting terms, of the Blankney theme:
horses in a fog that has no end. I arrived at last at the enormous
barracks, an exotic edifice of iron pillars and verandahs facing
north, that had been designed, it was said, for some swamp or
jungle in Jamaica, and by a typically imaginative, if erratic
gesture of the nineteenth-century War Office, had been erected
here instead. At present it could scarcely be seen, and remained a darker, sadder, denser bulk in the fog, but at the
same time one's ears detected signs of a dreary, ant-like
routine of bustle and fuss. Men shouted, sergeants commanded: bugles every now and then indulged in a brazen,
idiot bray; a band gave bursts of practice, too, from time to
time and, judged from the hollow melancholy of its hooting
and thumping, must be lost for ever in the fog, and yet, by the
same test, must be playing somewhere under the tinny resonance of corrugated iron; in a shed, which, colouring the music,
imparted to it the particular suggestion — except that the sound
was of much greater volume — of a rusty, superannuated
gramophone needle, grinding out a cracked record. Horses,
too, could be heard snorting derisively and stamping within
their iron temples. The fog, the enveloping, all-pervading,
barrack-coloured fog, here, at this point, produced a sort of
amnesia, so that I remember no single activity. I must, I
suppose, have reported my presence to the officer in charge,
but I can recall nothing more until I was in my room, changing
for dinner. To the thought of that meal I clung as to some fact
of accustomed life in uncharted seas or desert. Everything
else was unfamiliar; but dinner, one knew what that was — or
thought one did.

In getting ready for it, though, an antecedent note of
strangeness was struck for me by the difficulty I experienced in
arraying myself in a mess-uniform of the sort wherein both my
hosts and the Yeomanry Regiment to which I belonged, in
their different degrees of splendour, masqueraded. Every part
of the body had to be dragged and pinched and buttoned, and
the boots were so tight that one could neither pull them on nor
take them off, and remained for many minutes in a kind of

seal-like flipper-limbo as to the feet. Only by the kindness and perseverance of Robins — my new servant, who, as I write, some thirty-three years later, is still with me, and of whom I shall, therefore, have more to say — was I able to encase myself in this unaccustomed glory. At last, just in time, I left my room, walking with some difficulty — for this was the first occasion on which I had worn spurs and they kept on catching in my boots, my trousers, in anything with which it was possible to become entangled —, and hurried over to the Mess.

It was the leave season, and only two officers were present: one a taciturn, somnolent, mutely disagreeable Scottish cousin of mine, whom I had never hitherto met, the other a spry, pin-headed younger man, with a long, silky moustache and a cavalry lisp. I never discovered if my cousin had a lisp or not, for I never heard him utter sufficient words to make it possible for me to judge : since a routine of port and a fall on his head once a week from horseback kept him in that state of chronic, numb confusion which was then the aim of every cavalry officer. Yet he must, I realised from the first, be able in some way to receive and communicate ideas, for he had played a riding-on part, plainly enough, in the successful plan for my lassooing that had been engineered by my father and the General. . . . As neither of my companions spoke, either before the meal or at it, except to say, " How d'e do ? ", but ate on through many courses, not so much in gloomy silence — for gloom entails a prior process of feeling, or even of thought or reflection —, but in what is best termed a silence of bestial chaos, such as may have preceded the coming of the Word, and since I was of a sociable disposition and hated, too, to see people so plainly frustrated and unhappy, I determined to " make things go ". I talked on all kinds of interesting subjects and invented a number — on this I must insist — of first-rate jokes for their entertainment. But the surrounding and enveloping silence, an active silence, as it were, and not a mere negation of sound, made it seem gradually as if I were talking to myself in an enormous illuminated cavern, filled with sparkling silver objects. Gowk, my cousin, and Fribble-Sadler said nothing, but slowly drank their claret, and gave each other, from time to time, the sort of glance that the Gorgon Sisters must every now and then have exchanged among themselves when a stranger was present and as yet un-petrified. I talked on. For if complete silence came again, it would be worse, would signify defeat, and so I persisted, now giving my companions a lively and enthusiastic account of the Futurist Exhibition. Still I went on; I felt that I must somehow lift the atmosphere, which was becoming more and more like that of a dramatic monologue by Strindberg I had lately read, entitled *The Stronger*. Port, even port, brought no loosening of tongues, though it flushed the masks — or was that effect, could it have been, caused by anger? . . . It was not for a week that I fully comprehended how unfortunate an impression I had unwittingly created: because this listlessness and coma constituted a source of pride, a regimental tradition. For a period of two years at the least, no young officer must speak, except to his horse — and even then it would be more correct to pat the animal than to say a word to it. (How deeply my adoptive regiment would have resented The Talking Horse of Elberfeld!) When, after the conventional interval had elapsed, he was allowed, once or twice a week, to open his mouth — but only, of course, to an exact contemporary —, it must be to talk of horses, or, perhaps, for such a flight was sometimes, on festivals, allowed, of dogs. . . . Tribal Taboo, that was the meaning of the silence.

The next morning — it must have been morning, in spite of its night-darkness — the bugles, which seemed only just to have stopped, began to bray again, and set off barking, as invariably they did, the miscellaneous packs of dogs in the Officers' Quarters; a whole rasping chorus of bull-terriers, Irish setters, and half-wit, bandy-legged Sealyhams and Aberdeens. . . . Soon Robins was calling me, sidling swiftly about with his quick footsteps and alert movements, and soon we were once more struggling with my boots. Each morning, each day, precisely resembled the last. That year, fog and snow and ice continued for ten weeks, far into the spring, dimming buttons, and tattooing faces with red and blue marks, till they resembled, when you could see them, the masks of the native warriors of Australia or the furthest Pacific isles. Waited on, muzzle and hoof, the horses did not seem to mind the cold. Riding School, the first duty of the day's whole enjoyable round, took place at an hour still lost in the winter darkness — can it have been six o'clock or five ? At any rate, so dark was it still that one could only *feel* the snow, not see it. In the centre, under the arc-lamps, shining like moons through their circles of peat-dust that gave them aureoles, stood the riding-master, red-nosed, but silent, large-featured and stiff as an Easter Island figure. Though his chief criticised us little, the sergeant was voluble enough, his language vivid, as he shouted at the rolling, flustered recruits cantering round in a circle without saddles, " Stop bumping about on your bloody backsides there like a set of Piccadilly 'ores ". . . . In that high-roofed tin barn I learnt a whole repertory of helpful circus tricks *à la Russe*; such as jumping, without saddle or stirrups, over hurdles with my arms akimbo, or picking up at the gallop, from under the hoofs of the singularly vicious and oafish horse I had been allotted, a handkerchief which I had been obliged to throw down in the filthy peat-dust. To be able to perform this last feat, I was assured, would be of inestimable value, both to the country and to myself, in the next war, when it came.

At about 7.30, after, as it seemed, many hours, guided as to direction by instinct, I shuffled, as quickly as bruises and stiffness would allow, through the fog, across the darkness, to breakfast ; always a less talkative meal than dinner. . . . Again, bugles were braying, and already the band practice had started somewhere in the iron torture-chamber across the way. It continued all through every day ; bassoons, trombones, trumpets, droning on, drums thumping, steering an unpredictable course, until abruptly stopped by the enraged Bandmaster, but only to start again, through the intricacies of selections from *Véronique* and *Our Miss Gibbs*, or of a march by Sousa, equally complicated and subtle. Directly after breakfast, there followed pointless but elaborate manœuvres that continued for hours in the Long Valley, as it is called, which was at this season a white steppe. I could never get through these exercises without incurring public humiliation, since my horse, though odious, was well trained. Thus, when the Commanding Officer used to send for me, as he often did — and, I may add, with no view to congratulating me on my efforts —, this agile and vindictive beast would often set off towards him at the fastest gallop, meanwhile, by one of his tricks causing me to measure my length somewhere in the intervening wastes of snow and sand, and there abandoning me, would arrive, the cynosure of all eyes, the solitary half-centaur moving through this vast expanse, panting and foaming, in front of the great man.

When we returned to barracks, where the braying and droning still sounded, louder than ever, from under the tin roof, the officers, including myself, had to preside over *Stables*; a function which, comparable to the morning and evening services in church, took place twice a day. Similarly, the Stables in the morning were the most important, and all the hierarchy visited us, Major-General, Brigadier, and, without fail, the Commanding Officer, to see the equine gods being tended by their slaves. (Myself, I found the stench of ammonia within the precincts nauseating, and it induced in me a kind of asthma.) . . . When Matins were finished, came luncheon, and the munching of good food in silence; after which ensued two hours' drill on the Barrack Square, when the snow had melted, or, before that season at last arrived, in the shelter of one of the tropical verandahs that had been built originally, as I have said, to snare that rare bird, the North Wind. With blue noses, chattering teeth and frozen feet, we stuck it. Then came Evensong in the stables, followed, if we were fortunate, by a lecture on *The Care of the Horse Through the Ages, The Place of the Horse in the Twentieth Century, How the Horse will Replace Mechanical Means of Transport*, or some kindred subject.

In the course of these lectures, we did not hear much of the war that was being prepared for us, except that on occasion a lecturer would give us a discourse on *Cavalry Charges in the Coming War*. He would tell us that he hoped it would constitute no breach of trust if he informed us in strictest confidence that the authorities knew that a war was drawing near on the Continent, that we should become involved in it, and that it would be a Cavalry War. At last the Horse would, thank God, come into its own. . . . But we must be prepared, and must not think it was going to be a war after the style of the Peninsular War — that was a mistake we often made. We ought to thank our stars — that was the phrase he used — for the fact that the Boer War had been recently vouchsafed us as a model and dress-rehearsal for this approaching conflict. In many ways, Europe resembled the Great Veldt, and the people of the Veldt, too, resembled those of Europe — and from these premises, he would branch off into tactical and strategic discussions which I could not follow. . . . Otherwise, we heard little of the conflict that was just over time's horizon — and yet, people must have expected a war : and here let us draw a welcome breath away from Aldershot, for I find my old friend Major Viburne, whom, in the pages of *The Scarlet Tree*, the reader has already met several times, writing the letter reproduced below. But, before proceeding to read it, we must first pause to note the warning of Fascism which emerges from between its lines : a tone all the more unexpected, because this poor old man, physical no less than mental prototype of Low's stock figure, *Colonel Blimp*, had nothing, one would have said, to gain or hope for from Capitalism. Leading a threadbare existence, he yet showed himself an ardent champion of the system which condemned him to it. We may also wonder at his air of " being in the know " : whereas himself must have been aware — and have known I knew — that he was in no position to hear anything : because he possessed now, after being stranded there for fifty years, no acquaintance outside the town of Scarborough. Such news as was his, he derived from reading the two periodicals he took in, one the *Scarborough Post*, the other Horatio Bottomley's *John Bull*. . . . There is almost something gallant in the impudence with which he passes off his own views, founded on the reading of these two papers, as facts.

39 BULLER ROAD, SCARBOROUGH
Feb. 17, 1912

MY DEAR OSBERT,

I have just got back from Whitby, where I was addressing an audience mostly composed of working men, in the Old Town Hall

last night. I spoke on Home Rule and Current Topics. I wonder
if any good will come of Haldane's week-end visit to Berlin.[1]
Personally, I think there must be a war between this country and
Germany sooner or later, and it had better come sooner. A good
big war just now might do a lot of good in killing Socialist nonsense
and would probably put a stop to all this labour unrest. We are
within measurable distance of a coal strike which will cost quite
as much as a big war, besides paralysing trade, and making stagnant
the industries of the country.

The silly war in Tripoli is, I hear, costing the Italians a loss of
many men. The Italians cannot tackle it as it ought to be tackled,
and the Arabs and Turks are more than a match for them in the
open field.

I expect you will be out on strike duty next — at least your
regiment may be one of those sent from Aldershot if there is a big
strike.

The Government is suffering from internal schism — Asquith is
the stumbling block, and Lloyd George means to get rid of him if
he can. Then in that case probably for a time Sir Edward Grey
might be Premier, but of course Lloyd George wants the Premier-
ship himself. Winston also would like the post, so, for the present
possibly neither of them will get it. It is a nice muddle altogether,
and most deplorable. Bonar Law shows signs of fighting and hard
hitting. Much strength to his elbow.—Ever yrs, REGINALD W.
VIBURNE.

I particularly admire the manner in which the old gentleman deplores muddles that himself had only just invented,
and which thus existed only in his own head. Nevertheless,
through his letters runs, though entangled, as in the Oracles
of the Delphic Sibyl, with much nonsense, a true vein of
prophecy. In this he was representative of that class of old
gentlemen who, when I was young, used, since they had
nothing else to do, to sit in armchairs in club windows, making
prophecies to which, because of their patent absurdity, nobody
listened, and which yet always proved to be right in the end.

[1] The Haldane Mission. Lord Haldane, who had been educated partly in
Germany, and was in touch therefore with German thought, had been sent by
the Cabinet to Berlin, to see if the tension between England and Germany could
be reduced, and particularly to try to persuade that country to reconsider her
programme of great additions to the Imperial Navy. His mission, unfortunately,
did not succeed.

So, Major Viburne many times prophesied to me the coming of the World War, of the Russian Revolution, and, descending to smaller matters, that a certain great newspaper-proprietor would finally go mad.

But now I must return to Aldershot, to change: for at half-past seven a bugle-call announced that dinner was on its way, and at ten to eight another, that it was time to go across to the Mess-Room. . . . At moments I wondered if these braying tongues had only been instituted, out of a kind of vanity, to call attention to the silence that prevailed among the officers. Certainly music fulfilled for them some function of this order. When, for instance, guests from other cavalry regiments were fortunate enough to be invited to sample our particular brand of speechlessness, a small string orchestra would set the prevailing silence, as if it were a jewel, by playing selections from one of the musical comedies of the day. It was at these times that one felt loneliest. . . . And so it came about that one night, unable any longer to bear the insufferable boredom, I called for a bottle of champagne and discovered how the darkness could be artificially lightened. This was the first time I had drunk wine since the occasion described elsewhere, when, as a boy, recovering from a long illness, I had been so heartrendingly implored by the doctors to take to drink. Then I had not liked wine, but now it seemed to alter the whole of life, banishing worries about the following day, enclosing one in the golden circle of the present. I began at last to understand the chapter on port in *The Egoist*, a novel I had always much admired, except for these two pages, which had hitherto conveyed nothing to me. The Riding School at five the next morning receded into the distant and pleasant glow of the future; even the thought of the boxing contest in which, for the amusement of the mum and swollen faces round me, I had after dinner to take part, ceased to distress me. (But I had never realised, all the same, until then, how humiliating had been the lot of a gladiator.) And when the moment came I hit out with a will. Only physical force could impress these people, interest them, or lift them from the torpor whereto regimental tradition and years of training had brought them,

up to a height where once more they smiled, and almost framed
a syllable. Their tongues had become atrophied from disuse.

When the snows melted and the fogs dissipated, it was only
then that the whole horror of Aldershot, and the arid fantasy
of the life round me, grew visible. For the first time I could see
clearly, after ten weeks, the full uniform of the Regiment,
when occasion arose for the officers to wear it, a pseudo-
Hungarian caprice of frogs and flaps and feathers designed by
the Prince Consort in exotic mood, or perhaps merely in an
attempt to escape humdrum : for the first time I perceived the
endless array of yellow brick buildings and iron huts painted a
port-flushed purple, squatting among the trees in a perpetual
khaki mist of dust. Little Prussia in its very essence, all round
lay sand-dunes and fir trees, and indeed the only fit purpose
of such country seemed to be as a combined Reserve and No-
Man's-Land in which to collect obsolete types, and set up
rifle-ranges and targets. And with what precision has the
unrivalled genius of the English tongue found a name for the
place. . . . *Aldershot*, All-der-shot; how did such closely
fitting sounds come to be invented for this either bleak or
burning capital of English militarism ? (That the militarism
was inefficient I admit, but not that it was non-existent.) The
syllables *Alder* suggest, almost as if by magic formula, the universality of the boredom — while *shot* puts *finis* to the word
with the emblematic crack, as well as the meaning, of a rifle
bullet. It is a word smart and neat as men on parade, jejune
as a General's mind, desolate as a cavalry officer's pleasures ;
while, in addition, it has about it something appropriately
empty, hopelessly inept. . . . Yet to everyone the word does
not evoke the same images, for when, some years later, during
the season of Russian Ballet, which opened in October 1918 at
the Coliseum, my brother continually had to leave the theatre
early, explaining, as he got up, to Diaghilew, by whose side
we sometimes sat in the stalls, that he had " to return to
Aldershot by midnight ", the great impresario eventually
asked, " Qu'est-ce que c'est, cette Aldershot — c'est une
femme ? "

To me, certainly, Aldershot was a hard mistress. The climate, too, matched the name miraculously. And the Barracks, witheringly cold throughout the winter, red-hot in summer, completed the effect, so that scarlet, as for clowns' noses, was supplied by one extreme for half the year, and by the other for the rest of it. Moreover, once or twice the two combined in the same day, with the result that I contracted what I took to be frost-bite — but I suppose was merely an Aldershot super-chilblain — in the early morning, drilling on the Square, and, in the same place, a genuine sunstroke in the afternoon.

During this time, I was receiving almost daily letters from my father. He dismissed his secretaries now almost as soon as they reached the house from the station, and the poor men seemed to have only a single quality in common, an inability to learn shorthand or to use the typewriter, so that, in addition to other results, such as the irritable state of mind to which they reduced their employer and the fact that no correspondence was ever completed, one consequence was that the letters he dictated arrived for me every morning addressed in a different hand, thereby preventing me from realising, until I had opened the envelope and had begun to read the contents, from whom it came. Then my heart would start to bump, for I was already learning to dread these letters, and the instructions they gave me as to how to spend my allowance : most of which was apparently to be dedicated to the cult of the horse. Moreover, the financial details contained in them muddled me. The annual amount I was to receive had been calculated on an ingenious basis, the method employed being to strike an unhappy medium between the value — translated into terms of modern money, on a system also devised by my father — of the allowance customarily made to eldest sons by Lords of the Manor at the time of the Black Death (it worked out, I recollect, down to a groat) and that recommended to him by Major Gowk as a fitting sum for an officer of the present day. . . . First of all, before I pass to giving a letter of this time, so that the reader may judge for himself of the waste of money on things and animals I detested that my new career imposed on me, let me instance another, of a period some five years later, when he took a furnished house on lease from me for a few months, to show how closely he could make his letters resemble the old mathematical posers of school-days or of popular magazines : " Take a herring and a half, and divide by the number first thought of ".

My dearest Osbert,

 I have paid 6–10–0 for the telephone and 8–8–11 to the Gas Light and Coke Company. Total 14–18–11.

 We shall have the house from the 17th November to the 20th December ; 33 days — 4 weeks and five days, which, at twelve guineas a week, comes to 59–8–0. You have had £25–0–0, which with 14–18–11 makes 39–18–11 from 59–8–0, leaving 19–9–1 still to pay.

 I enclose cheque for this, but retain the £5 due for the cook, as other demands may come in.

 The first brief letter I received at Aldershot from my father contained orders for me to show him my cheque-book : commands repeated at frequent intervals during the ensuing years. But the second to which I have referred, and which follows, plainly affords clues to the life I was obliged to lead. Dated *Feb.* 12, 1912, it runs :

 . . . With regard to the clothes, they will be paid for by you out of the allowance. I will talk to you about the mackintosh. Archie Gowk's calculation was that the total amount of £530, which tallies near enough to yours and my own, should be made up as follows :

		£
(1)	Mess bills (including all subscriptions, sporting and otherwise)	170
(2)	First servant and laundry	30
(3)	Stable expenses	150
(4)	Clothes and Uniform upkeep	50
(5)	All other expenses	130
		530

 I have therefore arranged to pay you £530, but if you receive pay, you must pay back to me what you receive.

 Coutts and Co. may take as long as ten days from the date of the order, before you receive the cheque-book from them, but as you have plenty of time in which to pay your Mess bill, and as the ten days are nearly over, I think you can afford to wait.

And here, at the introduction of their name, I must take this opportunity of thanking Messrs. Coutts & Co. for their imaginative understanding of situations and individuals, and for the support they have afforded me from time to time, ever since I was eighteen and first became their customer. But for their coming to my rescue when it was necessary, I should now be working at some job for which I possessed no aptitude. Indeed, as I have frequently assured them, they have shown me more kindness and comprehension than did my own father. When businesses were content to lose everything except their profits, this great institution kept its soul alive. Throughout three centuries, those who work in it have maintained the same name for personal kindness and personal contact and, no doubt for that reason, have numbered among their clients many grateful artists and writers. In a day when it seems popular to attack the present methods of banking, I must state my opinion and experience, and add that, to my belief, there is more of character and rectitude, enterprise and independence contained in this one ancient house than in the whole of the attacking body. Not only the chiefs, but every one of Messrs. Coutts' clerks and employees, understands and takes pride in its traditions.

The dreary round of Aldershot continued. Hating every moment of it consumedly, in my turn I was much disliked. There could be no doubt that I was by a long head the most unpopular of the officers ; though several others among them were regarded, for one reason or another, with suspicion by their comrades. Usually, the unpopular emerged from this state after the passage of a few years. Even the Adjutant of the time — he had been away the night I arrived — had still the lingering cobwebs of unpopularity clinging to him : in his case, the reasons for it being that he was an unusually intelligent man, liked conversation and, worse yet, talked French as easily as he spoke English. Moreover, he paid a great deal of atten-

tion to his hands, in the way a foreign officer might, and this
made his brother-officers more uneasy. I used to watch his
shrewd, keen, rather thin face, as he pared his nails, much in
the way I have seen Italian officers do. We seldom, alas,
exchanged many words, for he was always busy. . . . This
officer was Louis Spears, later author of one of the best books
concerning the First World War, General, and first Minister
to the Republics of Syria and the Lebanon.

For the rest, a few young officers, like myself, attached from
the Yeomanry, or sent here for a course, and to whom, therefore,
since they did not belong to the Regiment, the taboo of silence
did not extend its magic, drifted in and out. Among them
were one or two old friends from Eton: Ednam,[1] whose genial
disposition, and keen sense of humour, seemed temporarily to
make this kind of life more bearable, because he was able to
impart the sense that things would go right if managed rightly,
and Alvary Gascoigne, whose generosity and zest for life have
consistently raised the tempo of it for others. He was, I
recollect, very active, and never wasted a moment of his leave,
being always ready to set off for Monte Carlo, or some equally
distant pleasure city, at a moment's notice, on Friday afternoon, travelling day and night, and returning to Aldershot,
without a night's rest, in time for early parade on Monday.
For myself, I appeared to get no leave (I suspect my father had
warned Gowk of his son's pleasure-loving nature, " inherited
from his mother's family "), and London was the place I
craved.

Ednam and Gascoigne would come sometimes to my room
to talk, for I had begun to avoid the silence of the Ante-Room as
much as possible. But usually we were kept too busy, and for
conversation and human contact I had to rely mostly on
Robins, my new servant: someone in whom it was possible to
place implicit trust. In any attempt to give a picture of him,
with his small, trim, energetic figure and shrewd green eyes, it
is his quickness, the rapidity of his movements and of his mind,
that in the first place must be emphasised; a quality made
more remarkable by the fact that his maternal grandfather

[1] Now 3rd Earl of Dudley.

had been a shepherd on the South Downs, a profession not usually associated with speed. No doubt from him Robins derived his accompanying steadiness. With great powers of hard work and a great liking for it, he was as thrifty as a French peasant, and I have often wondered whether French blood may not flow in his veins, for his mother's name was Duly, perhaps a corruption of Dulau, and her home was in Sussex, just across the water from France. Speed was certainly his element. In those days, in the Officers' Quarters, he often seemed to come down the stairs and be in my room almost before I had called him, and once there, he darted about with swift, crab-like movements. Even now, thirty-three years later, I often hear him take a flight of stairs with such a rush that his wife calls out to remonstrate with him, " Frederick, you darned fool, don't come down the stairs so fast. You'll break your neck one of these days. Remember, you're not twenty now." To which protest he always replies, " I'll jump over your head at ninety ! " He is, and always was, inclined to take a disillusioned view of mankind, saying " I *know* them ", for he began work at eleven years of age, and joined his mother's cousin in running a fish shop in Hailsham at fifteen. In this way, he came to understand people as well as know fish ; and his tongue, rapid as its master, is keen and can be cutting : but in action no kindness is too much trouble for him. And I am most grateful to him for his many years of service, and not least for his support and counsel while at Aldershot.

What little leisure I gained occasionally then, through some error in the official calculation of the time-table of duties, I spent in my room, reading. These were my most pleasant moments in the week, and even today I can remember what I read, particularly — for I had so few half-hours in which to read that one book lasted me for weeks — the *Clayhanger* series, in three volumes, by Arnold Bennett. I sat in an arm-chair by the fire, and got up out of it every two or three minutes to put a record on the large hornless gramophone, which had already made a twenty-pound hole in my allow-ance and hopelessly upset my father's calculations as to the ideal way of spending it. For many years subsequently he would refer to its purchase, as to some boundary-mark of iniquity: " It was at the time you bought that gramophone ". Meanwhile, it effectively protected me against the clamour of the Barracks. . . . And so it is, to this day, that the inappropriate rhythm of Viennese waltzes is mingled in my head with the grocer's or mercer's world of Arnold Bennett's novels. They seemed wonderful to me then, with their lists of facts and their painstaking analysis of materials. But, looking back, truth compels me to admit that, with one exception, the prophets of my young days seem from this distance to be an uninspiring band. There was Wells, a man of genius, with his naïf social paradise, served up many times, but unvaried in its ingredients : the scientific hero, who had discovered how to blow up old worlds in a new way, and his emancipated mistress, togged up in essential tweeds. Their appearance in the divorce court assumed in these novels the place of honour held, let us say, in the books of Charles Dickens, by a wedding in church : his earlier romances, such as *The Island of Dr. Moreau*, or *The Time Machine*, were drenched in nightmare, and contained, as do dreams, many twinges of future truth. There was Arnold Bennett, giving us detail after detail about life in the Siege of Paris, or about the way in which to run hotels ; there was Galsworthy, never a hero of mine, with his neat pictures of middle-class life, where the parlour-maid always knew her place, and with his sense of social injustice, which a little resembled the repulsion felt by a well-brought-up young girl on learning the facts of life. Only Shaw, with his genius and his laughter, towered then above his contemporaries and juniors, as he still does today, a lifetime later, a Prince and Cardinal of Literature, the greatest European figure and writer since Voltaire.

In the Ante-Room, it was, of course, impossible to read anything except the *Morning Post* or the *Pink 'Un*, and no-one spoke, except to mumble grumpily to himself. But one day, when I was sitting there, I watched a Major reading the newspaper, and noticed his face begin suddenly to swell, twitch and turn plum-purple. At last — I had not dared to break the silence and ask if I could be of any help — he threw down the rustling pages, and appeared to be making a struggle to frame words. Seeing this, a brother-officer came immediately to his aid, patting him on the back, and saying, " What's the matter, Snorter, old boy ? " — or Piggy, or Pongo, or whatever may have been his regimental, taboo nickname. I listened carefully, and gathered the gist of what he was trying to tell us. He had been reading, it appeared, the report of an incident on board a ship going to South Africa, when someone had insulted Paderewski. " I wish to God the feller'd killed him," the tongue-tied Major bellowed, that organ at last freed by emotion from its years of atrophy. " I don't believe he could play a choon if he wanted to ! He ought to be shot, that — Padder-oosky ! "

Such remarks as this, and the opportunities I was given to hear them, in the future afforded me, perhaps, a certain advantage as a writer. I have seen so many different types of human being : whereas other poets — and I say poets precisely, because I can claim never to have written a book, or a short story, or an essay that I did not conceive as if it were a poem, and in that resides the value, such as it is, of my work — have for the most part been able to spend their time with those of congenial disposition, whom they have elected of their own free will to see. A poet is, really, only interested in other poets. But I was obliged to get on as well as I could with those among whom I had been thrown. It is true that the process was bad for health and temper — which, again, with artists is the same thing —, but it enabled me to plumb the depths of the real and active hatred that the stupid in England, who often, because of their dumbness, could not express it except in action, cherish towards art and beauty in every form. About it there is something daemonic and elemental : as a force, a power, it must be treated with respect. This blind hatred of art contains something that almost partakes of art. The persecution of poets, the smashings by housemaids — when they existed —, the tidiness of Town Councils, with their cement edgings to woodland roads, the uprooting of wild flowers and then the throwing of them down where they have been plucked, the crusade against rare birds, the dumping of power-stations against cathedrals, the invention of open-cast coal-mining, and of ever more devastating weapons of warfare, all these are not isolated and sporadic phenomena, but part of the perpetual warfare between harmony and disharmony, between those who create beauty. and those who create chaos. The chipped plate, the banging door, the maimed animal, the bombed cathedral, are each, though different in degree, part of the constant rebellion against perfection. War, which is the crowning of chaos, war, with its squalid virtues of black-out, of jealousy (". . . he has more jam than me ! ") and of skin-flint thrift, always intensifies the innate Philistinism of every race : but the Philistine is stronger and more horrid, because armed with right, in northern countries where, as in England, there has been a Puritan reaction.

The artist has throughout his career to fight the Philistine. And my life in these early days at least enabled me to feel and appreciate the immense negative energy, if I may so term it, of the opposition. I, for one, never underrated it. I was able to realise — indeed, it was impossible to avoid doing so — the virulence of the feeling existing between those who hate beauty and those who love it. Yet perhaps it is this evil thing that has always given strength to English artists — those who survived. For the persecuted are apt to become strong in faith through persecution, and to conquer. Shelley, Byron and others, these reached through it an enriching of their quality — but that was not why the stupid persecuted them.

From time to time I still tried to reach London. Though only thirty-six miles away, the capital seemed infinitely distant. There were many things there this spring and summer that I wanted to see ; among them, the second Post-Impressionist Exhibition and a small show of drawings and paintings by Augustus John ; there were operas to hear, and concerts. I wanted, also, to keep in touch with the few friends I possessed, and from whom my incarceration at Aldershot cut me off no less effectually than a decree of banishment to Siberia. In June, therefore, I asked for the two or three days to which I had become entitled. . . . But when the Commanding Officer enquired where I wished to spend it, and received the reply

" *London* ", I could see the look of genuine consternation and amazement that passed over his face. " London ! " he plainly said to himself. " Imagine wishing to leave Aldershot, earthly paradise that it is, for so mean a city ! "

" But what can you do there ; what can you want to do ? There's nothing to do," he reiterated in a tortured voice, and with a soldier's simple vocabulary. When he had recovered sufficiently from the shock, he refused permission. But I think his story of " the Young Officer who wanted to go to *London* ! " went the rounds : for Generals, when they visited us, surveyed me carefully, as if I were a dangerous wild beast, and the senior regimental officers seemed to regard me with increased distaste. " What can be the state of mind ", their eyes clearly goggled the message, " of a young man who wishes to leave Aldershot to spend a few days in London ! " *London!* Why, you could not even kill anything there ! (It was tantalising, too, to see all those living creatures behind their bars, walking, pacing, climbing, swinging about in the Zoological Gardens, and not be able to get at them, not to be able to fire a single shot !) No huntin' : no shootin' : no polo, even. . . . Of course, there was always Tattersall's, that they admitted, but it need not occupy more than a single afternoon. You could be back in the dear old Mess in time for dinner.

I persisted in my efforts, however, and in the end, in late June, succeeded in reaching London one evening, with a day or two to spare. I had beforehand booked a seat for Covent Garden, where there was a season of Russian Ballet, as it was termed. I went out of curiosity, for I possessed no acquaintance with ballet — except that which I have described in *The Scarlet Tree*, when Henry conducted me, as a boy, to the Alhambra —, and little with opera. Indeed, I had only been inside Covent Garden once, the summer before, when I had first dined with my cousin, Irene Denison, at her father's London house, St. Dunstan's, a Regency palace, set in a vast circle of baked and honey-coloured lawns.[1] That occasion

[1] This fine house had belonged to the 3rd Marquess of Hertford, and was said to have been the mansion in which, in the pages of Thackeray's *Vanity Fair*, Lord Steyne's gay and equivocal parties took place. In the summer of 1909, Anna

still remains with me, for it was a golden, hazy evening in late July and the heat, I remember, had affected many of the animals in the Zoological Gardens near-by with a nostalgia for Africa, so that they were roaring and growling and braying their hearts out, and we seemed to be feasting among the swamps or deserts of the Equator. I recall that hour, too, because the only other person at dinner was the Kaiserin's Mistress of the Robes, a large Junkeress, tightly buttoned into pale velvet, the colour of German eyes, and all through the meal, with the persistence of her race and type, she slowly unfolded, beneath the tropical sounds of trumpeting and leonine bellows, in an unemphatic voice, but with a strong German accent, the plot of *Madame Butterfly*, the opera that was to be performed. Nothing could stem that relentless pressure. How well she knew the story, and no wonder, for she had been taken to Covent Garden many times that summer, and the same work had been given night after night, with scarcely a break! (The opera season should have been over long ago, but so many of its regular patrons had stayed on in London, and so many foreign visitors had been attracted to the capital this year for the Coronation, and had remained to enjoy the subsequent festivities, that the final night was 31st July.) When we reached the Londesboroughs' box the Junkeress had only got as far, in unrolling the story, as the beginning of Act II. But now she stopped to examine the crowded house.

The audience at Covent Garden was in a state of genteel excitement: since two famous stars of the day were performing, Bassi as Pinkerton, Destinn in the title rôle of Madame Butterfly. The very absurdity of the performance, its stilted realism, its playful cries and tears caught in a note, made it all the more memorable. Albeit we had entered King George V's

Pavlova had made her first appearance in England on a stage specially constructed in the ballroom here. She had been performing at the Châtelet in Paris, under Diaghilew, and my Aunt Londesborough engaged her to dance after dinner before King Edward and Queen Alexandra. It is probable that my uncle had seen her in Russia, which he had recently visited as head of the British Firemen. St. Dunstan's was pulled down just before the 1939 war by the Woolworth heiress, and a Woolworth-Georgian residence was run up in its stead. The garden in 1911 covered some eighteen acres, a very large space for London.

reign, this was the apogee of Edwardian opera, both in the music and in its rendering. In a sense, it was perhaps a pity that we did not, that evening, hear Caruso and Melba singing in *La Bohème* instead, as I heard them subsequently: but neither was performing in London that year. Destinn was certainly a finer artist, but Melba and Caruso, when, fat as two elderly thrushes, they trilled at each other over the hedges of tiaras, summed up in themselves the age, no less than Sargent netted it for others. Not only was Caruso as natural a singer as the thrush he resembled, the blackbird, or the conventional nightingale to which he was compared, but contradictorily, for all its lack of art, his voice, carrying in its strains, in the sound of those notes which he was able to attain and hold as could no other singer of that or of a later day, the warm breath of southern evenings in an orange grove, and of roses, caught in the hush of dusk at the water's edge, possessed, as well as a high degree of technique, a certain kind of art. Of Melba the same cannot be said. . . . Her magnificent voice was not invariably true, having about it something of the disproportion of the Australian continent from which she had emerged. But at least it can be claimed for her that, with her ample form lying on a couch, she made a surprising and unforgettable type of romantic consumptive.

In *Madame Butterfly*, Destinn was no less unusual as a Japanese geisha. Yet it would be idle to pretend that she was not effective and even moving in the part. *Madame Butterfly* is an absurd opera, the music has its own faults, but was there ever a score more vocal, or more permeated with the contemporary feeling? This was, as I have said, the first time I had heard an opera, and it was rendered even more interesting for me than it would otherwise have been by my recollection of having seen the composer, Puccini, the previous year, walking on the ramparts, the top of the stout walls — so broad that they support an avenue of full-grown trees — which enclose the little city of Lucca, and separate it from its prosperous and verdant plain. This town, so famous in the eighteenth century for its opera, had been his birthplace, and, as he strolled under the flowering chestnuts, with their pallid torches showing ivory white among the thick leaves, he was treated as if he were an Emperor. People went bare-headed in his presence.

Yet, for all the atmosphere that this performance, from the distance at which I stand today, brings back to me, it was, nevertheless, just one more theatrical entertainment. . . . And so, on this occasion, too, when I had booked a solitary seat for Covent Garden, I had expected, I suppose, something of the same kind : for I was aware that, as a rule, ballet was interpolated in operas, and I knew nothing of the programme. . . . Detained at Aldershot, I did not reach the theatre until the moment when the curtain was going up, for the first time in London, on *L'Oiseau de Feu*. I had been so tired by the day's riding that I had nearly decided not to go — but directly the overture began to be played, I came to life. Never until that evening had I heard Stravinsky's name ; but as the ballet developed, it was impossible to mistake the genius of the composer, or of the artist who had designed the setting ; a genius plainly shared, too, by the chief dancers and the choreographer. Genius ran through the whole of this ballet. Nevertheless, Stravinsky towered above the others, a master. It may be that today the music of this particular piece sounds almost traditional when compared with his later work, such as *Le Sacre du Printemps* or *Les Noces*, but as I heard it and watched the accompanying dances, I was aware that for the first time I had been given the opportunity of seeing presented upon the stage a work of art, imbued with originality and with the spirit of its own day ; not a tawdry glut of colour and rushing movement (like Reinhardt's spectacles, that had somehow burst right out of the theatre into enormous barns like Olympia — with them I was already acquainted), but a performance in which every gesture, every line, every tone, meant something ; a work of art that could not have existed before, and would cease to be given in its perfection, within the brief season of the dancers' finest span. Because, for the first time, I was able to watch, in addition, the dancing of great artists, Karsavina, and Adolf Bolm, who was superb in his part. Karsavina, so beautiful today, was then at the height of beauty and of her career, the greatest female dancer that Europe had seen for a century. The very poise of her lily-like neck was unforgettable, and there was about her shape and movements a perfection of grace that for the first time made me realise how near are the Russians, for all their hyperborean extravagances and childish glitter, to the ancient Greeks. Those working in the fields of art possess the same saturation with it that sets the Greeks apart as a race; and with Russians, as with Greeks, the theatre is the real dynamic centre of their arts. . . . The long, plangent ripple of the harpstrings as the Firebird entered appeared to offer to one some hidden meaning, just as the gathering of ogres and sinister satellites round the crouching, wasp-like figure of their baleful master, Koscheii (played that night by the great Cecchetti), seemed to bear some relation to life as I knew it. . . . The gates of life could be opened, if one possessed the key (what could I do?), and the powers of evil, chaotic and uncreated, ill-proportioned and anomalous, could be put to flight by one feather plucked from that rare bird. The raging of the old tyrant, and his sycophantic cronies and dependents, *could* be faced. Now I knew where I stood. I would be, for so long as I lived, on the side of the arts. (They needed champions as well as exponents; at least my life in Barracks had taught me that.) I would support the artist in every controversy, on every occasion. . . . And in my bones I felt that this opportunity would most frequently come my way: — but, thinking it over coolly, *how*? . . . To what could I turn my hand or eye? I possessed no gifts, no capacities, little perseverance, few friends, I was ill-educated, and found myself tied hand and foot to a way of life I detested. Among my own generation, I knew no-one of creative genius — except two most rare, but as yet unfledged artists, my own brother and sister. And their work still lay, like mine, embedded in the matrix of the future. . . . *What could I do?*

Book Six :: The Rose and The Thorn

> " The mind of man is far from the nature of a clear and
> equal glass . . . nay, it is rather like an enchanted glass, full
> of superstition and imposture . . ."
>
> FRANCIS BACON, *Advancement of Learning*

Chapter One
THE DOMINION OF THE SENSES

AT Aldershot, throughout suffocating summer days,
ice-cold sandstorms swept over the Long Valley, raising
high in the air strange khaki ghosts that sped subsequently
through the town, like the spectres that appear to travellers in
the Gobi Desert. Indeed, this English valley, which I so greatly
detested, might have belonged as easily to that dread and
distant region (in which, some instinct tells me, lies the whole
future of militarism) as to the Prussian plains, of which at
other times it seemed a part, physically no less than spiritually.
Further, a feeling of extreme antiquity, as well as of arid
military tradition, permeated the whole stretch of it, always
veiled though it was by a screen of grit that peppered and
numbed the senses, and, in consequence, it came to me as no
matter for wonder to learn, much later, that here in prehistoric
times neolithic man had fashioned his armouries — indeed, all
at which one could be surprised was that arrow-heads and stone
axes were not, two years later, being issued by the War Office
for use in the field against the enemy. Militarism, after the
fashion of many evil weeds, springs from deep roots in a shallow
soil.

In the Mess the silence, which, like a block of ice, contained
me, still persisted. The parades, the feasts, the junketings in
the open air, between the lifted bat's-wings of the sand, all these
seemed only to emphasise my unhappiness. No light, no hope,

was to be perceived. . . . One break, it is true, had occurred earlier in the summer, before the brief visit to London of which I have told. I had gone for a night to Renishaw, and the next morning had ridden thence to Sherwood Forest to join the Yeomanry Regiment in which I held a commission, and spend with it the annual ten days in camp. This period constituted my first experience of local military outings, a form of life in which the spirit of the late eighteenth and early nineteenth centuries, the fear of invasion by the troops of the King of France, or of landings by the great Napoleon, still joyously survived, outworn and demoded though it was by history. A certain fascination could be found in leading a life under the greenwood tree, in the very centre of Bonny Sweet Robin's wood, albeit clad in no Lincoln green, but, instead, attired at times in rustic versions of uniforms, such as had made splendid the Duchess of Richmond's ball on the eve of Waterloo, or had enlivened Vienna during the nights of the Congress. About our glitter, however, there was a comfortable provincial flavour which, had I then known them as well as I do now, would have made me turn for comparison to Rowlandson's drawings; not to the ravaged and hallucinatory heads, each distorted from its natural shape by some individual combination — never, in the infinite repertory of nature, to be repeated — of stupidity, greed, vice and disease, but to the reverse of them, the idyllic pastorals, inhabited only by the young, the men on horseback, the village girls carrying baskets of eggs and fruit, and bunches of flowers, these figures displayed against a background of crumbling stone and fading thatch, under gnarled and curly trees, with a pervasive sense of the lightest pinks and greens in the most buoyant summer weather, under clouds that play in the blue sky like fat and fleecy English lambs. Tents clumped like mushrooms at the foot of trees, Church Parade in the park of the squire, troops clattering, or rather thudding, on the drives that run through the great domains of Thoresby, Clumber and Welbeck, all these were local enough in flavour, yet sufficiently national to have presented subjects for the incomparable reed pen of that genius at its most feathery yet precise.

Good-humour reigned, partly because this short period constituted to the younger men their annual holiday, to the elder an escape from wives and families, partly because to all of them it was a masquerade. The whole of the youth of a county were playing at being soldiers: farmers, colliers, seed-merchants, squires, pawnbrokers, wool-manufacturers, gardeners, sweeps, iron-workers, all were engaged in the delightful game of make-believe. Even the horses seemed more amiable than elsewhere, full of fun, rounder, fatter, more countrified: perhaps because they, too, were pretending to be something they were not, battle-horses and Arab chargers. Just as at Aldershot, where the virus of militarism was continually at work, there was room for no feeling except malice, here, in this friendly atmosphere, obversely none could exist. Thus, when, for example, during the course of a long field-day, I laid claim, though unwittingly, to one of the traits said to have marked Napoleon out as a great military commander, that of being able when exhausted to fall asleep on horseback and retain his posture — indeed, I only tumbled off when I awoke —, even then my somnambulant exploit seemed to gain me nothing but good-will from my companions. . . . This is the place, too, to mention another incident of the same time, connected with the capacity to sleep if uninterested. By temperament I possessed, and through my experience, so far as it went, had acquired, a profound contempt for the Generals of that epoch — a contempt that was largely, it must be emphasised, to be justified by the conduct of the war that followed: and so, when one day we officers were assembled in a large tent to hear a cavalry commander of the most pronounced and stylised type, with thin legs, an eye-glass and a retrogressive chin, deliver a lecture on modern warfare, I at once went to sleep, but unobtrusively, as I had taught myself to do on similar occasions at Aldershot. However, my inner ear must have been alert and have decided that I ought to attend to what the General was telling us, for, to my own intense surprise, I suddenly found myself wide awake and listening with absorption to the only military lecture of real interest at which I had ever been privileged to be present. Here, nobody could fail to realise, was an original and resourceful mind at work; this singular little man must be a great soldier. He was, in fact, the future Field-Marshal Lord Plumer. . . . And at this point, in pursuance of what I have written a few lines earlier, let me explain : it was the Generals and War Office of *thirty years ago* that earned our contempt, and I, for one, like to think that the vast improvement in generalship and organisation which distinguished the British part in the Second World War and made our Generals revered by their men, and the War Office in its achievements a model of what it should be, may in some small part be due to the unceasing ridicule and criticism of the traditional hidebound military mind to which myself and many other writers who saw service in the 1914–18 struggle gave vent between the two conflicts.

The pleasure I had found in my outing with the Yeomanry, and still more in the ensuing few days which I spent at home again, yet only served to make captivity at Aldershot appear more bitter. . . . I suppose I had seldom, and certainly never during my school-days, seen Renishaw at this particular moment, the last days of May, the first of June, and this year I caught such an enchanted spell as only falls to us perhaps once in a decade, and, in the perfection it offers for its brief space, atones for the long, hard periods of our northern climate. During the hours it lasted, it seemed yet to offer a whole season, so pure, so essential, such sudden and uplifting freedom from the thrall of cloud and mist and cold as dwellers in sunnier countries can never know. The continued bitter weather of earlier months had kept back every kind of blossom, and now, in their old enclosures of red brick, all the fruit trees, pear and cherry and apple and quince and plum, had come out together, rearing their honeyed fountains high above the walls and, within them, let the petals, rose and gold and white, pour in torrents and cascades down to the aromatic ground, lying there in foamy, dappled pools. The freckled bees staggered home under their loads of sweetness, then turned to plunge again, drowsily, into their ivory towers. Beyond, nearer the house, on the upper lawns by the Gothic temple, the rhododendrons, planted a century before, were pitching, it seemed, above their enormous clumps of glittering, dark-green leaves whole awnings and marquees of the most luminous rose and lilac, under tall trees which themselves blazed from top to bottom with the smallest pennons and banners, dyed in the very sap of spring, to which the dark rugosity, due to age and smoke, of their trunks afforded the most touching contrast, because the leaves were so young, while the limes and elms which bore them were so old that each spring, one was certain, must put a last period to their glory. At their most glossy, too, were the yew hedges and grass lawns, refreshed by the thick snow under which for many weeks they had lain in the winter. The very shadows the few passing clouds cast down to race over these level green spaces, which appeared to have been created as an earthly record of their progress, in the same way that a dial is designed to clock the sun, now seemed eager to proclaim their own transitoriness, speeding and skimming happily over the grass, and the lake below now held, not strongly, but nevertheless permeating its whole essence, an Italian foundation. By this brief seasonal gaiety of climate and landscape I was astonished and baffled. Even the negro's cave [1] in the cliff beneath the Wilderness now showed itself to be merely a delicious, cool retreat : (perhaps it was in such a moment the outlander had first seen it and chosen it for his habitation). I was used to the leonine splendours of August and September, when heat brooded in the vistas until, far away over the luteous heads that stood with their braided beards in the stubble fields, vast mountains formed in sullen shapes on the furthest horizon, increasing in their bulk, until in one superb leap the lightning reached from hill to hill and filled the valleys with its thunder : I knew the great clouds of smoke that then occasionally ensued from heather set alight, and rolled over and scented this whole country : I was familiar, too, with the azure glades of earlier May, exhaling so great an odour of enticement, and was accustomed to the winter's polar pelt that blurred and softened every shape and merged the elements, air, water, earth ; but never before at Renishaw had I encountered such a golden moment of certainty. The world had been made for

[1] For a full account of this episode, refer to *Left Hand, Right Hand !* pp. 19-21.

man, the whole landscape sang, and for the senses of man, and — it seemed to add in an undertone — for young men, and in especial for the young men of my generation. . . . It was these fleeting hours, hybrid of spring and summer, as much as my later visit to London, that now made me resolve to leave Aldershot.

Towards the end of August, a stir in the atmosphere of the militarist capital could be perceived, and the reason for it soon became evident. The army was shortly proceeding on manoeuvres, and with it the cavalry regiment to which I was attached. I dreaded the prospect, because I was to accompany my tormentors. Fortunately, second thoughts in the Orderly Room eventually reached the sound, and indeed ineluctable, conclusion that, under the eyes of countless Generals, I should add no lustre to the reputations of those who had instructed me in the military art, and therefore, that since some officers had to be left behind in charge of barracks, I had better form one of this small group. . . . Of what followed I cannot be sure: for the kindly censorship which governs memory has expunged it from my records. I remember a few days, summer days free of Gowk and Fribble-Sadler; quiet days, for trumpet and drum no longer echoed under hot roofs, while beyond, in other barracks, in the more distant perspectives of low gables of corrugated iron, the bagpipes, too, had ceased their sinister whinings, so unsuited to these particular wastes. No batmen whistled. No horses whinnied. . . . Then, I went !

In effect, I ran away to Italy, to have a talk with my father, in order to try to persuade him to modify his plans for my future. But it seems plain that before leaving I must have obtained some sort of official sanction to go; otherwise I could neither have left the country nor later have entered a regiment. . . . Whatever may have happened, at any rate I left, bearing with me the sense of being held in dislike, and even in contempt; a feeling from which my brother-officers of the Grenadiers three months later rescued me at the Tower.

Even before this interval had elapsed, almost in a week, my spirits had renewed themselves, so strong at the age of nineteen is the natural recoil. The few days I spent in London completed the effect of contrast between England and Italy. It was only the middle of September, but this year the fog had already coffined the city for the winter, and the ragged, fiery manes of the gas-flares barely showed beyond the radius of a few yards. Through slow miles of murk I drove one night with some friends to a masked ball at Covent Garden Theatre. These public dances were then a feature of the London night in the autumn and winter months, and were singular in the general air of gaiety that prevailed; an air unusual in our capital at any time, and never to be observed perhaps, except in the carefree years immediately preceding the First World War, when the great, soft, headless, amorphous mob of rich people of indeterminate origin produced by the business activities of the previous century was bent on pleasure, though having, it seemed, little knowledge of how to obtain it or how to spend the accumulated millions. The old evangelical or nonconformist background was forgotten. . . . That night, the lightness of spirit appeared to gain from the wall after wall of darkness that the dancers knew to be enclosing them outside. Parties of masked figures watched from the tiers of boxes the glittering, shifting pattern made by the couples on the floor, spread above stalls, orchestra and stage. This — 1912 — was the year when syncopated dance-music first conquered England; soon the music-halls were to ring with moaning nostalgic prattle about Alabama and the Mason-Dixon Line, and already in a few advanced night-clubs a small negro band would hoot itself hoarse with whip-poor-will chuckles ; but here nineteenth-century waltzing still prevailed. The dancers crowded the space, slowly revolving, singing, and blowing paper trumpets. The company was recruited chiefly from the professional pleasure-lovers, the idle and dissolute, the stage-door hangers-on and bar-proppers, and I remember this was the first time I had seen men of education drunk. There were several of them, each dancing by himself in the lobby in a rapt and sullen *pas seul* that resembled in its solemn elaboration a tragic figure out of some ritual antique dance. (The sadness of the intoxicated is a theme never sufficiently emphasised.) . . . The very next day I escaped into Italy, then the garden of the world, full of a beauty and happiness that seemed to be an emanation from the soil itself, just as our fogs and damp pleasures appear to rise from the square miles of poisoned clay clamped under London pavements; I passed, moreover, straight from an English autumn into an Italian, then a season new to me, and perhaps the most beautiful and characteristic that any country offers, with its skies so clear, and of such a depth of blue transparency, showing between the great white clouds, flat-bottomed, that are evoked by the heat; the Italian autumn, with its pyramids of figs and peaches, its dust, its roses and oleanders, and brown, baked hills, spiky here and there with dark cypresses, and its terraces hung with opalescent, smoky bunches of white grapes, or the bloomy, jewelled clusters of the darker kinds.

In Florence, I found my mother and father were staying in a hotel, long established for foreigners, in the Piazza Santa Trinità. My father had greatly perturbed himself about an outbreak of cholera in Naples during the late summer. He suspected the Italian Government of suppressing news about the gravity of the epidemic, and had, in consequence, arranged with friends who lived in the afflicted city a private code, whereby he could read from day to day the progress or recession of the plague: thus, morning and evening, telegrams arrived for him. *Aunt Maria better* signalled an improvement clearly enough, *Calling in another doctor* was to be interpreted with equal ease to token a grave deterioration; whereas, perversely, the apparently comforting words *Aunt Maria had seven hours' sleep yesterday* meant, in reality, *seven hundred more deaths yesterday*. Unfortunately, the excitement these messages aroused in their receiver often caused him temporarily to forget the key to what they conveyed, or to read them in contrary, or even in both, senses. This aggravated his distress, and almost equally he tormented himself about one of the Balkan wars that were always current in those years, and in which he took a personal interest, recalling the lessons he had learnt — and taught — in the Volunteers. Nobody else in Florence appeared to be troubled in mind. Day after day, week after week, the weather offered the same tropical noons and fresh evenings, most plainly uncontaminated. It was impossible to remain there without beginning to enjoy life.

Even my dread of the little talks which I knew must ensue with my father, cast no shadow before them; though already long experience had taught me that in any matter touching money, or wherein money was indirectly concerned, or that appeared to infringe plans he had made — and these were so numerous, and himself changed them with such rapidity, that it was almost impossible not to transgress in this respect —, he would render any proposed discussion most awkward by countering at once with the familiar " No ! ", repeated thrice with great speed, like the firing of a machine-gun, or with the still more absolute " Certainly *Not* ! " In addition, he magnified in his own mind the difficulties which, when he so desired, he was able to detect at every point in the compass. Molehills reared their haunted summits and fantastic peaks in all directions : but the real mountains he failed ever to perceive. . . . Thus, the following year, when, while recovering from mumps, I wrote to tell him that the doctor ordered me to go to the seaside for a fortnight, he at once replied that unfortunately he could not afford to put me up in his house at Scarborough, much as he would have liked to do so, unless I agreed to pay him 4s. 9d. a day for board and lodging and a weekly sum for laundry. I could not resist saying in reply that I preferred to go somewhere cheaper and more amusing; but I regret my answer, for now I am convinced that he really believed what he stated, though at that very time engaged in his multitudinous activities of building and decorating, and making gardens ; and, further, I have come to think that had I been content to give up my life to it — and it would have proved a whole-time job, with never an hour off — I might have managed my relationship with him in a different way and with much less friction. . . . I did not realise this, however, until very much later, when a friend, both of my father's and of mine, Robin de la Condamine — who under the name of Robert Farquharson is known as so brilliant and skilful an actor, the only man who continues into the present day the particular tradition that in times past distinguished the English stage, and gives always a peculiarly mordant rendering of his part, as if it were outlined with fire — adumbrated for me with a perfect comprehension of character my father's attitude. For many years Robin owned an apartment in Florence, and I benefited much when there from his great knowledge, especially of all forms of beauty, and delighted in his vivid and singular talk, which again was all fire, smouldering for a while, with a train of sparks and little flames, until ever and again it would catch new material. . . . One day, then, a whole decade subsequent to the time of which I am writing, he pointed out to me that my father's tricks, all his deductions and small charges, arose from a childlike desire to play: it was his unique expression of it. Alas, neither shops, nor institutions like banks or colliery companies, nor individuals would respond in the spirit for which he hoped: he could find no-one willing, or perhaps with enough spare time, to join in the game. But this petty financial juggling, as it looked, was not solely symptomatic of meanness: on the contrary, he was capable — had I not seen it myself, as when, for example, he advanced to a friend of mine, a painter who was in money difficulties, a hundred pounds without demur, because he liked his work, though at other times he would create a tremendous rumpus about a sixpence he would allege to be owing to him! — he was capable, then, of great generosity. No, it was not stinginess as so many might mistakenly deem it: he wished other people to answer in similar vein, send him in a bill, deduct and counter-deduct, and charge him for meals to which they had invited him. Treated thus, he would have become a much happier man and, consequently, a more easy companion.

At first I was not convinced, but I put the matter to the proof. I was staying with him in Italy, and he had just served on me one of his extraordinary lists of small amounts he believed to be owing to him. Instead of refuting it in its entirety, on this occasion I took it away. I scrutinised the items minutely, struck out some, and entered others against him. Next, rushing into his room like a whirlwind, I waved the paper at him, and cried:

"I've had to make several small deductions from your

account. I've already knocked off three hundred and forty lire. I notice, by the way, that you've charged me for half Henry's board and lodging, but I'm afraid *I* can't afford to travel with a valet!"

I proceeded to challenge and debate every point, and at the end produced the counter-list. . . . It was plain that though my adaptation of his own methods had startled him, he was absolutely delighted. He spent many happy hours for several days, going over the whole thing again, and from time to time entered upon the little arguments he so much enjoyed, such as, "I notice you've paid 3d. for black coffee. A penny-halfpenny is quite enough. *I* should never dream of paying more."

In Florence, that autumn, though, I did not as yet realise the existence of such an alternative way of approaching his heart. I dreaded the talks with him: and even more than the financial discussions I knew they must include, trembled at the thought of having not only to try to persuade him to alter his mind, but, first, to confess my proved failure in life, of which he had long been so sure. It was a great mortification to be obliged to admit that I was unhappy in the life he had chosen for me: while, since he so firmly held the doctrine that weak points must be strengthened, rather than the strong be emphasised, the fact of my failure itself would perhaps only confirm him in the idea that, infallibly right in his choice, he had selected the one career which I ought to pursue. . . . Notwithstanding, I realised that I must make a start to tell him. I dared not delay.

My news, however, was by no means well received. Nearly every day, he would send for me to his room, and while he rested on the bed, festooned with a mosquito-net, so that, like the Deity, he remained only partially revealed, he would, from his cloudy cover, harangue me on my defects and delinquencies. As a rule, on my entry, he would rise from the bed, disengage himself for a moment from his floating gauze and, after creeping stealthily on tiptoe to the door, would open it suddenly, with a snap as it were, for he habitually suspected Henry of eavesdropping. This was part of the unusual relationship existing between them, of the way each studied the other, while never allowing it to distract him, or prevent him from playing his own hand to perfection. Each gave a most accomplished performance and when, in fact, from time to time the great man *was* found outside the door, he would make it signally clear that he was only there in pursuit of his calling, and occasionally, while my father and I were talking, we would be disturbed, after a brief period of utter, almost unnatural quiet, by clothes being brushed just outside, with so ostentatious a loudness that the sound seemed almost to frame its own meaning, " Here I am, Sir George, still at work in your interest, never a moment for my own pleasures, never an instant's rest ! Here I am, and don't pretend you can't hear me and don't know I'm outside ! " In any case, Henry was far too heavy to listen for long with comfort. No eavesdropper should weigh over eleven stone (as my father told him later, which Henry listed as one of the reasons for giving his notice the following winter) and at his sixteen the boards would creak and moan as though in pain. But if this did occur, very infrequently, it is true, then a transcendent noise of brushing, and even a whistled version of a hymn-tune, would quickly provide the innocent opposite of an alibi. . . . Having found or not found Henry there, as the case might be, and having in either case shut the door again with a loud decisive slam, my father would then lock it, to prevent anyone, and especially my mother, from rescuing me. This action had about it something symbolic : it was the sure portent of storm : after that, there could be no hope. . . . One day, the usual summons arrived. "You're in for it again, sir, I'm afraid," Henry announced. " *He* wants you at once. And he's humming to 'imself something terrible ! " (Humming — or what might be mistaken for it, an angry buzz-like sound, similar to that to be heard during the irascible dartings of a wasp hither and thither — was acknowledged to be the harbinger of the worst scenes.) I hastened to my father's room. He was in so great a hurry to begin what he had to say that he did not get up from the bed, but called out, " Come here immediately and lock the door ! I've an important matter I'm afraid I must discuss with you." My heart sank, and my mind ran swiftly, though heavily, over the list of my recent misdeeds; a bill for eight pounds for theatre tickets, a suit still unpaid for, a letter which I had been writing and had lost, in which I had revealed my feelings — no, it must be something worse. Foreboding settled in every finger-tip. After a momentous but poignant silence, he observed, in the even, carefully lowered tones which he reserved for family secrets and for accusations, but at great speed,

"Sit down! . . . Between ourselves, in *my* opinion, the Greeks have definitely beaten the Bulgarians!"

The relief of finding that only a major international complication was to be the subject of this confidential talk proved overwhelming. I could never have imagined so sweet a war.

Nothing, no amount of worry, could make one unhappy for long in Italy, at the age of nineteen. The country was too heartening, and the people, with their vital natures, too welcoming, to allow of more than a passing depression. The light alone was enough to enrapture anyone sensitive to beauty. Moreover, there were the private raptures, as yet incommunicable, which every artist in embryo experiences and which I had first known, as has been described, on the cliffs at Scarborough at the age of five: a sense of atonement, of being at one with Nature, of seeing great things in little, and the reflection of small things in great, of grasping for a moment something that is beyond comprehension: in fact, that special awareness of echoes, images, rhythms, of being part of Nature in a world created by God, and, in particular, of the scale of His universe, that, combined in their different proportions, is the business of every individual artist, whatever his medium may be. In stressing these emotions, and in setting them out as those common to artists, I am not staking for myself any claim to esteem. To be an artist is an accident of birth. Worldly fortune can perhaps be made a matter of desert, but the nervous equipment and explosive energy of the artist cannot be rationed: he must always have his extra portion of joy or torment, be always, by his nature, furthest from the abhorrent norm: above or below it in nearly every respect

This spiritual, physical and mental fusion I have attempted to identify contained, no doubt, the germ of poetry: but I was far too diffident to believe I could produce anything, or even to make a trial of doing so. . . . From one window, in a passage outside my bedroom, I could see the thin spire of a Tuscan cypress and part of a tiled dome, set in a perspective that, in the Florentine light, and of an evening especially, though so bare except in its essentials, seemed, while you looked at it, to offer the whole of Italy, together with the secret of its beauty. I would spend hours there, gazing at this view, in a kind of ecstasy, akin, perhaps, to what saints may feel when they contemplate the source of all virtue. Hardly less matter for wonder and excitement did I find in Montegufoni, which I saw for the first time during this visit to Florence, three years after it had been bought in my name. . . . And here I must state that, on this occasion, as, at the end of the twenty-mile drive, we motored down the steep hill between the stone lion and the stone greyhound — supporters of the Acciaiuoli coat of arms —, I was astonished to find that I not only knew, as I did from photographs, the garden façade, but that I also recognised the other, north side, so different in aspect and architecture, from having seen it in a dream. Indeed, on waking from it, I had thought immediately how poorly my subconscious mind had worked, where the background was concerned: for the building in no way resembled the photographs I had been shown, which were those of the other front only.

Twice or more every week, we would set out, rather early in the morning — since it takes an hour to drive there, through mountainous country, from Florence — to spend the day, returning to our hotel in time for my father to receive his evening telegram to the effect that Maria was better or worse. He would sit disconsolately, in a rocking-chair of thin, rather warped wood, under the central roof-lighting of the hall (he had, soon after I had arrived, quarrelled with the Swiss manageress of the first hotel we had been in, and moved to the dusty, echoing, thronged *salas* of a new Italian hotel), swinging up and down, and try to remember the code. Was IT better or was IT worse ? . . . Always his mind tended to the darker interpretation of the words. . . . In the days spent at Montegufoni, however, he seemed to be at his happiest. While we wandered through the high, cool rooms of the great house or, if it were not too hot, along the three sun-baked decks of the garden, Henry would be unpacking an ample luncheon of cold chicken, and Angelo Masti, the peasant in charge, would hurry in with a large, flat, cylindrical cheese, the *pecorino* of the neighbourhood, with a basket of figs and late peaches, tinged with green, and grapes, all still warm from the sun — some of these being of the kind called *fragole*, the small, plump, blue grapes, so different from others in their internal texture, and in their taste, which recalls that of the wood strawberry, that they might be fruit from the planet Mars or Venus — or a huge flask, covered in dry, dusty rushes, of the excellent red wine of the Castle itself. Presently, too, a very strong, pungent scent approaching us indicated that Angelo had just bought a large clothful of white truffles from a boy outside, who had been collecting them in the woods. (The white variety is only found, I believe, in Italy, and most commonly in Piedmont and Tuscany, and round Parma : it is coarser than the black, and, in its capacity to impregnate a dish, more resembles garlic, a fine grating of it on the top of any substance being sufficient.) His wife would cook for us, and send in a dish of rice or macaroni sprinkled with them. And these things to eat and drink would be placed on a table covered with the coarse white linen used by the *contadini*, under a ceiling painted with clouds and flying cupids, holding up in roseate air a coat of arms, a crown and a Cardinal's hat.

My mother seldom accompanied us on these expeditions, for she preferred to remain in Florence, reading the English papers, the arrival of which, though two days old, at an uncertain hour about midday, constituted her greatest excitement here —, then, a week or two after I had joined my parents, she returned to England. So, for the most part, my father and I were alone, and on these occasions, though still a little depressed by the Barone's stories of the impracticability of the place as a residence, he would seem to be in his least unaccommodating mood, full always of information, and often of pungent comments. I must emphasise here that, once he had emerged from his tower, he could be, when he wished — or when, perhaps, he forgot to be otherwise — a most interesting companion. . . . The comments are more difficult to recall, since naturally they were rooted in topical and personal matters. But the occasional superstitions of a man who prided himself on a total absence of them always amused me, and, therefore, I can recollect a prophecy of his at this time, which, alas, came true. He had been reading in the papers, I suppose, about the particularly top-heavy chariot of bronze which had lately been presented to the nation by its sculptor, Captain Adrian Jones, and erected on the top of the Arch on Constitution Hill, to celebrate the completion of a hundred years' peace between England and the United States ; or perhaps he had seen a photograph of it. At any rate, he remarked seriously, "Such a mistake to challenge the Fates! It means that both countries will be involved in a war within five years!" . . . However, such an idea was happily unthinkable.

I would like, as well, to give an impression of his talk in such a mood. . . . And two things I remember his telling me in the cool of a shuttered *sala*, while winged spots of light trembled over the ceiling like butterflies moving, and the drone of the heavy insects of the afternoon flowed in between the green slats. . . . In describing to me some of his travels in Italy, which for the last decade had been the mainspring of his life, he related an incident illustrative of the — until lately — seemingly almost inexhaustible artistic riches of Italy. Visiting Siena the previous year, to look for furniture and objects, he had several times been to see a jeweller from whom, finally, he purchased a Primitive, rather cheaply, for some hundreds of pounds. The old man — he was over eighty — had not brought it out until my father had already been to the shop on several occasions. It had been forgotten, he explained, being the last of eight hundred triptychs and altar-pieces he had bought half a century before. He had given five pennies each for them to a rag-and-bone man, who used to go round the churches, collecting them, and then pile them in the piazza and burn them for the sake of the gold he could extract from their frames and backgrounds by this method. The jeweller had sold them all — except this one, which he had mislaid — many years previously for 5 lire 60 centesimi each, and had congratulated himself then on a remarkably profitable transaction.

The second story, of a very different kind, concerned my father's friend of Oxford days, Carl von Buch, who in 1880 had helped him to expose Sir William Crookes's favourite medium on the premises of the British National Association of Spiritualists.[1] . . . Well, it appeared that this collaborator in the showing-up of human credulity had at last seen a ghost himself! . . . The tale he related to my father was this. Von Buch was connected with the Stock Exchange, and was worried, at the time of the happening, about a business deal. He had to go up to Norfolk, and at Norwich station got out of the carriage in which he was travelling with his wife, to buy a copy of the evening paper, so as to know the latest prices. When he reached the bookstall, he saw standing by it a relative, to whom he was much attached, and who, he noticed, was wearing the old brown suit and red tie he habitually affected. They talked for a few seconds, and then the cousin said to him, " Don't bother yourself about those shares. They'll turn out all right ! " As he said this, he disappeared. And at the same moment von Buch remembered, with overwhelming shock, that his interlocutor had been dead for twenty-three years. The conversation had taken a moment or two, but now, as he turned to go back to his carriage, the train began steaming out, and he only just had time to climb into the nearest compartment. When, at the next stop, he rejoined his wife, she at once asked him who the man was, with the brown suit and the red tie, to whom she had seen him talking at the Norwich bookstall. . . . A few days later, the shares recovered.

This story, since he knew von Buch to have possessed a stalwart lack of belief, similar to his own, came as a blow to my father. Perhaps, after all, one had better not be so certain ;

[1] For a full account of this episode, see *Left Hand, Right Hand !* Appendix A, p. 245.

there might be something in it! . . . And, in fact, from now onwards, his attitude began to crumble. But the process took many years, and he was at the moment busily employed in inventing explanations, equally improbable as the event. Nevertheless, to listen to these, and to the stories, interested me more than to hear the mock-Gothic details to which I was so often treated. He could see that I liked it, and, in consequence, these long afternoons spent with him thus were cordial, and perhaps helped me in my task of persuading him to relinquish his schemes for me as a cavalry officer. At any rate, we reached a compromise, by which I was to enter the Grenadiers. Persuasion at first was not easy; for, since life in the Brigade of Guards was known not to be cheap, he had to agree to an increase of allowance. Happily, he had been told that the discipline was very strict, and he warned me, formally, that I should not enjoy the life any better. He noticed in me very strongly, he added, the tendency visible in all my mother's family, to shirk disagreeable things! They seemed to perceive nothing wrong in enjoyment (*he enjoyed beauty*: but that was different), and, so long as people amused them, asked nothing better of them, never wondered whether the influence of such persons was frivolous or the reverse. . . . Such a mistake! . . . On the whole, however, he was in excellent humour, and, if sometimes he turned irritable, a mere glimpse at one of the numerous stone cannon-balls which encumbered the courtyards, or of some opening which might prove to be an oubliette, by exciting his passion for Gothic life — or, rather, death —, soon restored his mood. The happiest moment of all, perhaps, came with the discovery of a woman's skeleton at the bottom of the Castle well, said to be as deep as the tower is high.

The hours soon passed. Now moving on heavier, more uncertain feet, Henry would be packing up the empty dishes in the hamper. (Throughout the afternoon, shouts of laughter had swept up the stone stairs from the vaulted room where he had been drinking red wine and entertaining the peasants with his talk.) At six we would return along the slanting Tuscan roads that, before many weeks had passed, I came to know so well as to be able to recognise what point in the journey had been reached by the particular smell of pine or heath or olive-oil, or whatever it might be, appropriate to it. . . . At last the city lay before us, every church, of golden stone, or zebra-striped in black and white marble, every bridge, every dome of dusty terra-cotta tiles, every cypress tree and pine seemed long-settled in peace, fine and secure as did, similarly, the future before us : that two wars would sweep over Europe, and that this very city, among the two or three proudest flowers of European civilisation, the property of the world, would suffer damage from bombardment, within the brief boundaries of three decades, that was barred beyond the flight of the most evil imagination, and was no more within the realms of possibility, of things that happen, than the family disasters which were, too, so surely preparing themselves. Alone, one voice of earliest youth had pronounced the coming of doom upon the world, had cried it with a singular, whining persistency in the sombre darkness of the earliest northern morning, " Rags and Bones, Rags and Bones ! " or " Youth must die and Great Babylon will fall ! "

Though catastrophe of one sort and another was now so near as almost to be on the point of being precipitated among us, yet, so far as my sister and I and my brother had travelled, nothing seemed very much to have changed. . . . To take my own case : in the intervals of calling me to his rooms to rate me for my various misdemeanours, or to discuss imaginary terrors, such as the cholera epidemic, and the danger of catching malaria if you allowed your nose for one instant to be free of the mosquito-net, my father was still engaged in planning for his elder son — with a start he would remember that it was Osbert — the grandiose coming-of-age to which I have earlier referred : dragons in the lake, fireworks, stencilled cows, and all the rest of those ideas so long familiar to us. . . . He was fifty-two, and the alteration which the reader has watched taking place in his character, and which had been promoted no less by the long illness he had suffered than by the mere sculptural effect of the passage of time, was nearly complete. In future he did not alter very much, except physically : for he grew more impressive-looking every year. Now he was shut within his suit of Gothic armour, the vizor having been designed without slits for the eyes. No longer facing life at all, he saw it as he wished to see it, and had learned to apply his mountain-ash-berry technique to every phase of life and every event in it. If he did not like what was going on round him, he just refused to perceive it, and then it could no longer exist. His consolations and his sorrows, his frequent fault-findings and rare compliments, all grew from imagined roots, and in their culmination these processes entailed terrible suffering for himself and all those connected with him, and led to happenings as tragic and disastrous on a big scale as they were diverting and ludicrous on a small.

My mother's troubles had already started: my father remained blind to them. The miasmas of Borstal air are as contagious as were the prison fevers of former times, and one of the friends I had made at my crammer's, a gay if perhaps vapid young man who spent his days in an endless fatigued fog of cigarette-smoke, had come, a year or so previously, to stay with us for a few days. He was amiable and so I liked him, and he most certainly harboured no evil intention towards us, but while in the house, my mother mentioned to him how worried she was about money affairs, and he gave her the name and address of a financial adviser he had found, who had helped him out of all sorts of trouble; a benefactor, who seemed to be able to arrange almost anything for one. . . . Soon after, my mother went to consult this invaluable adviser at his office, and from that moment she was unable to escape from the web he spun. Of the consequences of this meeting, the young man — he must have been just twenty-one — who had given her the name and address of the moneylender was the first victim. . . . It was after this fashion that she fell into the toils of a notorious miscreant.

His very appearance constituted a danger-signal, and should have been sufficient warning — and then, had any enquiries been made about him, his antecedents would have been made plain. His stunted, stooping, paunchy body, with over-delicate hands and feet, carried a heavy head, as though he was wearing a mask, with a beak like that of an octopus, which spiritually he so much resembled, and a small imperial and moustache that were dyed, as was his hair, a total and un-natural black. This gave him a slightly foreign mien; there was just a suggestion of Napoleon III, or perhaps, too, there may have been a touch of oriental or of creole in his blood. Certainly there was about him an emanation of evil. As a rule — and I saw him several times — he wore striped trousers, a frock-coat, and a grey top-hat that, like his face, had acquired a tinge of yellow in it from wear, or as if in some way tainted. In the street, as he walked, at a rather slow, self-important pace, he would glance shiftily from side to side, nervous no doubt of meeting some of the hundreds of victims he had blackmailed and squeezed in his time, and who might, in the desperate straits to which he had reduced them, use physical force upon him.

It has sometimes seemed strange to me, in connection with the calamity he brought upon my family, that even this man, who during his long lifetime must have caused the most intense anguish to thousands of foolish persons and their rela-tions, and whose criminal capacity — I write with deliberation — it would be difficult to overrate, just as it would be by no means easy to single out any kind of crime or sin and be certain that he was innocent of it, had possessed a literary background and ambitions. It may be of interest, therefore, because, except in so far as all crime is ordinary and, indeed, vulgar, this man was no ordinary man in his wickedness, and because I believe that the perfection of this type of evil will cease to exist, yielding to other forms in a poor and levelled world where there is no money to spare for parasites to thrive upon, to tabulate what can be found out about him. In a way, the facts are singular; while his origin, and his friendships of earlier days, serve to mark the depth of his fall.

Field — Julian Osgood Field, to give him his full name — was born in New York in 1849, the third son of Maunsell Bradhurst Field. The Fields, of aristocratic American origin, had settled at Bayside, Flushing, New York, in 1638, and were a cadet branch of the old and respected English family of Field, of Horton, Heaton, Shipley and Ardsley, in the West

Riding of Yorkshire. The American branch had thriven, and many of the Fields, and of the similar families into which they married, had held high and honourable posts in the administration. Thus, Field's father had been Assistant Secretary of the United States Treasury, and his maternal great-grandfather, Osgood, had been Commissioner of the United States Treasury, and at another time Postmaster-General. Julian Field went to Harrow, to Mr. Middlemist's house, in September '67, and left in December '68. He matriculated at the age of nineteen at Merton College, Oxford. He became acquainted with Swinburne, who stayed with him on several occasions between 1869 and '71, just at the time when the poet was at the height of his fame. And I have seen it stated that Jowett thought highly of him. . . . After '71; we hear no more of him until the 'nineties. Almost exactly twenty years after he left Oxford, he published the first of his three books — of which I have seen two —, assuming as an author the signature " X.L." This volume, consisting of short stories, several of which had already been printed in magazines of literary repute such as *Macmillan's* and *Blackwood's*, was entitled, appropriately enough, *Aut Diabolus, Aut Nihil*, and at the time of its appearance enjoyed a certain vogue, and for several years was in demand at the libraries. It is dedicated " as a friend " to Walter Besant, and in a footnote to one of the stories, the author claims to possess " very numerous letters " from Victor Hugo. (He also, probably truthfully, represented himself as a friend of Maupassant's.) The first and title story — it is to be noticed that the titles of his books are, as a rule, connected with Satan — recounts how the Devil manifested his presence to an Abbé who had allowed himself to be taken to a Black Mass. In the preface, Field claims that " the only real portrait . . . is that of His Satanic Majesty himself ". But this avowal both overrates the book and underrates the aura of his personality wafted at the reader between the pages. In the press-cuttings at the back of one book, a reviewer in *The Athenæum* is quoted as saying that *Aut Diabolus, Aut Nihil* had excited great interest in Paris, " where people are eagerly seeking to identify the characters ", while a writer in the *Evening News and Post* declares that the story is " either the work of a cynic who has given his imagination full rein, or a lurid glimpse into an undreamt-of nook of Parisian life. The literary quality is undeniable." . . . In fact it is almost unreadable, dull as sin. But the second is duller, and no less evil. Named *The Limb*, and inscribed to Charles Gounod, as *souvenir affectueux*, it is concerned chiefly with scenes of Russian life. In the Harrow School Register, the entry under Field's name, and obviously revised by him, states him to have been the author of numerous plays, and to be the only foreigner who ever had a play accepted by the Comédie-Française. . . . What can be deduced from these facts, and from the books, of the man's life between 1871 and the 'nineties, is that he had lived much in Paris, in the company of writers, painters and musicians, that he had witnessed a public execution in France (he describes it in a story), and that he had visited Russia. . . . The rest of his life, more clearly documented, can be read in old numbers of *Truth*, and in *Truth's Cautionary List*: that of a swindler who ruined numberless people.[1]

At first, it seemed merely as though my mother had got herself into a scrape of the kind in which any unthinking woman, not versed in business, might find herself involved.

One might have expected my father, whose lack of faith could so easily convert molehills into mountains, not to have been unaware of what was going on. He could not, you would have thought, have remained in ignorance of how distracted with worry she was, or of the reason for it. But so it proved — and in fairness to him, it must be remembered that his letters were tampered with, so that no warning should reach him, and that, further, at no stage until the very end was the full extent and depth of the pit which Field had dug to swallow her up, and her family with her, visible. Out of each small lawsuit sprouted another, more grave ; beyond each vista lay one further, and more calamitous. With each new revelation the seriousness of the whole affair became emphasised. She told us nothing. Even if she had wished to remember the various promises by which she had been led on, the various traps into which she had been so easily lured, she could not have done so. Once a thing

[1] See Appendix E, p. 315.

had happened, it died for her. Besides, she did not wish to remember : she wished to forget.

The few benevolent people who knew what had been happening, did not venture to interfere or to enlighten my father ; for, as the reader will have understood, he was not an easy man to approach. . . . One morning, after my mother had returned to England, I received a letter from my friend who had been at the same crammer's, and whom I have mentioned as having introduced her to Field. He had now been for some months gazetted as an officer to a well-known regiment, and wrote to inform me that he had backed certain bills for my mother at Field's instigation, that they had fallen due and had not been met, and the solicitors had written to warn him that unless they were paid immediately, the Colonel would be told, and he would have to leave the regiment. . . . I at once decided that the only thing to do was to inform my father — as I write, the scene rises up before me. I persuaded him to come for a walk with me, saying that I particularly wished to talk with him. We started out, and after an uneasy silence of a moment or two, I said, " I'm afraid I must tell you that Mother has got into the hands of a moneylender " : to which he replied, " I never heard such nonsense : if she were, *I* should have known about it ! " — which was, in fact, the very reverse of the truth. However, I persisted and, in the end, my words, together with the unfortunate course of events, which could not be made to vanish by a pure process of contradiction, persuaded him of the truth.

The reader has patiently watched the shaping of character and events. . . . My mother, the daughter of an enormously rich man, had been married from the schoolroom. Money held no meaning for her. It was as if, as I have suggested earlier, the exertions made by her ancestor, the founder of the Denison family — exertions inherent in his rise from abject poverty to great wealth, from being a destitute youth unable to read or write, tramping the roads, to becoming the most famous of English bankers—, had placed too great a strain upon the financial sense, upon the faculties of reckoning, economy and caution, leading to the complete atrophy of them in his descendants. Even the simplest sums were beyond her computation. Further, she had reached an age when reason is apt to lose its sway. . . . Her debts amounted to some two thousand pounds. She signed papers that made her responsible in all for thirty thousand. By these processes she received a total amount of six hundred. Field and his accomplices swallowed the rest, and he aimed, beyond her, at her relations with their great wealth. His plans were in essence those of a blackmailer more than of a moneylender. And in his calculations he showed the typical conventionality of the cramped criminal mind. His schemes were all based on the assumption that the husband would pay without demur the money to be extorted from him, rather than allow his wife to face the case to be instituted against her, and in which the moneylender had arranged so that it would appear as if she were the culpable person. It had never struck him that my father would refuse to settle — and up till the last moment he could not believe it. My father, however, was a more unconventional and combative type than he had met so far in his professional life. He steadfastly refused to pay : all the more resolutely because he now found that Field had a year or two before entangled a young cousin of ours — a boy of nineteen or twenty — in his toils. Had the moneylender then been shown up, my father maintained, had the young man's parents declined to pay the sums levied on them, and instead, allowed the case to come into court, Field would have been exposed, and, consequently, my mother would never have fallen into his clutches. The only way, therefore, to render Field harmless for the future and unable to ruin thoughtless people, he argued, was to allow the cases against my mother to proceed. It was a duty. . . . No doubt, other reasons helped him, some consciously, others unconsciously, to this decision. And he never, I think, understood how black the cases against her would appear to those who did not know her. As it was, every familiar turn of speech in her letters, everything that could count against her, told remorselessly. Even a phrase quoted from a letter to myself, in which she said, " Can you get hold of So-and-so ? " — words she habitually used if she wanted to send for anybody, as

" Can you get hold of your Father ? " — were taken to mean that she had wished me to lay a trap for him.

The main and subsidiary lawsuits often came one after another, with a deadly iteration though conflicting in tendency and results. Thus I find that Sir George Lewis — of Messrs. Lewis & Lewis, who acted for my mother — in writing to thank me for a letter of congratulation I had sent him on having won an action for her, says how great a comfort it must be to me to think of the entire matter being ended : while a month later, just as I was going to the Front, my father writes to tell me that the whole thing has started again. And I have a letter written from Eton by my young brother, in great misery of spirit, at the age of seventeen, reminding me that at least one of these sordid lawsuits had taken place every single half since he had arrived there ; and it was true, the series lasted from the spring of 1913 — and already the worry of it had taken root at the time of which I write, in 1912 — until the appalling culmination in March 1915. . . . So henceforth, for years, life carried this terrible duality for us, a development and continuation of the double thread of life that had in earlier days taken so heavy a toll of childish nerves : the apparently prosperous, traditional life stretched over and disguising the frenetic disputes, the rages and the cold hardness. . . . Now, however, this duality had assumed a more objective, purposeful and evil embodiment. It coloured every day for each of us, and made us fear the next, and the new revelations it might bring. Everything had to it this sad and horrible aroma. And, as usual, my sister, who was most at home, bore the greatest share of the suffering. In my own case, youthful spirits proved irrepressible : it was not conceivable, even now, that family affairs should take so grievous and desolating a turn as in fact they took. For though my mother was of so unpractical a nature, so undeveloped in certain respects, my father was an undeniably clever and capable man, of considerable experience. With some degree of ease, therefore, I was able to support possible misfortunes in which I could not quite bring myself to believe. Nevertheless, when this has been allowed for, and though, as I have said, my physical and nervous make-up did not permit me to remain depressed for more than forty-eight hours at a stretch, yet in the account of my life that follows, this undertone of sorrow and apprehension must be borne in mind. I shall say little more of this squalid business, the materialisation of the dark shadow that the reader has seen at times clouding the sunnier early years. I shall mention the climax in its place, without comment : for in the preface to this book as a whole, I indicated the scope of the work I am attempting, and declared its aim : to beguile the mind. So I shall only here ask the reader to imagine the contaminating sense of insecurity, that occasionally retreated, but only, always, to come back with greater force, a feeling that underlay all these years, and their beauty and laughter, and to picture for himself the difficulty sometimes experienced in meeting old friends again, because of the chasm caused by explanations or the lack of them. And I must also add that the personal kindness I received from, and the tact and trust shown by, my brother-officers and the regimental authorities in circumstances of great difficulty for me and for them, were beyond anything that I could, or that the reader could, have expected. I should, indeed, be churlish if, writing of my life in the next few years, I did not acknowledge their generosity.

Ten days or so after I had told my father of Field's existence, he returned to London. At present these affairs still looked as if they would easily be put right : this was the first time I had been left abroad by myself — and it seemed as if the whole world were opening to me. That Florence and Aldershot could be situated in the same globe was scarcely to be believed. Never had people looked so beautiful or appeared so interesting as in this city. And the kind of youthful ecstasy I experienced here and later in London, as opposed to what I felt at Aldershot and at home, is the effect I must try to capture and present in the next pages. . . . Ambitions were not mine. I had no wish to be a General, an Ambassador, a Prime Minister (though after that last position, I did, if the truth is to be told, from time to time a little hanker — my father used to say that if I entered the army, I expected at once to be promoted to

Field-Marshal), least of all a captain of industry or finance. If only, if *only*, people would leave me alone, would cease to tell me what to do and how to do it, what a wonderful, exciting place the world would be! Perhaps, if I had realised it, that is an embryonic or transitional stage of every writer's mind, which must be for many years steeped in its own quality. In any case, I found I could be happy all day, visiting galleries, or walking round the streets of Florence. And it was only then, after some years' acquaintance with it, that I began first to comprehend the strangeness of this city, which, passing itself off as one of many European cities, is yet in its being as remote from them as would be medieval Timbuctoo or Aleppo. In the palaces and churches, there is an unexpected tilt to every roof, an unexpected angle to every wall, especially to be noticed in the earlier buildings — the edifices of striped and chequered marble are in their surroundings as exotic as would be giraffe or okapi. The universality of the Renaissance itself never succeeded in banishing this alien element that had accompanied the inheritance of Etruscan blood ; for who knows, even today, the ancestry of that mysterious race, or whence came the originals of those enigmatic effigies that can still be seen reclining upon their funerary urns in rock-sepulchre and museum? — figures with slanting eyebrows and brooding, incalculable smiles : characteristics to be repeated, over and over again, many hundreds of years later, in the Florentine pictures, and to be observed to this day, exemplified in the eager, rustic faces of the Tuscan peasants. . . . Even better than a day spent in wandering about the city, were the long, sunny hours at Montegufoni : which, during the ensuing weeks, I really grew to know and love.

Now, in mid-October, the gardens resembled those of an English June ; not only were they filled with roses and carnations, not only with an exaggeration and profusion of plants already known to one in England, so that the little green bushes of lemon-scented verbena, that in favoured positions, and draped with sackcloth, may survive our winter, were here grown almost to trees, showing tawny, flaking trunks, covered with spikes of grey-blue blossom (quite a handsome flower,

169

though at home only one or two of these, and in a wilting condition, grace the most prosperous and sheltered of these shrubs), as well as with their aromatic green leaves, but there were also other and more unfamiliar flowers. With *Ranunculus asiaticus*, of course, one was acquainted, but not as grows the *Rosellina di Firenze*,[1] with a feathery lolling fullness, speckled and powdered, that was altogether lacking in the north. Though the chief season for it is April and May, it flowers also in the autumn, as do so many Italian plants. One could see it, moreover, painted on the ceilings of many villas in the neighbourhood, for it was introduced into Tuscany during the last period of the Middle Ages by the merchant princes of Florence, who brought it from the Levant, and it was specially cultivated in the gardens of the Grand Dukes. It had, therefore, been first acclimatised in this very countryside and was said still to flourish here with a particular luxuriance, its papery flowers segmental and circular, as though drawn with a compass, dappled and tipped and spotted and veined as though composed of the wings of swallow-tailed butterflies rather than of petals. Then, too, on the first terrace, against the walls of the building, in the high, narrow flower-beds, stone-bordered — the dark, blue-grey stone of Volterra is used here for all cornering of rubble, brick and stucco —, the clustered, light azure heads of the plumbago rioted with an exuberance unknown to its delicate sisters in English hot-houses. Further,

---

[1] Species *Ragionieri* — see *Le Roselline di Firenze*, by Dr. Attilio Ragionieri, privately printed at Florence in 1923 for Count Giulio Guicciardini.

Dr. Ragionieri states that the Sultan Mahommed IV, who was an invalid, solaced himself with the cultivation of *Ranunculus asiaticus* in the grounds of the Grand Seraglio at Constantinople : but he reigned as late as the mid-seventeenth century, and though the credit for introducing this plant into Europe has sometimes been given him, Father Agostino del Riccio in a manuscript in the Florentine library, dated 1592, lists the flower as then usual in the spring gardens of that city.

The author of this learned treatise, who names the Acciaiuoli as among the families particularly devoted to fine gardening and rare plants, is an hereditary authority on the *Ranunculus*. From 1790 to 1822, Gaetano Gheri was head-gardener at the Royal Villa of Castello, where the plant was specially cultivated. As his son, Gheri adopted a nephew, Giovanni Ragionieri, who succeeded to the post, and was followed in it by his two sons Ferdinando and Francesco. Giovanni Ragionieri was the most famous specialist in *Ranunculi*, and Dr. Attilio Ragionieri is his grandson.

since I had never previously been in Italy in September and
October, there were fruits, as well as flowers, new to my eyes
in the guise of growing, living things : lemons, no longer
wrapped in their twists of tissue paper as in a shop in London,
but here displayed at each step in their redolent and simultaneous developing, as if the old, glossy-leafed and fragrant
trees — still standing in huge seventeenth-century jars of dusty
terra-cotta that yet bore a shield of the arms of the Acciaiuoli
Cardinal, surmounted by the wide, tasselled hat of his office :
treasures of which such care was taken that they were carried
out from the vast old lemon-house at the end of the second
terrace in the spring, and back there in the late autumn, when
they were further protected by scaffolds hung with screens of
straw ; as if, then, these trees, spangled with ivory-white buds
and rosettes of gold-flecked, perfumed blossom, as well as
bearing fruit at every stage, from small, dark shapes, no bigger
than a hazel-nut, to fruit of green bronze, and then gradually
coloured and shaped by the sun, to the finely-drawn elliptical
ripe lemon, painted with so gay a brush, were engaged in
giving an all-the-year-round exhibition of their powers.

The garden offered reptilian and entomological, as well as
floral, wonders. To comprehend the character of the place,
the reader must be reminded that these great stone terraces,
into which the sixteenth- and seventeenth-century owners of
the Castle had converted the ramparts and bastions of a
medieval fortress, carried their own systems of minute life.
These worlds possessed their own interest. There were, for
example, the colonies of ants, marking the worn and tawny
tiles with an invariable streak of moving sepia, as they followed
the monotonous routine of their socialist and boy-scout utopia ;
and there were two kinds of lizards, blue-green and emerald-
green, living like capitalists in their warm crevices, behind
south walls, which are sprinkled with tufts of rose-coloured
snapdragon and the blossoms of the wild caper, a little resembling a passion-flower. From their retreats, the lizards
would dart out every now and then to sun themselves and
flicker a tongue in the direction of some working insect, and if,
when they rested thus, the sun glowing down on the living

green of their bodies, you regarded them for long, isolated against walls, they took on the heroic proportions of the pre-historic. There were wild bees, too, bringing with them, like the former owners of the Castle, many a fable from the blue seas, white-crested, from the broken marble pillars and thyme-clad hills of Greece, and the taste, even, of their honey was legendary, fragrant beyond any to be found in hives; there were cicadas, playing selections, day and night, from their voluptuous repertory of music, though, for all the lure it held for others of the species, to us it sounds a dry and arid music, a scraping, scratching jangle from among crackling, baked grasses; there were butterflies, large and small, and huge moths, like those drawn by Beardsley, and — but this was earlier in the year — there were the flickering illumina-tions of the fire-flies. (In this connection, I remember that Henry described to me how one evening, some years later, my father had hurriedly risen and jumped from his mosquito-net, fearing that a fire-fly, which had succeeded in penetrating his gauzy protection, would set it alight!) Then, in the afternoon sun, when everything was at its fullest and largest, the roses wide open, the heliotrope scintillating with its particular glitter in the light, there would sound the comforting buzz and bump of beetles, not the dragging kitchen-beetles of England, with their obsequious insolence, but bold scarabs, armoured warriors or priests in their robes of blue and green and purple. And, too, one would obtain occasionally a glimpse of sidling, poisonous creatures, sad, bad and dangerous to know; tarantulas, or elongated, parchment-coloured scorpions that were said to have waxed thin upon the bones of the Saints who reposed in the Chapel.

This building contrasted with the vegetable excesses of the garden, as if it were a Christian symbol of suffering opposed to a pagan fertility emblem. You reached it across the length of the Great Court, where the large blue pavers lay reverberant in the heat, but its immediate approach was sheltered, from the direction of the living-rooms, by a graceful three-spanned arcade, contrived behind the Castle's east front, with a façade that, on the other side, resembled a three-leaved screen, with the middle leaf straight, and those of the other two set at an angle. When you entered the Chapel, a small, cool, stone-vaulted chamber, its very compactness brought home the facts of death, of man's — and even holy man's — mortality, with an unequalled force, just as, obversely, the landscape that glowed through the grilles of its windows, in spite of its gentle sweetness, emphasised, with its prosperous vineyards, orchards and fructiferous terraces, the facts of life. Within these cubic feet of space contained by marble flooring, frescoed ceiling and the walls with their richly carved panels of white and gold, there rested a remarkable concentration of holiness, the finest collection of Saints' relics in Tuscany. It had been formed in medieval times by an Acciaiuoli prelate, and had no doubt been originally assembled in a chapel of earlier date. Under the altar you could see, if you lifted the cloth, reposing behind glass, the skeleton of San Donato, while the panels, in spite of their thick and handsome decoration, slid down with ease into the floor, to reveal shelf after gilded shelf, laden with elaborate caskets of gold and crystal, displaying sacred bones, vellum-coloured or ashen, adorned with rosettes of pink paper, and sprinkled with flowers of artificial orange blossom. Here one could attain to a kind of peace, in contemplation of other than fleshly aspects of mankind.

In this resembling the village church, a stone-throw away — a little building (though it seemed a cathedral compared with the Castle Chapel), which lay just under the prow of the Cardinal's Garden, hanging, wreathed with roses and oleanders, above it in the air —, the Chapel possessed its own bell. The two competed and on specially holy days divided between them the lordship of sound over the landscape. The sound of the bell from the church was cracked, dryly joyous as the music of the cicada, and with an echo that hid high up in it. It rang at all hours and seemed sometimes to be working in an inexplicable, whining, wheezing frenzy of preparation, for, above all, it carried the sound of announcing some exciting message. Come here! Come here! Hither, hither, it called unmistakably; whereas the sound of the bell from the Chapel was, on the contrary, cold, mournful, sweet, solemn, infrequent, and telling with well-bred composure a story, you would have said, of the past. And perhaps, not inappropriately, for this bell bore on it an inscription in Latin, relating how it had been cast after the Battle of Manfredonia, with the planning and outcome of which one of the Acciaiuoli had been greatly concerned. This song of jangling bells, together with the punctuation of it by the little owls, who remain immured all day and night, through the spring to the late autumn, in their fragrant dark-green spires, hooting at each other in the most captivating manner, dominated the atmosphere of the Castle at this season : (of its vernal ecstasy of sound I hope later to tell the reader). It constituted its natural music, just as the sour but vital odour of must, rising from the wine-vats in the cellars below, impregnating the air of the whole vast fabric, was its natural scent.

Over a hundred people — men, women and children — were still living in the house, yet every day new features came to light in rooms that had recently been quitted and were beginning to be restored. For the next twenty-eight years, except at the very climax of the two wars, the noise of hammering, scratching and scraping was to rise up from dawn to dusk at my father's command. Already many of the rooms echoed with it, and a cloud of dust hung over the Court of the Dukes of Athens ; the existence of which, for it had been filled up with a warren of rooms, had only lately been revealed. On one wall, with its artificial stucco pattern to copy stonework just as fresh as it is often shown in the background of Italian primitives, was found, still hanging in place, the azure-painted shield, with its carved stone lilies, that formed the coat of arms of the Prince of Taranto, son of Joanna of Naples. Niccolo Acciaiuoli had been Grand Seneschal of the Realm, and Joanna's son had taken refuge here in 1348, bringing with him in his suite Boccaccio. . . . This court was just behind the tower, which rose from one corner of the Great Court, and had been built, so the tradition of the neighbourhood alleged, in imitation of that of the Palazzo Vecchio. The story was that an owner of the Castle in the thirteenth century had publicly sworn that if a certain prayer were granted by St. Anthony, he would never live out of sight of the Palazzo Vecchio tower. Not long afterwards, he obtained his desire, but since he was greatly devoted to his country estate, had meanly sought to avoid the payment of his oath by constructing at Montegufoni this counterfeit.

The Muses, then, — Clio not least of them — had often brushed this romantic residence with their wings. Its fault, in so far as it had one, was that apart from the Grotto, with the surmounting balustraded outside staircase, apart from the tower and the baroque eastern façade, it possessed no features of supreme architectural interest. The statues were not by the great sculptors, nor the frescoed ceilings by the great decorative painters of the period — albeit as yet we were not sure what might not be revealed, for in some instances the large halls had been divided into four, by the insertion of an extra floor and partition walls, and the frescoed ceilings had been covered over and were only just beginning to show above my father's dust-storms. Montegufoni atoned for its deficiencies, however, in other ways. The vistas of painted rooms were splendid and pleasant: the terraces an enchantment: but above all, the general atmosphere was overwhelmingly touched with poetry. As plainly as the grapes of the valley belonged to the vats in the vast old cellars, the Castle — a construction, rather than a house — belonged to the landscape, dulcet but poignant, in which it stood, crowning a little hill in a wide valley that rose on all sides again toward the horizon. Below, in the trough of the valley, a small, clear stream ran through a wood of cypress, clothed in its perpetual sweetness, so easily in-breathed, and here, too, one could listen to the music of the few Italian singing-birds that, being small enough to have escaped the Italian sportsman's shot, if not his aim, survive to sing ; while the country, as if to compensate for so much delicacy by adding strength, offered a romantic and rugged landscape to the north, so that, across the Great Court, from the windows of the state dining-room — a very long, narrow room with a pretty Tiepolesque ceiling, a painting of cupids carrying away the Crown of Athens — could be seen a cool, blue vista of distant mountains, crowned, as a rule, with snow. . . . But it was the number of small pointillist touches

— so hard to reproduce — that in their sum gave the house its character. . . . For instance, in the space under the Cardinal's Garden, which sailed so high in the air, was a little vaulted room with a balcony. This chamber had been used in the late seventeenth and eighteenth centuries for distilling scents, and in it I found stored in a dark corner large sacks of shells, rose-pink, lilac, pearly, fresh as if the sea had just receded from them, that must have been placed here two hundred and fifty years before, when the Grotto was made, in case it should ever be necessary to patch or repair the mosaics of the interior walls.

The cellars, replacing medieval dungeons — though some of these still existed —, reached to a great depth beneath the structure. Each contained two or more vats : and one of the dark, vaulted rooms, lit by a grating and the light from an open door, offered music as well as wine. . . . The very first letter I had received addressed to me at the Castle came from *La Società Filarmonica di Montegufoni* — in other words, the village band : for the inhabitants were still sufficiently numerous to support an institution of this kind, just as, similarly, they had their own tailor's, cobbler's and carpenter's shops. The letter contained a warmly-phrased request to me to become patron and president, and I was delighted with it, though my father, who noticed me reading it, and at once enquired, " How are they ? " (a ruse he had lately worked out, and now always adopted to find from whom a letter came, by the pretence that he recognised the handwriting, and also by the distraction he caused you, in the middle of reading, because in order to obtain silence you were inclined to blurt things out), when I told him about the invitation, rather skimmed the joy from it by remarking, " Such a mistake ! They only want twenty-five lire from you ! " His comment arose from his distrust of all music — except that which occurred in the medieval times of Sir Walter Scott's novels : he had nothing to say against troubadours, minstrels of all kinds, and merry fiddlers — and too, because, no doubt, he imagined the music, from the high-sounding title assumed by its players, to be better than it was. . . . Howbeit, I accepted the proffered honour, and, now that my father had returned to England, I would sometimes, of an afternoon or evening, attend a rehearsal, and it must be admitted that those hours offered some of the strongest and strangest physical sensations of a lifetime.

From above, from the courtyard, or the room adjoining it, only a little muffled rhythm, a bumping and squeaking, could be distinguished, but once you entered the inmost and deepest stone chamber in which the band was playing, the sound conquered and prevailed over every other feeling. The effect, I think, owed its resonance to the fact that the cellar was surrounded, at each side and above and below, by similar echoing apartments, and that there were several storeys or depths of them. Be the cause what it may, the volume of droning and buzzing and clattering was so tremendous as to seem to add an element to Nature herself, as you breathed the sound, inhaled it, drew it in through the very pores of the skin, lived in it, as fish in water. The music might not be good, but you were plunged and immersed in it. The sound vibrated through every cell in the body, so that you felt a part of it and that it was a part of you. The tunes, exclamatory, dramatic, old-fashioned, possessed a rusticity, both in their kind and in the playing of them, that I have nowhere else encountered, yet it cannot be denied that they were powerful, and rendered with power. . . . The scene, too, was memorable : the grace-fully-vaulted, rather low room, with its walls stained by age, draped with cobwebs, as though it were a hall in the Palace of the Sleeping Beauty, and lit, for the daylight scarcely entered through door and narrow window, by a single acetylene flare, which threw into one corner the huge distorted cylinders of shadow cast by the vats. Moreover, the solemnity and intentness with which the *Società Filarmonica* played, was worthy of a more notable body : these men, at other times vivacious, cared for nothing now but the score in front of them. The conductor, with gleaming, bead-like eyes, wore an elegantly cut dark suit and a cap with a patent-leather peak. Standing on a box in the middle of the cellar, with resolution he beat the air, and round him, as near as their instruments allowed, were clustered the members of the band, the majority of them blowing and writhing in the grip of enormous brazen serpents, now extinct save in the most remote and secluded Latin communities. Some of the coils showed signs of the perpetual Laocoön-like struggle, by large dents, but, notwithstanding, the huge gold mouths bellowed.

What, the reader may enquire, was the reason for this constant, arduous practice? . . . The answer is: it led, for one thing, to the most enjoyable band contests, when on a fine evening the crest of every knoll in the broad valley would rise up, crowned by its own din and brazen blare; for another, and more important, it was necessary as prelude for the supreme event of the year, at Montegufoni itself, the *festa* in the Great Court on the day of the Patron Saint of the Castle, late in the autumn. Everyone of importance among the peasants of the neighbourhood, as well as all the *contadini* of the place itself, would attend. Among them, perhaps in opposition to dead Saints, was included a living witch; for the landscape, though barely twenty miles from Florence, was remote enough to harbour an old woman belonging to this ancient cult, who claimed to tell the future, to cause or cure illnesses, and to cast spells upon men and beasts, and her rights to covencraft were clear, for she was the seventh child of a seventh child. In this resembling many of her kind, she liked festivities, and would rather be present at holy revels than at none at all. I saw her often as a unit — though an isolated unit, for people feared her — in a crowd, but I only spoke to her once, to say good-afternoon: still, that occasion was sufficiently fantastic for me to hope later to describe the episode and to introduce the reader to her. . . . Very early did the morning of the *festa* begin, with an unprecedented metallic clatter of bells. An altar, with a fine silver front, and carrying four silver candlesticks emblazoned with the Cardinal's arms, was set up in the open air under the shadow of the tower, which fell across the Great Court in the image of an enormous lily. After mass had been celebrated and the altar moved, the band would start to play and would continue its music all day. The tawny-skinned girls, who resembled gypsies, except for their stouter build and the straightness of their glances, would begin to move in abrupt, staccato waltzes, held at arm's length by that part of the adult male community not wrestling with serpents in the *Società Filarmonica*. Hour after hour they revolved, while, all round the Court, the older peasants, by now a little flushed with wine — which stood in large, reed-covered flasks by their side on the window-ledges —, watched their dancing. Through the dusty glass of other windows could be seen white grapes hanging in bunches from long bamboo canes, stretched one above another on a rack, so that the fruit could reach the degree of almost rotten ripeness requisite for the making of *Vino di Pasto*, while split figs, half dried, lay spread on straw mats on the tiled floor. . . . But still the smell of must prevailed over every other scent.

The *festa* came later, a little later, in the year. At present the band were only practising. The trumpets roared. The whole place shook. In a way, I loved to watch the members of the band even more than to hear them. It was not easy, though, to sort out the individuals and to memorise them, apart from the conductor : for they seemed to adhere very strongly to two or three types. The families of the inhabitants of the Castle, who had lived in it for more than eighty years, had intermarried to an unusual extent, but this seemed to have entailed no evil consequences, one saw no dwarfs, idiots or deformities ; on the contrary, a stranger's attention would be attracted by the good looks and quick intelligence of these peasants. The only visible result of the inbreeding appeared to be that the young men were more precisely like their fathers, whose place they would soon take, and the fathers more like the grandfathers, than any people I have known. They seemed to form a race, a family, more than a chance collection of persons. . . . So must have been the tribes in the days of the Patriarchs.

The sunset hour was at hand, and it was time to return to Florence. As with the particular speed, or sense of it, that comes before dusk, we rushed along the ridge road and then descended into the nearest valley, the cool air rising from the narrow stream that ran through a wide, stony bed greeted us

already with a breath of evening freshness. By a bridge —
about two miles from Montegufoni — stood the remains of a
chapel that had once been frescoed by Giotto. A shaggy
white dog, belonging to the special breed that so noisily guard
the broad farm-buildings of the Val di Pesa, barked at us
ferociously from the middle of the road : even the approach
of the motor would scarcely persuade him to move. In the
adjoining village, the pallid surfaces of the walls, in light greys
and parchment and ash colour, caught a glow from the scarlet
pennons that streamed across the sky. A child threw a stone,
which rattled on the side of the machine : yet, though so poor,
the place was peaceful, and the inhabitants friendly. Who
could have foreseen that here some thirty years later would
be fought one of the fiercest battles of modern times, the Battle
of the Bridgehead, as it was called, when throughout twenty-
four hours New Zealand and Indian regiments stormed,
again and again, the position held by the German troops
across the river, on the Florentine side of the trickle of summer
water ? Or, again, who would have believed that, during this
bitter fighting, to our *Castello*, so short a distance behind the
line, would fall the honour of entertaining perhaps the most
extraordinary collection of art-treasures ever assembled together in a private residence : for these ancient walls gave
refuge to the majority of the great pictures removed from the
Florentine galleries, and then stacked in the rooms here, one
against another, by the Fascist Government, under the illusion
that this was a safe retreat, far out of the world and away from
any possibility of trouble ? [1] . . . But that is a different story,
and I plan to tell it later : this is still the evening, the very
evening hour of peace. The white dog slinks away and the walls
assume a deeper tinge of rose before they are swallowed up
by the grey blanket of dust that we leave behind us on the
road. The peasants are now coming home, following or leading

[1] To indicate the sort of pictures the house contained from 1941 until the
end of 1945, I should perhaps say here that Botticelli's *Primavera*, as well as the
great Giotto from the Uffizi and the Uccello *Battle of San Romano* were among
them. The value placed upon them, in vulgar terms of money, by the Italian
Government for insurance purposes was 320,000,000 dollars, or in English money,
£80,000,000.

their milk-white bullocks, wreathed with vermilion flowers and traceries of leather, and they talk to them, as the animals plod on. When the beasts strain, going up the abruptly climbing roads, the voices rise louder, to a cry, and when they reach the top of the hill, the bells sound more gaily. In each village now, lights shine in the wine-shops, through the windows of which can be seen, hanging from the ceiling, Bologna sausages of many shapes and sizes, cheeses — *pecorino*, and the huge drums of cheese from Parma —, and the rush-covered bottles of wine. . . . After passing through the villages, we come to a clear tract of country, the motor accelerates, and races up the hills among the rocks, stone-pines and cypresses. This is plainly the same landscape as that depicted by Benozzo Gozzoli on the walls of the Riccardi Palace; where he shows us the Princes of the House of Medici riding in procession to meet the Emperor of the East, on his melancholy errand of trying to organise an effective barrier to the inroads of the Turkish hordes. That visit was a portent of catastrophe, resembling the futile and fruitless dartings to and fro of the politicians before the last war. But in 1912 there was no breath of the coming change. We were still in the trough of peace that had lasted for a hundred years between two great conflicts. In it, such wars as arose were not general, but only a brief armed version of the Olympic Games. You won a round; the enemy won the next. There was no more talk of extermination or of Fights to a Finish than would occur in a boxing-match. But then as yet the vast, headless, collapsible, rudderless mob, running tic-tac from one extreme to another, and dedicated to its own extermination, had not been let loose to rule. At present, everything was peaceful.

Soon the famous monastery of the Certosa, disposed upon its cypress-pointed hill, lay below us, seeming by its size an ancient town rather than a single building. And then came Florence itself. When we reached it, the dark streets were sprinkled with lights and the hard golden palaces and dazzling, striped marble churches of the city held within them a certain mystery and sadness, as well as their usual hubbub and confusion. We crossed the Arno by the Ponte Santa Trinità. But this venerable bridge, by far the most beautiful of the three, with its four tall stone figures, holding baskets of fruit and flowers, that had been carved by Francavilla and presented to the city by the Acciaiuoli family, was destined, though it had already lasted for more than two centuries, to perish before many of those who were now crossing it. It would have been impossible to believe that so great a preventable disaster would be allowed to overtake this famous and distinguished monument. . . . There was no cloud, no threat, except men's folly, which often can be an agreeable thing. . . . And even when I got out at the hotel and went upstairs, I had no unpleasantness to fear. For the first time in my life I was enjoying a period which ran counter to my father's dictum that you should do at least one distasteful thing a day.

Having returned to England at the end of November 1912, I joined the Grenadier Guards and, a week later, was posted to the battalion stationed at the Tower of London. Towards this purpose, I had been obliged, directly I reached London, to present myself for an interview at the Regimental Orderly Room. From the distance of thirty years later, I can comprehend, what I did not altogether realise at the time, the extreme accomplishment of the group of persons forming this entity, and that the head of it was more expert than anyone I have ever met in wrapping himself round with an air of quasi-benevolent authority, and by this means obtaining an absolute and unquestioned obedience. And, since there have been modifications — for example, the chief would now be a young man, freshly versed in war, instead of being over sixty —, let me give some account of this organisation, as it was; though it survives and can still be studied to this day.

The effective head, " the Lieutenant-Colonel ", as he was known, of each of the four regiments of the Brigade as then constituted — Grenadiers, Coldstream, Scots Guards, Irish Guards —, possessed as his headquarters or appropriate shrine a kind of small Greek temple in stucco, with fluted pillars and capitals of the Doric order, placed, as if for the sake of inviolability, behind the stout, spear-like iron railings of Birdcage Walk. Besides being so important a military mandarin, the Lieutenant-Colonel was, as well, an institution comparable to that of an Elder in the monasteries of the Russian Orthodox Church, healing, and bestowing advice or reprimands. In other respects, he more nearly, perhaps, resembled an idol. Summoned hither, to the temple of the particular cult to whose worship he had been dedicated, the neophyte, not yet fledged or newly-joined ensign — or as for that, any officer who had conducted himself in a manner contrary to, or perhaps, even, only exaggerating, regimental tradition —, would find himself first involved in a flurry of stamping sentries and saluting orderlies (a process which, singularly enough, only served, by the apparent aura of respect it with such irony produced for him, to make his own feeling of inner instability the worse). Then, ushered almost at once into the august presence, he would be obliged to salute, in his turn and as smartly as he could, the idol seated at a desk, behind the cloud of incense composed of his own cigarette smoke. Directly the ensign beheld the old image, who would be puffing at a substantial but delicately aromatic Turkish or Egyptian cigarette, he would realise that here, before him, was the improbable realisation of an ideal; an ideal cherished by a considerable number of contemporaries, including most officers and all the best tailors and haberdashers, hosiers, shoemakers and barbers in London, indeed in England. And this quality, or rather, the subconscious knowledge in the image that he embodied it, produced in him something of the genial, smiling impartiality of royal personages passing through the wards of a charitable institution. The English always put substance first, rather than its treatment; and just as roast beef is — or, alas, was — their principal dish, so everything here, also, was of prime material: and thus, though too restrained to suggest dandyism, yet everything about him was immaculate, of the finest quality and cut: cloth, linen, and the man encased in them. Every pore of the skin, every hair of his grey moustache and eyebrows, was unemphatically — for emphasis would smack of ostentation — in its right place, and showed in miniature the same kind of order and beautiful military precision that the regimental parades exhibited on the grand scale. His manners, too, imbued though they were by their quality of rather impersonal affability — and though it was quite evident, as well, that the idol realised that affability was not his whole practice and that at times it was his duty to instil awe —, were memorable in their perfection. At a single glance it might be deemed possible by the inexperienced, such was the apparent sincerity and straightforwardness of his self-presentation, to know all about him, even to write a testimonial, *strong sense of duty, hard-playing (golf, cricket, polo), generous, brave, fine shot, adequate rider, man of the world, C. of E.* These same attributes, too, seemed to belong to the objects on his desk, the photographs, in simple silver frames or leather — the best photographs of the best people, in the best frames —, the silver cigarette-lighter, made in the shape of a grenade, the silver pen-tray and rack, the pens and pencils, the regimental trophies and presentations, even the blotting-paper which lay spread out under his hand without a stain. (How did he ever contrive to dry the ink on a letter? one asked oneself.) But where it would be easy for the young officer to go astray in the estimate he was making, would be if he were to dismiss the fine and benevolent old gentleman in front of him as at all remote, or out of touch with the true business of his regiment : for, as if the position he held bestowed upon him special powers of divination, he could, at one pounce, show himself singularly, surprisingly, frighteningly well-informed.

When I compared this polished, kindly and agreeable individual, of unfailing courtesy, with Major Gowk of the cavalry regiment from which I had just made my escape, I understood my good fortune. The realisation of an ideal always, no doubt, carries with it its weak points, but of one thing you could rest assured : the idol before you would never treat any man, especially one younger than himself, with unfairness : nor, you could be equally certain, would his predecessor have done it in the past, or his successor do it in the future. For the type was fast. When the time came for this elderly man to retire, another, almost identical in appearance, would reign with the same elegant ease in his stead, behind the same cloud of cigarette smoke, at the same table, covered, it might seem, with the same photographs, the same objects. Very seldom did these skilful old gentlemen, so well versed in the behaviour of the young male of their sort, make a mistake. They knew their job. . . . Sometimes, however, the military mind, engaged in its own world of stiff, Euclidean calculation, leads even its finest exemplars to reach false conclusions. But if I relate first an incident of this kind, I must, to render the correct balance, counter it, immediately after, with another

of opposite tendency, to show the quality of delicate understanding that a machine of such military efficiency could on
occasion, and most unexpectedly, reveal. In both cases, I
jump ahead five years, towards the end of the First World War.
By that time, I was twenty-four, and a Captain.

Late one morning, I was sent for to the Regimental Orderly
Room. Hastening as quickly as I could to the temple, I was
commanded to proceed at once, with the regulation escort of
a lieutenant and ensign, to St. Pancras Station, and there arrest,
as he stepped out of the train on to the platform, a " young
officer ". The charge against him was unspecified, but, I was
given to understand, of a serious nature. In fact, I must use
force, if necessary, to nab him : for he might prove a battling
captive. And in this connection, let me remind the reader that
the term " young officer " was technical, youth consisting in
short regimental service rather than in lack of years, and that,
during the 1914–18 war, when many were already middle-
aged before they took commissions, the accused might be
old enough to be my father. And so, indeed, he proved. The
poor old chap seemed very surprised when, placing his hat on
his grey hair, he stepped out of the carriage and found two
other officers and myself waiting for him, with, if I remember
correctly military procedure, our swords drawn. He enquired,
with an engaging air of puzzlement and timidity, what we could
have against him. I replied that he would shortly learn, in the
Regimental Orderly Room. According to orders, we marched
there in fine style, and were received with considerable dis-
ciplinary pomp.

" Mr. Crouchend," the Lieutenant-Colonel observed, looking over the top of a pair of beautifully made spectacles with a
terrifying mildness, " there is a serious charge against you ! "

" Sir ! " Mr. Crouchend replied dutifully, in the sacrificial
monosyllable that is the correct reply to a superior officer in
the Brigade of Guards.

" You gave a false address when on leave last week," the
Lieutenant-Colonel continued in the voice of an oracle. " You
wrote in the book 42 Clarges Street : we have evidence that
you were staying at 12 Half Moon Street."

With the cry of a wild animal that has been snared, poor Mr. Crouchend broke away from tradition and wailed,

"But it's the same building, sir! It's Fleming's Hotel!"

Silence of a rather portentous kind followed this disclosure, and the junior officers of the escort, I observed, stared in front of them with peculiarly unseeing eyes. Already the mind's ear could detect the thunder of reprimand and rebuke that would, when we had departed, roll through the room: for the idol would speak, of that there could be no doubt. At last he roused himself from the coma into which he seemed to be descending, and called,

"March that officer out at once! I will go into the matter later."

The reverse of this story indicates the flexibility of regimental tradition. A very strict rule existed that no officer should be seen, except on duty, in the company of a private soldier. . . . One day, soon after this other occurrence, an officer who had joined the regiment since the war started, and was fighting it out in the corridors of the War Office, reported to the Regimental Orderly Room that he had seen me having a drink with a private soldier in the Café Royal. When summoned to the presence, I explained that the private soldier in question was Jacob Epstein, and that I refused to cut a distinguished sculptor who was a friend of mine, just because he happened to have enlisted. To my surprise the Lieutenant-Colonel, purely out of a sense of decency — for it can be imagined that Epstein's sculpture was not numbered among the Regimental Orderly Room's ideals —, took my part. He saw the point perfectly, and called to order the officer who had reported me. . . . Such was the wise latitude at times allowed.

To go back to earlier years, after the initial interview with the Lieutenant-Colonel and the joining the battalion to which I was attached at the Tower, my next duty was typical of the War Office of those days. As if in London, a city containing seven million inhabitants, no doctor was to be found, I received one afternoon official instructions to report to Lichfield for medical examination the following morning at eleven. To accomplish this, I had to catch a train at 5 A.M. at Euston, and my journey to Dr. Johnson's birthplace and back, first-class, was charged to the nation! . . . I spent a happy morning wandering round the Cathedral, with its Tennysonian-Gothic bearded kings and Victorian *grande-dame* queens, and paying my respects to the Doctor's statue. I had luncheon at an inn, where the neighbouring farmers, I remember, gathered after the market — and in those days farmers still engaged in a topiary of whisker that made their faces extremely interesting and characteristic —, and returned to the Tower in the afternoon.

Throughout the months that ensued between December 1912 and the outbreak of war, my background varied constantly: the Tower, Aldershot once more — but after the town I had known, how strangely different and comparatively pleasant an Aldershot this seemed! —, several months of leave, Pirbright, Purfleet and Wellington Barracks. . . . It was eight o'clock in the morning. School was finished with. Though finding myself a member of a profession for which I showed no aptitude, and though aware of my deficiency in this respect, yet now the lines would begin to be engraved on my right hand, differently from my left. December 1912 was the month in which my life, my own life, began. . . . As I looked at my home, I could see how quickly things were altering. In April 1913, while I was still at the Tower, Henry quitted my father's service for ten years. That, in itself, marked the end of an epoch. Robins now took his place, and had, in his turn, to get to know all the points of The System: that plan for the better ordering of his life which my father had devised. At their first interview, my father had looked at him and said,

" I know *some people* make out I'm difficult to get on with, but *I* don't agree with them ! "

And, indeed, at first everything went most smoothly. One day, though, referring — because one was to be made up — to a book in which my father kept all his prescriptions, Robins saw a reproachful note newly entered, " *Potassium Bicarbonate* (or whatever the name of the drug was), *this should be taken in a level tea-spoon: but Robins has several times given me a heaped-up spoonful of it* ".

Many changes, as I was saying, were evident. . . . It was not difficult to perceive the trend and accent of things or to notice how the various shadows had come out into the open, and were now parading themselves, their blackness touching the dawn and dusk of each day, of each day in each week. Life, however, in spite of it, seemed so welcoming, so enchanting, that these patches of moving dark would surely disappear : though my instincts never allowed me to accept the burgess view, so often proffered, that " the worst never happens ", and so, for moments that in their horror stretched to hours, and for so long as my physical cheerfulness would allow me, I would wonder whether the shadows, now in part materialised, might not take on full substance. . . . As I looked back at the view sweeping to so great a distance behind me, I could see nothing of the sort, nothing to offer a warning by parallel. Shadows, of course, must have existed when one had been down there, but how swiftly they had vanished. Similarly, life lay spread before me, stretching on all sides toward a horizon, peaceful, golden and illimitable. But what kind of life ? I asked myself. That for which I must look, and which heredity itself had taught me to seek, was a continuation of that of my father — and still more of that of his father, less exceptional ; in the same houses, in the same county, in the same country ; the same kind of existence, domestic and official, the same professions, the same posts.

All this was inscribed in my left hand, but what there was in my right, I could not tell. It was easier to deduce from frame, appearance and trend of mind what characteristics I had inherited and from what direction. It was plain at this age, I think, that I embodied two chief strains, Sitwell and Somerset : from them comes what, in combination, gives me any particular quality I may possess as a writer ; a way of seeing things, a mind that loves and comprehends modern art, a faculty for enjoyment, and a natural demand for it, or gusto, qualities that are allied with or rise out of the physical constitution ; to them, of all my relatives, I am chiefly drawn by inclination, though our tastes are so different, and it seems to me that in my reflection in the looking-glass I could — and can —

observe the traits that I know from portraits, just as, very clearly, I can identify in my sister the traces of Plantagenet blood, so that she might by her cast of face, in the mould of body and in the shape of her wrists and hands, have sat for the portrait of Lady Elizabeth or Katherine Somerset,[1] or their cousin Queen Elizabeth, or for the golden effigy in the Abbey of their ancestress, Queen Eleanor. Looking at myself, as I was then, I recognised the height, and breadth of shoulder, the straight, fair hair, the long, bridged nose, with winged nostrils, the rather florid, fair colouring; these I had seen in portraits at Renishaw and elsewhere. But there were other things, besides, and to take wit, if I may claim it, that is always a personal possession, an accident of birth or upbringing, a power never fully under control, in essence explosive and anarchic, composed of diverse and unresolved elements. My mind, I believe, was modern, in accord in many respects with the age in which I live, but it may be remembered that I have also in me the blood of a family which today yet bears, as it should, the old Royal Arms of England, quartering still the lilies of France — which George III surrendered — with the leopards, and carrying under the shield the words *I disdain to change or fear*; blood which in its very pulsing ever showed steadfastness and a peculiar loyalty to tradition.

The view, then, which I saw ahead of me was one of which I was not altogether worthy: but that did not prevent it from being golden or very different from today's dun-coloured plains, full of ant-like turmoil under the gigantic rocks that have been hurled down. . . . What was the lie of the road in front ? . . . Before I reached the climax of my life and became a candidate for, or member of, Parliament, as my father, his grandfather and great-grandfather had been before me, or found myself in some position of trust and responsibility, it led to two whole worlds (two worlds, again; for " Gemini rising gives a dual impetus "), for me to explore, if not to conquer. But so far, throughout my school-days and the years that had followed, I had shown myself to be a failure; of this I was fully aware. There was the inner regimental world, the

[1] See *Left Hand, Right Hand !* p. 76.

brother-officers I must learn to know and understand, and the officers, beyond that, of the whole Brigade of Guards, who formed the mass out of whom to choose one's friends : with whom one must associate, expecting to meet them every day at restaurants and theatres, at dinners and dances in private houses ; and, outside, the second, the fashionable world, of whom, apart from relatives, I knew singularly few members.

I must mention, for he belonged to this first world, one young officer in the Irish Guards, a friend and exact contemporary of mine. This was " Alex " : the future Field-Marshal Viscount Alexander of Tunis, the greatest soldier Britain has produced since Wellington, who came, too, of a precisely similar family and origin. . . . In the days of which I write, he was a charming and elegant young man, with then, as now, a seriousness underlying his gaiety of disposition, and a quick and easy smile. Since he was also stationed at Wellington Barracks while I was there, I saw a good deal of him, and I recollect that he and a great friend and brother-officer of his, Eric Greer, who was killed in the 1914 conflict, were unlike others of my friends in their enthusiastic study of military history, to which they devoted themselves for hours ; though quietly, and without giving their views on it to the rest of us. I did not take part in such recreations, for just in the same way that the illiterati protest that they cannot understand modern poetry, so I find military history, strategy and tactics obscure and disappointing. Of such matters I cannot understand a word I read. On the other hand, in this resembling those who are wont to declare that they " know a tune when they hear one ", I am not enough of a military Philistine to fail to recognise a great soldier when I see one ; though, when Alex and I met, as we did frequently, we discussed people, and things pertaining to them, more often than strategy or modern literature ; because to mention a subject of any consequence in the environment in which we found ourselves would not have been well looked upon. Enjoyment was the aim of life, and gaiety and high spirits the links that bound us. I remember many long walks back to Wellington Barracks late at night in his company, from some dance or supper-party, down the graceful yellow sickle of the Nash Regent Street, and down Lower Regent Street to the Mall, across the Iron Bridge that spans St. James's Lake, and so home to Wellington Barracks. Sometimes, the conversation would take a more thoughtful turn, ill suited to our attire; for we were dressed, with the dandyism of a time when in England cleanliness was really believed to be next to godliness — instead of being regarded, as now it is, as an unjustifiable and anti-social extravagance —, in evening clothes, wearing broad-braided black trousers, white waistcoats, starched shirts and white ties, white kid gloves, with a white carnation or gardenia in the buttonhole of our coats, and carried gold- or tortoise-shell-topped Malacca canes. Such was the convention, and, strange as it seems now in the shabby, broken-down London of today, we walked for miles clad in this manner, and, moreover, crowned either with a silk hat or a gibus, the mode for which alternated every few months with startling rapidity: (though it struck me as strange that a gibus should ever be fashionable, for, in spite of its Jack-in-the-box fascination — so essentially that of a toy —, it was the only instance to be found of mechanism applied to clothing).

If we talked rather seldom of grave affairs, and never of professional, it must be granted, notwithstanding, that somehow or other I succeeded in divining Alex's capacity. Shortly after the end of the 1914–18 fracas, it so happened that I met him on a cross-Channel steamer bound for Boulogne. I had scarcely seen him to talk to, since the days of peace, and I greeted him with the words,

" Hullo, Alex! . . . You are *really* a very intelligent man, aren't you ? "

He replied, with his usual spontaneity and frankness, but with an air at once modest and somewhat taken aback at the discovery of a secret long concealed,

" Well, yes . . . I suppose I am ! "

At the time of which I write, however, we still maintained a conspiratorial silence on the matter, growing, as it were, even less serious as we approached the Barracks and took the sentry's salute. . . . Nor, as we drew nearer, did the prospect of the Barracks, or of the life it contained, depress me. In my memory I still recall the time I spent there as the first period of my life that I enjoyed with a full sweep, and fortunately I recognised my happiness while it lasted. A thousand small things, as well as greater, contributed to this result. Even to leave the Barracks on foot or return to them, offered its own pleasures : because, for example, to walk by day or night across the Iron Bridge in St. James's Park provided a never-failing moment of delighted surprise, by the view it afforded, across the length of water, of Whitehall and the Foreign Office : a vista as spectacular as any in Venice or Pera, in its conglomeration of domes and towers and belfries, in their styles unassimilable except by the poetic mist that the London atmosphere alone contributes, to unify and bestow its own enchantment.

I went to Wellington Barracks in September 1913 — at the end of Army Manœuvres, on which I had proceeded with the 1st Battalion from Aldershot. Each day, we marched some twenty to thirty miles, and by dark I was usually too exhausted to know or care where I might be. My incapacity as a soldier must, indeed, have been conspicuous ; if sent out, as sometimes one was, with a map, to find the way for the battalion, expeditions inevitably had to be sent out before long, in their turn, to find me. And I still remember the shock of recognition with which, the sun and breeze suddenly lifting a light fog, I discovered myself to be by the side of the formal canal, among the herds of deer and piebald flocks of Jacob's sheep, in Sir Alfred Dryden's famous but secluded estate of Canons Ashby, about two miles from Weston, my grandmother's old home. I had possessed no conception that I was within a hundred miles of it ! . . . In these Manœuvres, though, some friends of mine distinguished themselves as much as I disgraced myself : but it all came to the same thing ; for in those days to spring a surprise on the Staff by doing too well was equivalent to doing badly. To be over-zealous and super-successful was a fault ! Thus I well remember the consternation caused when, the Intelligence Officer falling ill, my friend Geoffrey Moss temporarily took over his work, and since he possesses an acute and untrammelled mind, nearly put an end to Manœuvres by capturing two motor-cars full of " enemy " Generals. They had hurriedly to be released, for they had envisaged no such move on the part of a junior officer, and their faces flamed red as the tabs they wore, with anger.

Another feature of that ten days I recall with more appreciation. One Saturday night to Monday, the Brigade of Guards camped in the park of Mr. Alfred de Rothschild, at Halton in Buckinghamshire, and officers and men were given many treats by the generous owner, who most sumptuously entertained the officers. This fragile, beautifully neat old gentleman with an anxious expression, who seemed to sum up in his own person a century of luxurious living and sly financial domination, inhabited a large yellow stone house, with lofty French slate roofs and towers and turrets, that stood at the top of a hill, well screened under the higher Chilterns, among acres and sweeping acres of carefully mown grass. The first afternoon, he gave us a performance of his private circus. It was a somewhat grotesque occasion. The little old man, dressed in a blue suit and wearing a blue bowler hat above the minute white screw-curl on each temple, acted as circus-master himself, and stood holding a whip in the middle of a miniature ring at the top of one of his poodle-smooth lawns. Round his feet, the performing animals leapt through their hoops and pranced and danced on their back legs, and went through all kinds of ingenious tricks, while, with a flick of his lash that touched no dogs, not one of them — for he possessed the genuine and excessive tenderness for pets that often characterises the millionaire —, he explained that all was done by kindness. But it was fortunate for his peace of mind that he was deaf — this accounted for the anxious concentration of his glance —, and so could not hear, as we could, the yelping protests of the poor little beasts off-stage, in the hands of their trainers. . . . Tiring of this circus, I walked away, I remember, to examine the rustic details of a summer-house near-by, attracted to it by the curious rattling sound it emitted in the golden breeze of mid-September: but the mystery was quickly solved, for the ivy that covered this retreat proved to be made of painted metal, and so clanked faintly against the walls with each breath. But no doubt it always remained neat. . . . Inside, stood on a table a telephone of ivory and gold. . . . The interior of Halton, spacious and ugly, contained many superb objects, mostly of French derivation. I climbed a few steps up one side of the double staircase, to examine more closely a Watteau, hanging on the wall above. But soon I felt someone was following — and sure enough, at a few paces behind, a hefty stranger, of what is known as " respectable appearance", was watching me intently. This proved to be Mr. Alfred de Rothschild's private detective. And in the house at the same time, I was told, there resided as well a doctor and a lawyer, in case the old gentleman fell ill or wished to add a codicil to his last testament. To such lengths, such heights or depths, can great wealth lead a being endowed with a highly strung nervous system and some imagination. In addition to his own lawyer, doctor and detective, Mr. Alfred de Rothschild possessed a private orchestra of string instruments, which played during and after dinner. And if the programme of music it discoursed was on this occasion rather banal, it may have been chosen to suit the military taste. The dinner itself was a masterpiece of French art, and the accompanying wines were memorable.

Alas! the life we led, in bivouacs, with noses blue from cold at night, and with sausages or herrings as the pinnacle of every meal, was not so luxurious, and it was with joy that I found myself in London again, at Wellington Barracks, where I remained until shortly before the outbreak of the war in 1914. I occupied a room on the second floor, overlooking the Parade Ground — from this height almost hidden — and, beyond it, the trees and water of St. James's Park. On the left, one could not, during those years, see Buckingham Palace, because the front was entirely screened by a criss-cross of scaffolding and canvas, behind which the new, hard, Portland-stone façade, a soulless model, was growing, stiffly as a cactus, to replace the rather charming but dingy confusion of that by Blore. This temporary, many-storeyed maze of poles and planks and platforms and screens was impressive and interesting in the manner of a drawing by Piranesi. But, at night, the view in general from my windows became transformed, for then the thousands of lights across the St. James's and the Green Park, and as far as you could see, dyed the ragged edges of the clouds, suffusing the whole vast vault with a flush of rose and orange, and made anyone who looked beyond the dark surrounding banks and mounds of the leaves become conscious that he was, indeed, in the quiet heart of the greatest and most famous of cities, the light of which could thus enflame a whole sky to its apex. . . . Here you did not, it is true, have the feeling of the continuous traditions of a thousand years of fierce life, or of the desultory and savage outbreaks of history, that assailed you at the Tower, but merely of having access to every pleasure, every mystery, every whisper, of the town. . . . Moreover, unlike the Tower again, there was no Officers' Mess, and so no official regimental feasts occurred : *Belshazzars*, as they were called, which, because of their habitual length and dullness, as well as for their occasional horseplay, young officers rather dreaded. Here private rather than regimental life prevailed, and every evening could be spent where or with whom you chose, except when the duties of Picquet Officer confined you to barracks for a day and night, or for the twenty-four hours spent on King's Guard, or the fifteen on guard at the Bank of England.

So far as I know, though it has been for so long one of the spectacles most familiar to inhabitants of London, and most loved by visitors, little has been written about the Changing of the Guard : to the crowd, the performers in the ceremony cease to exist when they have marched away : and so I propose to give for a page or two an account of the very individual life led by the officers on this duty, who, after the manner of monks, albeit for twenty-four hours only, are immured in the seclusion of a brick building from which, though situated in the very centre of the capital, you can scarcely hear the passing of traffic. . . . First, the new Guard marches to the ceremony, just as later the old Guard returns to barracks, to the military music of the drums and fifes of the battalion from which it is drawn. If the King is in London, the ceremony takes place, as all Londoners know, at about ten minutes to eleven, in the Fore Court of Buckingham Palace, or, in the monarch's absence from London, on the Colour Court at St. James's : but, as a spectacle, Buckingham Palace is to be preferred as a background, because of the greater space it affords. The drill exhibited has many of the merits of a work of art, such as only the most accomplished forms of dancing or skating display. But of all the difficult tasks, the Ensign — the youngest officer present — has the most awkward allotted to him : marching just behind the Captain and Lieutenant of King's Guard and in front of the detachment of men composing it, the whole body progressing in slow time — an exercise which itself requires the greatest skill — at right angles to the Palace, he must lower the Colour in salute to the Colour of the King's Guard relieving or being relieved, and hold it stretched out in that position for some twenty paces. Many weeks of practice on the barrack square are required before perfection is attained — if ever it is — in this stately ceremonial crawl to the solemn and inspiring strains of the March from Handel's *Scipio*, which the Grenadiers have adopted as their own, in the same way that the Coldstream use the March from *Figaro*. After this part of the performance has been concluded and the new Guard has taken over, and while the sentries are being posted and the detachments placed in position, the officers of the King's Guard mounting and dismounting walk up and down together in twos, according to the military rank they hold, while whichever regimental band may be playing gives selections from its repertory. Each of the four, naturally, had its own specialities, and in those days the band of the Grenadiers used often, rather unexpectedly, but always to my delight, to break into contemporary Spanish marches and selections from current *zarzuelas* : for Prince Alexander of Battenberg,[1] the Queen of Spain's brother, who was in the Grenadiers at the time and possessed that love of music which, since the days of George I, so many members of the Royal Family have shown, used to bring back the scores with him from his visits to Andalusia and Madrid. And these were airs which a musician could like, in no way resembling the popular tunes of Paris and London, cities in this respect so badly served for more than a century, though the tunes whistled and hummed by the people at work, and played at street corners by bands and barrel

[1] Now Marquess of Carisbrooke.

organs, should form so important an ingredient in the communal happiness and afford its own characteristic rhythm to each city, as they do — or did — in, let us say, Palermo and Seville. Other innovations were not so successful as the Spanish marches. Sometimes the band grew ambitious, and I remember Williams, for many years Bandmaster of the Grenadiers, telling me of how he had made an arrangement for his men of part of the score of *Electra* by Richard Strauss, and of what happened when first he played it. It had taken them many months to learn, and they had just given it in public for the first time during this long interval in the Changing of the Guard at Buckingham Palace, and had experienced a due sense of elation at their own audacity and at the success that had crowned it, when — a rare event — a scarlet-coated page came out from the Palace with a personal message for Williams from King George V. The note was brief and ran, " His Majesty does not know what the Band has just played, but it is *never* to be played again." . . . For some twenty minutes or half an hour, then, the band would lift the spirits of the watching crowd, ox-eyed at the railings, and by the end of that time every sentry would be in his place, and the rest of the oncoming Guard be free to march away to its quarters in St. James's Palace, and the old Guard to return home.

The oncoming Guard was on duty until relieved twenty-four hours later. During this space of time, the officers had to remain in the part of St. James's Palace allotted to them — an inner section, built of stout, dark brick, more nearly recalling, save that there were no trees, part of some college or close than the centre of a palace : this haven they were not allowed to leave, except for tours of duty and inspection, when they visited the sentries at Buckingham Palace and Marlborough House, and except for a few minutes in the afternoon when they were permitted, if they wished, to walk across to the Guards' Club or the Marlborough Club, then both situated within a stone's-throw, in Pall Mall. (All officers serving in the Brigade joined automatically the Guards' Club, though not the Marlborough.) As the Ensign had to go out on a tour of inspection at 2 A.M. it made a long day for him, and life in the guardroom with its view of lead flats and dingy crenellations, though it possessed an air, and seemed the very core of St. James's, became a little monotonous and might, indeed, have grown insupportably to resemble a prison, had it not been for the munificence of King George IV, who had directed that, after his death, an annual sum should be paid to the officers on guard. It was not enough to defray the whole of the expense, but it certainly enabled them to entertain their friends to dinner in a handsome manner, and, in consequence, the long room, in the evening, with its table arranged with silver trophies, and its food, celebrated for its excellence, as no doubt that gourmet, King George IV, would have wished, became a place where many distinguished — and undistinguished — people could pass a most pleasant evening. The quality of the company depended chiefly on the Captain of King's Guard and his range of friends : certainly I passed many delightful hours in congenial company there : and among my own friends who dined with me in later years, when from time to time I was Captain, were Sir Edmund Gosse, Sickert and Robert Ross.

I shall not now write of this room, nor of Paul, the old French waiter, for several decades its chief ornament ; since I have written of both at some length. in the series of characters — a book as yet unchristened — with which I design to bring this autobiography to an end : but, at least, I may here mention Edouard, who does not figure later in these volumes. Some twenty years before, he had been the chef of Willis's Rooms,[1] the most famous and fashionable restaurant in the London of the 'nineties, and a place much frequented by Whistler, Wilde, Frank Harris and other celebrities of the epoch. Edouard, now retired from the active labours of cooking, and presiding, instead, over the catering of King's Guard, was a plump, rather unwieldy Frenchman, who still retained the face of a chef : though rather pale, the mask of one who had spent his life near fires and ovens, and had inhaled the essences of a thousand famous dishes. Perhaps

[1] Willis's Rooms, in King Street, St. James's, subsequently became the Auction Rooms of Messrs. Robinson & Foster. Unfortunately, the premises were bombed in 1941 ; but, at the moment of writing, one fragment of a plaster frieze still survives, and can be noticed by curious sightseers high up on a blackened wall.

because of this, he suffered from gout, and occupied habitually a large chair — shaped to his body like a snail's shell, so that he rose with difficulty — in a diminutive room on the ground floor at the side of the narrow staircase. There was hardly space for him and his chair and his desk in it, let alone for his papers, his keys — he seemed always to be jangling keys, like the Chief Eunuch in *Schéhérazade* —, his sample bottles of wine and brandy, the cloves of garlic and bunches of dried herbs on a shelf, and his books of recipes and accounts. (The account-books were the same long, stiff-covered books, full of faintly pencilled scrawls, that you see in provincial cafés in France.) In this den, he planned all the meals and the marketing — and, no doubt, the rattle and jingle of his keys was the sign that he was thinking out some problem of the palate. He would hobble up the narrow stairs, only just wide enough for him, several times a day for consultation on culinary points : but I preferred to talk to him in his own surroundings, to go and find him at his desk. There, however, his attention would be less easy to engage, for he would be sure to be looking at his accounts, and he seemed always to experience that same difficulty in adding them up that one notices, too, in restaurant-keepers abroad. The sums seemed to haunt him, even when talking of other matters, and his lips would move in invisible addition. He may, perhaps, in his time have been an extravagant chef, but he was a thrifty man : and his interest now was divided between the art of cooking, the choice of fine wines and the amassing of money. With the national sense of fitness, he objected as strongly as he could to the buying of anything out of season, of early, forced asparagus or strawberries, and would always try to prevail on the Captain of King's Guard to order whatever constituted the best and cheapest material, and that most poetically typical of its moment. In subsequent days, when I had got to know him well, even when not on guard, I would often call in to seek his advice and more generally because I enjoyed hearing him talk English with his throaty French accent, and because he held for me the atmosphere of a past period, of Willis's Rooms and of the 'nineties, which seemed already remote as the times of the Atridae. . . . The dinners he provided constituted, without a doubt, the high light of these claustrophobic hours : whether the guests were amusing or whether they were dull, it was always with regret that the younger officers saw them leave — they were obliged by custom to be out by ten minutes to eleven. Soon the Ensign would be left alone, with nothing to read except the evening papers — of which, then, there were six or seven, in their various shades of pink and green, as well as white — until his final tour of inspection, when he marched through the garden, very large and dark and full of shadows, of Buckingham Palace — or " Buck House " as shibboleth decreed it should be called : an abbreviation, no doubt, remaining from before 1825 when the former Buckingham House first became known as Buckingham Palace.

The days spent on King's Guard were of so special a nature as perhaps to resemble a little those spent by Catholics during a Retreat, though, of course, devoted to more material pursuits and duties. The resemblance consisted of the way in which the days added up and each fresh period joined on to the preceding, to make, as one looks back, a separate small lifetime of a month or two months in all, but in their quality completely unlike any other kind of existence the same individual has led. The things which afforded a sense of continuity with the life of the world outside could, moreover, be counted on the fingers of the hand. But, in addition to the few I have mentioned, one other link existed : it was permissible to have your hair cut ; and, all the more because there was less reason on those occasions for my native impatience to frustrate entirely the hairdresser's art, as it so often did, and because, on the contrary, it constituted a most pleasant diversion, I always arranged for an appointment. Accordingly at about 5.30 in the evening and carrying a black bag of instruments, Mr. G. F. Trumper, hairdresser to King George V, would come to attend me.

Trumper was already an old friend of mine, for I had by chance, when as a small boy of eleven or twelve I was staying for a few days in London, and was, as small boys are, being plagued to get my hair cut, selected the shop in which he worked as a likely place for the purpose. I had been fortunate enough to find his chair vacant, and we had soon become friends. He had not then acquired control of the business which bears his name, but he was already the prevailing personality in it. First of all, before proceeding to describe him, I must make it clear that he was an exceptionally good hairdresser. I have always been interested in the predispositional factors that induce a man to adopt any particular profession, and I believe very often, whatever the trade, from dentist to dustman, you will find a sense of vocation has been the chief cause.[1] Certainly Trumper was as much of a character in his profession as outside it, in talk. He had invented the method of thinning the hair with a razor, and of brushing the hair straight back from the forehead, which governed the fashion for men in my youth. And I remember that, in one of the few instances in which I visited another firm, I extracted from his rival the somewhat unwilling admission that " Mr. Trumper has done more to raise the status of the whole profession than any man living". It would be true, then, to say that he was a born hairdresser : but no-one could have been less like the classical Figaro in his make-up. I grew to know him well, for friendship requires a basis of time for one of its dimensions, and since I went to be shaved and have my hair brushed by him every morning when in London, I spent at least a quarter of an hour of each day with him, and, of course, much longer when my hair was cut as well, during many months a year, over a period of some three decades at least ; a fair allowance of time, longer, indeed, than that bestowed on many friends. But, even at that, his personality offered a field of study which could not be covered in the time. From the first it would be evident, however, that this lean, direct man, with his greying hair, his correct clothes and tie, in which was always a pin carrying the royal cypher — a gift from the King — had none of the traditional *allegro*, happy-go-lucky ways of that runner of messages, that formerly the name of

[1] Among the various data I can offer, without any attempt at deduction therefrom, is the curiously inconsequential fact that enquiries usually elicit that members of the dental profession originally wished to join the Navy, but were prevented by one reason or another ; and that they are apt to retain a great devotion to the sea and sailing.

barber summoned up. The members of this profession had the reputation also of being vain, as well as sycophantic and inclined to chatter as they plied the scissors or razor; but, I take it, a hairdresser's practice might equally conduce to constraint, cynicism and silence, for who else, except a lawyer, sees so many unpleasant or absurd traits revealed unequivocally by his clients, from the silly pretensions of the boy, who comes to have his non-existent moustache curled, to the faint but persistent hopes of the elderly *beau*, who demands a dye, under the disguise of some other name, for his hair? Trumper's level but humorous glance, and rather severe look, except when he smiled, and the jut of his jaw, which was somewhat aggressive, certainly suggested a love of truth, and a willingness to maintain it as opposed to flattery. Indeed, far from seeking to ingratiate himself with a customer, he was inclined to behave despotically, treating some with unaccountable fury (at times, his richest and most influential customers would be ordered out of the shop, and it can be imagined what a spectacle this made for the young, as elderly gentlemen, hardly able to believe what their ears told them, hurriedly shuffled out) and according to others an equally arbitrary favour. Those he liked, or disliked, offered a wide range from the trainers of race-horses to poets : and the qualities he appreciated were simplicity, politeness, want of affectation of any sort or of a sense of personal importance, and, I think, originality in whatever it consisted. Especially Trumper hated what he termed *swagger*. (Except in the drama, for he always, when talking of the theatre, used to say " What I like is *costume*, with lots of swagger and romance ".) Once, when a celebrated man, a Minister of the Crown, sent for Trumper, and was having his hair cut, he demanded :

" Well, Trumper, what do they say of me in the country, now? "

" Never so much as mention your name, m'lord. They don't know who you are."

After this application of cooling lotion, the talk collapsed.

I remember an incident which occurred in 1913. A little, over-dressed customer, a rich man, intensely self-satisfied, and with the typical self-importance of the dwarf, used to come every day to the shop. His casual but agreeable likeness to Little Tich had in the first place drawn my attention to him, and I had begun to take an interest in him. Almost the only engaging quality he possessed was an exaggerated nervousness about his health. For some weeks, or perhaps months, I had come to the conclusion that matters were mounting to a climax; especially when this very wealthy client spent the whole of one morning trying to sell Trumper (who in any case did not want it, and never dealt in such things) a case of Roumanian brandy, instead of buying hair-lotions or cigars, as he should have done. And the outbursts of " swagger " too, which were frequent, were not, I could see, to Trumper's liking. One day, I was present in the shop waiting for Trumper, who was just dusting his customer's coat with a brush, after giving him a hair-cut and shampoo and thus emphasising his odious air of spruceness, when the foolish little man turned to him and asked with complacency : " How do you think I'm looking now, Trumper ? "

Trumper summed him up carefully with his eyes, and pronounced judgement :

" Shocking, sir ! You've fallen away terribly at the back of the neck. It's a bad sign. I should say you'd be for it soon ! "

The effect was instantaneous. The little man fairly scuttled out of the shop, home to bed, and Trumper's reply — or it may have been death ! — removed this customer for ever from the shop.

On certain days Trumper would be engaged downstairs, distilling his own secret preparations, lotions and balms, with names like those of nymphs, Floreka, Eucris, and others : or he might be in the closet, half way down the shop, where he kept his stock of Havana cigars, piled up in boxes (though many were already sold and bore on them labels with his clients' names). He was a great judge of cigars, and had built up a noted trade in them. Occasionally, the sound of a violent altercation would come over the top of the partition which formed the walls of this sanctum : but it was equally probable that the customer would be given a box of cigars, of so fine a quality that they could not be bought. And often, when he came round to cut my hair on King's Guard, he would bring me a cigar or two as a present.

The half-hour he spent in attending me would pass all too quickly for my taste, for it took me back to the outside world. . . . He would talk of many things, and I would ask him for news of his customers, and of what had been taking place in the shop, for I have always liked to know by sight and by name a whole diverse range of people not known to me personally but whose ways can be studied — and the ways of men during the quarter of an hour spent in a barber's chair are singularly unselfconscious and much can be learnt from watching. . . . In return for my questions, Trumper would make enquiries from me about my father, who (though, until he was an old gentleman, he would never enter the shop) would be sure when I saw him similarly to show his curiosity concerning Trumper. The reason for this display of mutual interest was that during one of the raids my father conducted from time to time on my expenditure and mode of life, he had written to Trumper, with whom he had found out that I dealt, to demand whether I had an account at his shop : in reply, he had received a real rouser, which, without any attempt at polite evasion, told him to mind his own business. This correspondence had left a great impression on both of them. . . . Trumper would also, when he came to wait on me, talk to me of his early days. He had come from Manchester to London in the early 'nineties and had first worked in a shop in the City Road. In front of the shop was a pit, sunk in the pavement and securely barred at the top, and in it lumbered and grunted a live bear, as an advertisement for bear's-grease, to flatten and give brilliance to the hair. It was thus still in use in such quarters of the town, though its chief vogue had obtained some fifty years before. It had been a great struggle then to live, for the assistants were shockingly badly paid, and threepence was the biggest tip to be earned. He told me that on news of his first promotion, he had taken out two of his colleagues and they had had a memorable evening on grocer's port, followed the next day by consequences as unforgettable. He had been passionately fond of dancing as a young man, and I would make him tell me about the dances, the halls in which they took place, and the conversations of his partners. He also alleged that his first real chance in life had come from a bet, a lucky double which had enabled him to buy and furnish a house. He remained faithful to gambling and must have won and lost considerable sums, and his favourite holidays were, till the end of his life in 1944, still spent on the race-course.

Though the hours spent on King's Guard had been long, and the night was to be short, yet the routine afforded a complete break which removed, as it were, this space of time far from the run of London days, and made it seem both longer and shorter than it was. The Guard at the Bank of England, on the other hand, provided a very different existence. The Ensign was the only officer on duty, and he had to start from Wellington or Chelsea Barracks, without drums or fifes to support the faltering rhythm of his footsteps and those of his small detachment of men, on a long march through the hard, endless streets of the city, at about five or six o'clock in the evening, and to remain at the Bank till 9.30 or 10 the next morning. The Brigade of Guards had first been called in in the year 1780, at the time of the Gordon riots, to protect the original building — before Sir John Soane's edifice was in being — when the Government had thought it to be in danger from the drunken mob. And though cries of " No Popery ! " no longer rent the air of Threadneedle Street, day by day the Guard was still posted there. For, just as tricks of speech lingered, relating to past times, so did many obsolete customs survive. And in this connection I must record that a year or two subsequently, when the shortage of man-power first evinced itself after the great slaughter of 1914 and '15, and forced the authorities to examine the placing of sentries, with a view to abolishing all those not strictly necessary, I was told how it was discovered that two guardsmen were always on duty at a certain spot in Whitehall where the reason for their presence was not immediately obvious. On enquiries being made, and the records inspected, it became plain that when Sir Robert Walpole had been Prime Minister, he had formed a habit of walking from Downing Street, near-by, and of sitting on a garden-bench there for a while to rest and take the air, and that, because his life had been threatened, sentries had eventually been posted on each side, at the suggestion of Queen Caroline, to ensure his safety. . . . Walpole had resigned in 1742, the bench had crumbled to dust over a century ago, but the duties of the men, and their successors, had continued.

Similarly, the Bank and its Guard remained singularly unaltered. In 1913, it had not yet been added to, and remained almost unmodified since the time of Soane. After the business of the day had been finished, at the hour at which we arrived, this one-storey building, emptied altogether of life, and with its garden-courts and cloisters, resembled a monastery or a deserted temple rather than the most famous financial institution in the world. By one of the passionate paradoxes of its creator — surely the most original of all English architects —, it seemed to offer a quiet, leafy, well-kept retreat from the world. And, to one on guard, the most striking feature of it was the absolute silence, even deeper than that of St. James's, that prevailed during the hours of duty. At dusk, it was true, there would be the chirruping of thousands of starlings who dunly sprinkled the branches of the trees, temporarily communicating to them the liveliness and mobility of watch-springs: but, after darkness had penned these flocks, there would be no sound, except the very distant rumble of traffic, and the dragging footsteps, from time to time, of the peripatetic night-watchman. . . . Officers and men received a special fee for duty here, and the Ensign was allowed to have two guests to dine with him. The serving of dinner, the silver and linen, were just what they should have been; grilled sole, and fillet of beef to eat, and rats'-tail spoons and eighteenth-century forks with curving ends, to eat them with; all sound, un-adventurous, irreproachable — safe, in fact, as the Bank of England. But in the space of a year or two, this atmosphere was to be destroyed, and a top-heavy Tower of Babel, perhaps typifying post-war insecurity and the instability of its finances, was designed by Sir Herbert Baker to blot out Sir John Soane's restrained courts and screens, and to extinguish the peace of its cloisters by the substitution of heavy stone-work for fresh air.

How different in their quietness and, indeed, solemnity, were these evenings from others spent with the friends I had made lately! Hitherto I had scarcely been aware that such people existed as those whose houses I was now for choice to frequent, who lived for amusement and for things of the mind, eye, ear; a world of drawing-rooms, it is true, but drawing-rooms where it was at least possible to catch sight of such figures as Debussy and Richard Strauss, Chaliapin and Nijinsky, Delius and Sargent and Diaghilew. (It will, however, be noticed that even now the majority of artists whom I met belonged to entertainment, rather than offering a purely creative type.) This, my second world, offered me a wide choice of friends. My locale varied from Wellington Barracks or the Tower of London to Downing Street, from the cab-shelter, where sometimes I had supper after a dance, to Lambeth Palace — in a technical, L.C.C. sense, by no means a place of entertainment —, from my Aunt Londesborough's house to the Cabaret Club, where the lesser artistes of the theatre, as well as the greater, mixed with painters, writers, and their opposite, officers in the Brigade of Guards. This low-ceilinged night-club, appropriately sunk below the pavement of Beak Street, and hideously but relevantly frescoed by the painter, Percy Wyndham Lewis, appeared in the small hours to be a super-heated Vorticist garden of gesticulating figures, dancing and talking, while the rhythm of the primitive forms of ragtime throbbed through the wide room. Over it presided Madame Strindberg, the third and not least exceptional of the great writer's wives. I remember her as a small, pale, determined woman, but Augustus John, in his memoirs, gives a rather different and more spirited account of her. When not engaged in organising the club, this lady busied herself in discovering pictures by Whistler, a pursuit in which she was singularly, almost unnaturally, successful. . . . Dancing more than conversation was the art which occupied the young men of the time in the Cabaret Club: (I had taken with ease and delight to modern ballroom dancing). Indeed, I only remember one fragment of conversation. Late at night, I was introduced to the mother — or, as some said, merely the duenna —

of a girl who, though still young, had for some years been confidently expecting to make her début on the stage; a purpose that had been furthered by several notable friendships. In appearance the daughter — if such she was — recalled the convivial female intimates of Hogarth and Captain Laroon; she belonged to a type almost extinct today, rotund and highly-coloured, having about her a kind of full-blown, rustic but frowzy freshness, like that of a dewy, but lolling and drooping rose, of an early morning, and an air at the same time sullen and good-natured, quick to smile and equally to take offence. On this occasion, however, her long course of professional disappointment had, perhaps, overcome her, and she could not speak a word. Her mother, in more expansive, if sentimental, mood, looked at her fondly and remarked to me — " Poor child . . . she's thinking of her dad who was killed. . . . He was an Admiral, in the Army ! "

For talk, however, I found other resorts more interesting, and I have always preferred private houses to restaurants, and conversation to shouting. . . . Mrs. Asquith,[1] by nature no less than by habit ever hospitable, used to invite me to Downing Street, then a centre of such an abundance and intensity of life as it had not seen for a hundred years and is never likely to see again : for at that time it contained a social dynamo as hostess. Alas, her example, and the influence it exercised on politics, was sufficient to enjoin, for the future, carefulness, and to exalt a contrary model, of primness, smugness, sealed lips and *Punch* humour. Mrs. Asquith's audacious comments, those called forth from a witty and original mind, were governed, in spite of their apparent sharpness, by invariable standards — though standards not of taste, but of truth. In the first place it must be borne in mind that she was an extremely religious woman. It has been related, for example, that at the time of the Armistice in November 1918, she went down on her knees in a crowded omnibus, to say a prayer. If this be true, it will have been a genuine demonstration of feeling, for she lacked all self-consciousness or pretence. She got on well with the simple : the silly and the flighty, the

[1] Afterwards Countess of Oxford and Asquith.

greedy and the mean were her quarry; but even the barbs she directed verbally against these, though outspoken, were ruled by the strictest Scottish moral sense. In art and life, she was always on the right side; just as her politics, too — though not every reader may agree with them — were generous and inspired by Christian charity.

In Downing Street, as, indeed, in every house over which she presided, she was superb. She knew how to make the interior of a house lovely, and always imparted to it a particular atmosphere, impossible to mistake, so that entering it, you would at once have recognised whose home it was. Her conversation was inspiring: in the common phrase, she spoke her mind: or, at any rate, with the utmost rapidity she thought of things she would like to say, and said them. Nor was she in the least troubled by that bugbear of the polite, where to speak them (one must not be rude in one's own house, or in anyone else's, and I remember my father adding another prohibition to the list by remarking to me once, with a glance severe and reproachful — " I'm surprised! Rude to me in my own motor-car! ") But Mrs. Asquith would say what came into her head — often difficult to couch in civil language — in her own house, in your house, in the house of a friend, in the streets, in church, in shops, in theatres, in motor-cars and in buses. . . . For example, when she came to stay with me in Scarborough a few years later, meeting my father for the first time, she glanced at him critically, and, pressing my arm, remarked in a sympathetic, hissing and over-audible whisper, " Oh, Osbert, what a look in the eye! *Cold* as *ice*! But if you want help, let me know, and I'll talk to him! " And of dinner-parties in her own house, it was remarked that there was no-one present who did not leave the dining-room a better man or woman than he or she had entered it — the guests, their souls purged by pity and by terror, because of what their hostess had said to them; the hostess, for what she had said to the guests. Thus, it was always either with regret or relief that her friends saw her entomb herself at the bridge-table, to which she was an addict, and to which, as the years went on, she devoted all too much time.

Her kindness — active, as opposed to the negative quality that often passes for it — was as frequent and touching as her faults were obvious. She was even more generous than extravagant, even more kind than sharp. Her face, her profile — so characteristic —, her voice, her trim, small figure, which she retained until the end of her life, her clothes, were all the vehicle of an intense personality. Extremely feminine in her composition, she was always dressed in what seemed by the extremity of its modishness to be a caricature of the latest fashion, yet the taste responsible for it — even if it were ill-suited to her own structure, so much more dependent on bones than on flesh — was obviously her own. Thus, the indefinable and clear-cut style of her individuality permeated the whole of her outward appearance and carried her through errors of judgement and through exaggerations to a singular sort of perfection, that of a drawing by Callot or Stefano della Bella. She loved the young, revered the old, but had little patience with those in middle life, of middling mind or character. Yet, with all this, and in spite of her striking experience of the world, she remained naïve, shrewd, uneducated, though to a degree well-read and versed in humanity; a child of brilliant perspicacity, wandering through the world, saying exactly what she thought and felt, telling others, too, what they ought to feel and think, in language that by its vivid inspiration, its gift of the art of summary, could lay a drawing-room waste. She never, I think, intended to be unkind, and often remained — for in some ways she was insensitive — unconscious of unkindness when she had been guilty of it. Her daemon, wit, the voice that like an oracle uncovers the hidden truth, the voice that speaks in spite of itself or its owner, and is nearer to nature than either, drove her to the most incisive utterance. She spoke, in those tones so personally stressed, before she had time to regret it : as when, on one occasion taken to see the Corotesque work of a young painter who dabbled in willow trees and silver sunrises, all caught in mist, she pronounced before she could choke back her judgement, " A mouse's sneeze ! "; a remark which would somehow reduce the afflatus of any artist.

For many years, Mrs. Asquith slept badly and, waking early in the morning, would write a collection of pencilled notes to her friends (how well, on reading this, they will recall the angular handwriting on the yellow-white envelope!) — about various topics that had caught her attention or were occupying her mind. These would be headed 4.30 A.M. or 5 A.M., and would usually run to some pages. I have still in my possession one of them — though this time quite short — which she sent me in later years. She had been annoyed by the judgement Mrs. Woodrow Wilson had passed on her in a recent book, and had telephoned one evening to ask me urgently to come round the following morning at 12.15 to have half an hour's consultation with her. Accordingly, the next day, I arrived at 44 Bedford Square at the hour indicated. Lady Oxford was expected down in a moment, and meanwhile the butler handed me a letter. The envelope was unfastened: on the outside were instructions to the butler.

> *Whitmore.*
> Give this letter to Mr. O. Sitwell *before* he comes into the library at 12.30 today.

Taking out the contents, I found two single sheets written in pencil, and glancing first, as often I do, at the signature, was surprised, because the handwriting was so pleasantly different from my own, to find it signed with my own name! It was dated, " 5 A.M. the 22nd Sept: '37 ", and ran,

DEAREST OSBERT,

To save you the trouble of reading the lies written about me by Mrs. Woodrow Wilson (in a book you will never read) I would like you to write a letter to *The Times* or the *Daily Telegraph*, to say that your attention has been drawn to a paragraph in a book . . . lately published by Putnam. That you have been a friend of mine all your life, and resent what she has written, and even doubt whether it is accurate. You can add " Lady Oxford has *never* spoken ill of *anyone*, and though she has known many members of the Royal Family, she is not a snob : nor is she as vulgar as Mrs. Woodrow Wilson portrays her.—Yours, etc., OSBERT SITWELL."

All this, Lady Oxford thought was the truth. It was certainly correct to say she was not a snob : indeed, the fact that when Mr. Asquith was Prime Minister, twenty years before, she used occasionally (a fact that earned much censure) to insist on the butler taking part in charades in the drawing-room at The Wharf, in order to impersonate the more ponderous members of the Cabinet — rôles for which he showed an undoubted flair — was, in a way, proof of it. But it was more difficult, I thought, to declare so roundly that she had never spoken ill of anyone: though, again, it was true that her character was devoid of malice and it would have been accurate, I believe, to have said that she had never made an unkind remark for the sake of its unkindness. . . . I spent the half-hour that ensued after she appeared, therefore, in trying to convince her of that of which others, when I am angry, have so often tried to persuade me: that such statements as those of Mrs. Woodrow Wilson carry no weight, and that to write a letter to the Press in refutation of them will only serve to call attention to the words and opinions to which you are objecting. . . . But I do not know that, in a part so new to me, I was altogether successful.

I received also much kindness from Lady Brougham and her family. Lady Brougham was older than Lady Oxford, belonged, indeed, to a previous generation and to an opposite school. Earlier in this book I mentioned her as outshining even Lady Colvin in the art of fan manipulation, and she was certainly the most vivacious wielder of that instrument that it was ever my good fortune to meet. She fanned herself with an inimitable allurement, born of restlessness, and perhaps of a certain shyness of disposition, though this was the last quality one would have suspected in so accomplished, so finished a product of her age. More than that, she was an old lady of real beauty and of infinite charm, carrying with her, right through her old age to the day of her death, not only her winning air but the looks for which she had been famous. Her circle, too, was as different from that of Lady Oxford as from that of Lady Colvin: neither the political nor the literary world was hers: intellectuals and writers would have frightened her, or she would have expected that they would. She had been mistress of two great houses, Brougham and the Château Éléonore at Cannes : she belonged to private and not to public life, so essentially that it seems scarcely fair to write about her. On the other hand, she possessed so much fascination, both as a personality and as a type that no longer exists, that it would be impossible for a writer who had known her to leave her out of a book of reminiscences. In days when private life was an art, she raised it even higher in the scale, and, as an old lady, her life was largely spent in her own house, for, apart from driving about in a brougham — to the use of which vehicle, named after the first Lord Brougham, she still adhered solely —, she seldom went out in London. And no wonder! For everything in her house was beautifully ordered, maintained and arranged, and even when not exactly beautiful, formed part, as it were, of an engrossing work of art : full of character, even down to the huge eighteenth-century volume of coloured engravings of flowers which stood propped open on an eighteenth-century chair, on the landing at the top of the stairs, as if to refresh you after the climb. These plates showed *strelitzia* and other exotic blossoms, and nearly every day were different, the book being changed, or opened at a different page.

In the 'seventies, Lady Brougham had been one of the first of her generation to take an interest in furniture and decoration, and her large mansion in Chesham Place, though naturally in the idiom of her day, and not in that of ours, manifested an impeccable and individual style, just as did her personal adornments : the diminutive piece of lace she wore on the top of her head, like a small cap, her earrings, and lace and black silk dress. There was something about her of the freshness of a vivid-hued carnation, even in old age. She remained debonair and jaunty, and though she must have had cares and sorrows of her own, appeared more interested in the worries of other people. It was the greatest pleasure to see her, to talk to her, to have luncheon with her — even the food was unlike, and better than, that elsewhere —, or to sit for a few minutes talking to her at tea, in her room, so imbued with individuality, with its chairs, covered in chintz of a narrow red and white stripe, and its flowers, that were never to be seen in other houses, huge arching sprays of green *cymbidium* with scarlet centres, or the coralline shields of the *anthurium*. She owned many lovely pieces of furniture, inherited from her father, who had been one of the celebrated connoisseurs residing in Florence in the second quarter of the nineteenth century. But these objects could constitute a source of embarrassment as well as of delight to her guests, because she possessed, too, a standard of generosity that was innate in her, but completely her own. If someone admired, let us say, an Italian tortoise-shell cabinet of the seventeenth century, she would cry with the impetuosity that she had plainly preserved from her youth, but combined with an odd humility, a genuine surprise that you should like anything belonging to her, " Do you really think it pretty ? . . . You must have it ! " . . . This sounded merely one of the phrases that some people use ; but in her mouth these words were sincere and later acquired reality : for, as likely as not, by the time the visitor returned home in the evening, he would find it waiting for him in the hall. In her leisure, she embroidered beautifully ; and she painted china, but unlike others I have mentioned in *The Scarlet Tree*, this she did, too, in an expert manner, and so that many of the jars that carried her designs were beautiful objects. Further, just as she could infuse gaiety into other people by her presence, so, too, she could be witty, witty, as a rule, in a self-depreciating way, for though sure of herself, she thought nothing of her attainments or qualities (though, in fact, no-one could have known her, or even met her, without entertaining a warm regard for her) : and this gave an added point to the things she said, which, for their value, depended usually on two things : her unfailing shrewdness of judgement, and her use of the appropriate but unexpected adjective. In illustration of this aptitude, I was told by a friend that when King Edward VII went to stay at Brougham, he arrived in a mood that rendered him difficult to please. Plainly something had gone wrong. At dinner, the King was still silent, so Lady Brougham began to talk, asking,

" Did you notice, sir, the soap in Your Majesty's bath-room ? "

" No ! "

" I thought you might, sir. . . . It has such an amorous lather ! "

After that, the King's geniality returned.

To Lady Brougham, Lord Brougham, nephew of the celebrated lawyer and statesman, made a perfect foil. Older than she — he had been born in 1836 —, he was now nearly eighty, and lived to be ninety-one. Massive and imposing, everything about him was large, dignified, and a little gruff. They plainly adored each other, and Lady Brougham, in gay mood, used to refer to him in his presence, but never, of course, behind his back, as " my old Rock of Ages " — and there was something of the enduring quality of rock about him. Lady Brougham's restless quickness, the way she moved and fanned herself, used to worry him for fear she would overtire herself. Even his clothes had a fine solidity about them : he was the last man in London to wear starched collars and striped shirts made in one piece — and this, though so small, indeed trivial a point, nevertheless both a little illustrates him for the reader, and is worthy to be recorded as a small note to the history of male attire. He was altogether the type of an Englishman — he could be nothing but that —, but of a former age with determined, pronounced features, and carried into the post-war world the feel, the certainty, the steadiness and purpose of the Victorian Age, just as Lady Brougham showed the charm, taste and gaiety which this great epoch, reputedly stern and philistine, could manifest.

My Aunt Londesborough, on the other hand, though only some fifteen years younger than Lady Brougham, offered, in appearance, manner, and in her houses, as distinctive an epitome of the Edwardian Age, even though some of the Victorian tenets still survived in her : as, for example, that of being kind to the young people of the family, for whose benefit or advancement, as she saw it, she would take a rather nebulous infinity of trouble. She had now disposed of St. Dunstan's, and was established in a marble-lined mansion in Green Street, where, though the background was a little more confined, the same lavishness and air of splendour as formerly still marked the numerous parties she gave. She had not long returned from the Durbar, laden with large presentation portraits of jewelled and dusky potentates, which, in spite of their colour, resembled white elephants in size and usefulness, and were discreetly hung in the country. She had also brought back with her an Indian boy, Bimbi, and when she gave a dance, he would stand, in his native robes and high pink turban, on one of the landings of the marble staircase, directing the guests in the manner of an eighteenth-century page. Here, too, as at Mrs. Asquith's, you met many foreigners, albeit of a different kind — not foreign diplomats, politicians, artists or musicians, but Hungarians and Austrians of the hunting sort. In addition, there was always a solid mass of relatives. Among them my cousin, the Duchess of Beaufort, and her two daughters, Blanche and Diana Somerset : gay and delightful girls, full of zest, with an ability to instil amusement and liveliness into their surroundings, into all they touched — into the hunting-field itself, I suppose : for I believe they were always eager, even when in London, to return to Badminton, and to resume a life spent largely in the saddle, anxious, however much they might be enjoying themselves, for the autumn to bring back cubbing, and for the winter to allow them whole months pursuing the fox. With a tolerance that, as I had learnt when attached to the cavalry regiment at Aldershot, not all those who seem to have been born on horseback can show, they teased me, in their warm, luxuriant voices, so typical of their family, and laughed at me, but did not in the least mind my being interested in other things. So I could talk to my Uncle Londesborough about various modern composers of whom few of the guests in the house had heard, for the majority of them were kept too busy toeing the monotonous gilded line that led from Ascot to Goodwood and to Cowes, to have time to hear any composers but Puccini and Verdi. They were not believers in experiment. But with him I could discuss Chabrier—still then unknown in England, though many years dead—, Stravinsky, Schönberg, Debussy and Ravel.

Another house at which I was a frequent visitor during these and ensuing years was Mrs. George Keppel's, in Grosvenor Street, surely one of the most remarkable houses in

London. Its high façade, dignified and unpretentious as only
that of a London Georgian mansion can be, very effectively
disguised its immense size. Within existed an unusual air of
spaciousness and light, an atmosphere of luxury, for Mrs.
Keppel possessed an instinct for splendour, and not only were
the rooms beautiful, with their grey walls, red lacquer cabinets,
English eighteenth-century portraits of people in red coats,
huge porcelain pagodas, and thick, magnificent carpets, but
the hostess conducted the running of her house as a work of art
in itself. I liked greatly to listen to her talking; if it were
possible to lure her away from the bridge-table, she would
remove from her mouth for a moment the cigarette which she
would be smoking with an air of determination, through a
long holder, and turn upon the person to whom she was
speaking her large, humorous, kindly, peculiarly discerning
eyes. Her conversation was lit by humour, insight and the
utmost good-nature : a rare and valuable attribute in one who
had never had — or, at any rate, never felt — much patience
with fools. Moreover, a vein of fantasy, a power of enhancement
would often lift what she was saying, and served to emphasise the
exactness of most of her opinions, and her frankness. Her talk
had about it a boldness, an absence of all pettiness, that
helped to make her a memorable figure in the fashionable
world. The company of her two daughters added to the
pleasures of frequenting her house : Violet, cosmopolitan and
exotic from her earliest years, with a vivid intelligence, a quick
eye for character, which had bestowed on her an irresistible
gift of mimicry and the ability to gather unexpected pieces of
information about people and things, which she was wont to
impart in a voice, eager but pitched in so low a tone as sometimes to be inaudible; Sonia, though still in the schoolroom,
with a very strong personality, too. She was tall for her age,
and down her back swept a mane of golden hair, like that to
be seen in some of Renoir's paintings : while her manners were
exquisite, her views were still definite as only those of a child
can be, and she expressed them in a voice full of the most
caressing charm.

With the sumptuousness of the entertainments at my Aunt

Londesborough's and at Mrs. Keppel's I could contrast the archiepiscopal austerities of Lambeth, with its cohorts of curates devouring the modern equivalent of locusts and wild honey. But even the wild honey would have proved, I apprehend, to be tame. After dinner, at 10.15 or 10.30 in the evening, many guests repaired to the Chapel, which had been so hideously frescoed in the time of my Tait relative. I remember with what relief — for the company of the clergy sometimes intimidates me, who am frightened by no other men — I used to ask for a taxi, and tell the driver to take me to the Alhambra, where I arrived just in time to hear the last half-hour of a revue, entitled, if I remember rightly, *Swat That Fly!* And there I would meet all my friends from the Brigade, admiring the serried ranks of beauties on the stage, the curls and legs and eyes in line. Or else I would hurry away from Lambeth in order to see the performance of Gaby Deslys at the Palace Theatre or elsewhere — a star, in her kind, of European celebrity. And here the reader and I will escape for an instant to discuss her — though there is a connection in memory between her and the Church, as will become evident in a moment, for this artiste held strict views on the clergy, or, at any rate, on Bishops. Though she possessed a house in London, facing the Park, with a tall, demure-looking painted façade, the window-boxes of which blazed with formal flowers, geraniums and their predecessors and successors throughout the spring and summer months, and though she was often to be seen driving in a motor, Paris was her headquarters and her appearances on the London stage were short in duration and infrequent. They occupied about ten minutes or a quarter of an hour each night for a special engagement of ten days or a fortnight, every few months. Moreover, it must be admitted that when she essayed a bigger act on the English stage, and a longer run — as, for example, when Sir James Barrie wrote for her the whole of a revue, entitled *Rosy Rapture*, which was produced at His Majesty's Theatre in 1915 —, she was not so successful. But in her brief songs, dances, and scraps of acting and conversation, all of which she entered upon and executed with a sort of casual deliberateness, she was curiously effective.

There was no-one to approach her in her own form of stage glamour, and strange yet banal allurement. To a flourish of elementary ragtime, very French in its accent, on the part of the theatre orchestra — usually to *The Gaby Glide*, a tune possessed of a peculiarly inappropriate and naïve gaiety — would come from the wings a flutter of silk, feathers, flesh and jewels, drenched in light, and the star would have arrived to join her partner Harry Pilcer, who, by a convention, would already be looking for her (" Where can she be? ", " Where is she? ") everywhere except in the direction from which she advanced. The moment she was there, rather heavy-shouldered for her body, and crested like a bird, for she was wearing on her head a tight-fitting cap loaded with ostrich feathers, she seemed, with her fair hair and tawny fair skin, to absorb every ray of light in the theatre, to exist only in that flaring, sputtering brightness of another world, to be outlined with the icy fires of a diamond. She would sing a little, dance for a moment, as if she were almost too fragile, and too much in need of protection, to execute the steps, sing in her voice with the rolling r's of her French throat, unmusical but provocative, and the whole result was perfect of its kind, a work of art, but specialised as the courtship-dance of a bird, with the same glittering and drumming vanity, except that here the female and not the male played the chief rôle.

Though both Gaby Deslys and Harry Pilcer could, in their looks and their personality, no less than in the turn they gave, have belonged to no other period than their own, and albeit Gaby Deslys was so famous a music-hall artiste, yet, in addition, there pertained to her the interest of a specimen: the last surviving example — though the type, no doubt, is recurrent — of a certain kind of almost legendary stage figure, most usually to be seen in the Paris of the Second Empire and more generally to be found in the Europe of the nineteenth century. In this resembling Lola Montez, she had helped to upset a throne, and famous as an artiste, was no less notorious for the part she had played, and for which Fate had cast her, in the downfall of the Braganza dynasty. The infatuation of the youthful King Manoel — who had become sovereign after the terrible assassination in a Lisbon thorough-fare of his father King Carlos, and of an elder brother — had, a year or two before, been for many months the subject of eager but condemnatory report in the Press of the world, and in Portugal the stories that the new King was lavishing money on a French dancer, and had bestowed upon her pearl neck-laces and gems said to be heirlooms, had certainly done much to enflame Portuguese opinion against him. Now, the King was an exile in Twickenham; and as for Gaby Deslys, it can be imagined that while the stories had increased her notoriety in England, they had by no means influenced the Noncon-formist flocks or the Anglican congregations in her favour. On the first morning after her reappearance on the London stage, a Bishop, I recollect, made a public protest in an inter-view, against her performance, alleging that her clothes were too scanty (though actually it was in the precise opposite, in the richness and style of her clothing, that the whole essence of her appeal resided). Ten days subsequently, on her return journey to Paris, Gaby Deslys, too, gave an interview to journal-ists assembled at Dover, in which she would only say, "Tell your Bishops, I love them — but they show too much leg!"

After her death, some ten years later, she was found to have left a large fortune to the poor of Marseilles, which she declared to be her native city : though when her will was published several French papers contained statements that she had been brought to France at a very early age from a town in Roumania, where she had been born, and in which still lived various relations of hers who intended to claim their inheritance, under the *Code Napoléon*. This origin, however, has never been established, and would seem for her an improbable one — since nobody more French, in her way of moving, speaking, or wearing clothes, can be imagined. Let us avert our gaze, and return to Lambeth, and its more dim, if less worldly, lights. Spiritual rather than fleshly graces were to be sought here, and were said to endure longer. . . .

I recollect very clearly the first occasion on which I accom-panied my sister to dine at Lambeth. It was an immense dinner-party, and, on leaving, the hall was full of fellow-guests waiting

for vehicles to take them away. The butler had on this occasion
with great trouble procured us a taxi, and I can see now my
sister's expression of anguish, when, in the press, wishing to
reward him, I inadvertently clamped half a crown instead into
the inexpectant palm of Mr. Laurence Binyon, who, like us, was
waiting for a cab. He remained for some moments, holding it
in his hand, with a rapt gaze : and I always considered it most
generous of him in after years never to mention the incident to
me. . . . The circumstances, too, of another evening when I
dined in the same hospitable precincts come back to me. There
were, in all, about twenty of us in the dining-hall at Lambeth,
including, unless I telescope two dinner-parties, the then
Bishop of Zanzibar, famous in Church circles for something
that, like the Differential Calculus, remains ever outside the
bounds of my comprehension : the Kikuyu Controversy. The
occasion must have taken place during the 1914 war, when
there was first talk of rationing, because the Archbishop always
genuinely believed, as fitted his great position, in setting an
example, and I seem to remember, with our lemonade, a
token cutlet and a representative cheese-straw. Suddenly
upon our discreet and innocent merry-making, there broke
in a series of appalling, high, dervish howls and screams,
mingled with a faint metallic clinking. The Archbishop
looked surprised, started up, and hurried out, accompanied
by a chaplain or two. In an instant, the ululation reached
a climax of pandemonium, and then subsided to a sound that
was like the recitative of an opera, when the members of the
chorus turn inward, one toward another, and whisper with
a resonant persistence, " Ah ! What will *he* do ? What shall
we say ? " . . . After that, clinking only, and then silence.
. . . The Archbishop returned, looking rather shaken, and
said, " It really is most inconsiderate of the Bishop of London.
The Suffragettes went to visit him at Fulham, and though I
have repeatedly told him that I refused to see them, he advised
them — and without telephoning to me — to come on here.
The police were just having their tea, when the poor, misguided
women broke in, and padlocked themselves to the railing."
. . . One of the chaplains added in a deep, slow, sombre

voice, " And one of them struck a policeman with a dog-whip ! " . . . The curate next to me spoke out. " I do not like to set myself up in judgement on my fellow-men," he said, ' But the Bishop of London should *never* have *done* it." . . . ' *Never* ", we all agreed. . . . Meanwhile, the Suffragettes had dispersed. It was the only occasion on which they demonstrated during the 1914–18 war.

Among relatives whom I often went to see, there was my cousin Mrs. George Swinton : of her I have written earlier. Her house was full of painters and musicians, and the most intelligent of their audience. Though I had known her for many years, this was a friendship I had chosen, as well as inherited, belonging to the right hand as well as the left. Her glorious voice was at its height, and she was unchallenged as a singer in her own line ; and I would often go with her to concerts where she was performing. . . . Of more recent friends, and with a very different personality, there was Lady Sackville, certainly one of the remarkable characters of the period. From time to time, I would go to dine with her alone. I would find her, before dinner, sitting in the Persian Room : a small panelled room that, though inappropriate for England, was not without a certain fitness for her, because the arabesques, and small tightly painted roses and cypresses blazoned on the walls recalled Granada and Andalusia, and thus the strain in her own blood from which sprang the particular strange quality she possessed. Though she was now middle-aged and fat, the lines of her face were pretty with an almost classical prettiness, and her expression could be extremely seductive. The long, hollow, hooded upper lids, that so clearly mark those of Sackville descent, and, as a rule, show beneath them eyes of a sombre melancholy, in her case displayed eyes, rather prominent, of a living, changing but rather shallower fire, for to all her gifts she had given a material direction. Peasant and aristocrat, she combined many curious and conflicting traits, lived in magnificence and could live in squalor, was capable of creating both, was the slave of beautiful things, and yet must always change her surroundings, however splendid they might be, so that even Knole, which she had so greatly loved, became too static for

her. Or, perhaps, it offered too strong, too concrete a personality of its own, and of her family's making, until at last she
came to resent it; for she liked houses to be adaptable, Regency
mansions that she could make blossom within, into Renaissance
palaces, or caprices of her own design, with sunken, unexpected
courts and gardens. Furthermore, she liked to be able to
surprise, to convert objects to other purposes than those for
which they had been intended. The decoration of her houses,
indeed, mirrored her personality; yet the ancestral cave in the
Albaicin was to be detected in it, no less than the ancestral
palace. The large windows, full of objects in coloured glass,
gave a living warmth to the rooms, the rugs, the tortoise-shell
and lapis furniture, all imparted an air of luxury and of invention. Indeed, Lady Sackville lived in a world almost entirely
imaginary. She never told one the same story twice; for,
to her, truth was relative and depended on how she felt when
she was talking: and while the tales often retained the same
features, in each new version these would be rearranged, albeit
with a surprising ease, grasp and power of conviction. But
there was nothing petty about her: she was capable of acts
of imaginative kindness and of cruelty, she was clever and
cunning and silly and brave and timid and avaricious, extravagant and most generous, possessed the best taste and the
worst, and was, in all, one of the most vivid personalities I
have ever met. And I am sure that she never afforded her
friends, still less those nearest to her, a dull moment; the
opposition in her character of aristocrat and Spanish dancer,
gypsy and woman of taste, was too pronounced to allow of it.

Occasionally, I would be taken to supper, too, at All
Souls' Place — that piazza consisting of one house behind All
Souls' Church in Langham Place — by Felicity Tree and by her
sister Iris, who was then very young, but possessed a honey-
coloured beauty of hair and skin that I have never observed
in anyone else. Viola Tree, and her husband, Alan Parsons,
would often be there as well, Viola contributing her own
particular vein of warm-hearted vagueness and humour, and
her spontaneous and inexhaustible gift of mimicry; while
singly or together, Sir Herbert and Lady Tree could be de-

pended upon to supply an entertainment of the most delicious
personal fantasy, based on the flimsiest and most delicate
foundation of sense. Though I, with the rest of the world,
have seen quoted and heard repeated so many of Sir Herbert's
remarks and exploits — as, when, for example, he went to a
post-office and asked for a penny stamp, and on being given
one, demanded, " Have you no others ? ", and, after a sheet
of them had been produced, considered it exhaustively, head
by head, and then, selecting a stamp in the very middle, pointed
at it, and remarked with decision, " I will take that one " ;
and though, equally, I have read, heard, or been told of many
of Lady Tree's epigrams, such as when, being offered two
kinds of fish at a dinner-party, she remarked, " Ye cannot
serve both Cod and Salmon ", or when — another ichthyo-
phagous bon-mot — on a similar occasion haddock was handed
to her, and she exclaimed joyously " Cry ' Haddock ! ', and
let slip the dogs of war ", yet nothing can do justice to the
captivating absurdity with which they both invested everyday
life. Moreover, just as Sir Herbert's eminence on the stage
a little overshadowed the exquisite virtuosity of Lady Tree's
acting, so, erudite in many subjects as she was — in an earlier
age she would have been a celebrated blue-stocking —, not
enough attention has been paid to her talk, her ability to save
almost any situation or conversation by injecting into it the germ
of nonsense, or to her masterly choice of the inappropriate adjective. Thus, in after years, when she came to stay with me in
Scarborough, I took her during a tremendous storm for a drive
round the foot of the Castle Hill, which juts far out into the
sea. The breakers pounded the great walls of rock, and sent
their wings hundreds of feet into the air, to drop with the sound
of lead upon the pavement quite near us. In an interval
between the roaring and the tumbling when at last a voice
could be heard, Lady Tree clasped her hands together, and
pronounced, " How sweet, how *roguish* ! " . . . This remark,
of course, was a form of fun, more than of humour, and
depended a little for its effect on the deftness of the concurrent
action, the expression of surprise and pleasure, as of a child's
outburst on receiving a playful kitten as a birthday present.

But further, by her dazzling mastery of the pun, in some mouths so lumpish an accomplishment, she showed her great feeling for words, and the delight to be extracted from them. Wit, indeed, veined the whole substance of Lady Tree's life, and even during her last illness, at most a day or two before she died, when, realising her extremity, she sent for her lawyer, in order to sign her will or add a codicil, she observed to those round her, when his name was announced, " My darlings, here comes my solicitor, to teach me my Death-Duties ".

The world seemed enchanting to me. Albeit, perhaps, all the persons I saw in these years had attaching to them the freshness of my own youth, and of a moment when I was consciously enjoying myself for the first time, yet surely life in the decade preceding the First World War offered something that no other period had given — a quality pleasantly grotesque (it was to grow even more, but less pleasantly, grotesque after 1918) : a richness, above all a variety, lacking in previous epochs. In age it was as mixed as in other respects. In instance of this detail I remember seeing a great-aunt and her nephew, in their appearance of the same time of life, setting off together to a ball, both of them determined to enjoy every moment until they returned home at four in the morning, and on completely equal terms in spite of the sixty years that separated their births, and I recollect wondering then whether such a combination could ever have occurred before. But this was, indeed, the reign of the *Vieillesse Dorée*. The belles of the Edwardian summer survived in a kind September splendour, like the ephemerids that haunt the roses and rich autumn daisies until the first blast of winter is to be felt in the air. Their spirits were higher than — or as high as — those of the young, their appetite for amusement quenchless. I can boast that at the age of twenty, I was taught the tango by Mrs. Hwfa Williams, a woman already for three generations famous for her chic. And she danced with spirit, with a sense of fun and joy ! It is not easy for someone afflicted with deafness to be amusing, it calls for unceasing alertness which must be a great tax on energy, and it will be understood that she was no longer a young woman : nor was she rich, so she could not entertain : but the sense of the pleasure she found in every moment of the company she was in, and her amusing comments, gave her a unique position. At every dance to which she went, she was surrounded by a crowd of young men, waiting for her arrival, and they always addressed her as Madam. This reception must surely, in itself, have constituted some sort of reward for the trouble she took. The chief disadvantage she suffered from her deafness was that, until she caught a chance word or two, she had to adapt her expression in sympathy with the reputation of the person speaking — a smile for the whimsical, a laugh for the witty, a striking look of interest for the dealer in the dramatic, a tear for those who wore their hearts on their sleeves. Sometimes this method, imposed upon her by her disability, misled her for a while as to the trend of the conversation, but once she grasped a word, she would right herself in an instant, so quick was she.

The social world, I was saying, was more miscellaneously composed than ever it had been : it offered the most singular contrasts, while the ready friendliness found in so many places provided for me a lively intoxication. Indeed, the London of which I talk possessed such warmth and life, and existed, comparatively, so short a time ago, that I am continually surprised at its complete disappearance and extinction. Equally, the sight of a survivor from it astonishes me.

As if to make this life — and I give a fuller account of it in the next chapter — complete for me, I now fell in love for the first time since I had grown up. And this, the atmosphere of it, tinges all those years for me, and unites the various backgrounds with the same thread of gold. . . . Under a staircase, at a dance — my liking for dancing had become a passion — I saw a young girl sitting, talking to her partner with a curious, distant, wide-eyed solemnity, and the impression of her small golden head and small, child-like, rather expressionless face, — eyes that were like a gap because of their light colour, but full of appraisal and meaning —, and of her long, slender neck, and long, delicate figure, as first I thus saw her, was with me for many years, so that, whenever I scribbled on a piece of paper without thinking, it was her face that, however clumsily, I drew. (Indeed, I recall my surprise when one day I was scribbling and my companion — it was in the trenches — saw what I had drawn, recognised the likeness, and said, " I know who that is ! ") . . . As I had passed, her glance had rested on me — or so I like to think — and when we met, later that evening, we soon became friends. I was, indeed, fortunate that in the next few years she chose to give me so much of her time and company. Though two years younger than myself — she was barely eighteen — she was not only extremely original in her point of view, but already most decided in character. She found herself as naturally at home in the modern world as I did : while, unlike me, she had enjoyed, and been clever enough to take advantage of, a superb education of the traditional kind. She accepted no ready-made way of thinking or feeling, was naturally a rebel — and, who can say, even perhaps, in spite of her love of pleasure, a saint — in her heart ; and she possessed a natural comprehension of the esthetic standards of the day. In no other period would young people have been allowed to see so much of each other, without interference by their elders. She and I, and a band of friends of the same age, used always to go about together, forming our own nucleus at every party. Besides frequenting the ballrooms of the rich, we would find our own amusements, going to dance at the White City or Earl's Court, visiting suburban music-halls, theatres in the East End, and a music-hall in White-chapel where all the turns were fresh — if the term *fresh* can be used about them — from Cernauti, and spoke only Yiddish. Thus, we became lost in the strange proletarian cosmopolis of the twentieth century, the inexorable pattern of the future. Many miles of City, East End and suburb we traversed in our walks at night.

For the following five years, I saw her, except when I was staying with my family or abroad, almost every day. I grew to know her every look, every way of expressing herself, every aspect of her character. To her, companion of my youth, I owe an inestimable amount of happiness and sorrow, of joy and regret.

How is it possible to capture the sweet and care-free atmosphere of 1913, and of 1914 until the outbreak of the First World War? Never had Europe been so prosperous and gay. Never had the world gone so well for all classes of the community: especially in England, where an ambitious programme of Social Reform had just been carried through, and Old Age Pensions and Insurance schemes had removed from the poor the most bitter of the spectres that haunted them. (Even more far-reaching reforms were introduced in subsequent years, but by that time the feeling of ease had vanished: Europe had lost half her sons, and in England unemployment was an established feature of life. But in 1913 and the next few months, young men could face the future with confidence.) In Western Europe there had been no war of any sort for nearly two generations, and for a thousand years, if an outbreak had occurred, standards of chivalry prevailed. And I remember from my own childhood, what must have been a common experience with members of my generation, reading the Bible, and books of Greek, Roman, and English history, and reflecting how wonderful it was to think that, with the growth of commerce and civilisation, mass captivities and executions were things of the rabid past, and that never again would man be liable to persecution for his political or religious opinions. This belief, inculcated in the majority, led to an infinite sweetness in the air we breathed. Even if war came one day — and it was unthinkable, the point of greatest danger having passed in 1911 —, it would be played according to the rules: the loss of life would be on the Boer War scale: (in no war had there existed the incidence of mortality to which the two great conflicts have inured us, and of which the first was in this respect the more dreadful). There was, as yet, no hint to be detected of the sorrows and terrors that lay in front of the most highly cultured races of the world. In England, the political warfare that existed, and then only at the level of drawing-rooms, merely added to them a breath of excitement. If Lady Londonderry cut, let us say, Mrs. Asquith, on account of the Home Rule Bill, the world in general yet sped toward its ultimate re-creation or perfection. All classes still believed in absolute progress — and the loss of this certainty has whittled down, more than anything else, the feeling of life's joy. Then it existed, and appeared on all sides to be justified. There was no disillusionment. Happier, wealthier, wiser — and younger, too, for our age — every day, we were being conducted by the benevolent popes of science into a Paradise, but of the most comfortably material kind : a Paradise where each man and woman, even if no longer born with an immortal soul, could by means of such devices as false teeth and monkey glands have conferred upon them a sort of animal and mechanic immortality of this world, and where, even if not destined for angelic honours, they could at least aspire to the monetary eminence of a Rockefeller or Roth-schild. Not only did the future, which to every age appears golden, seem without measure enticing : but, if a moment's doubt ever intervened, we could examine, too, the solid merits and achievements of the present, in themselves a sure gauge of the years to come. Look at Sir Thomas Lipton ; look at turbine engines ! How could you doubt ? . . . Rich and poor became richer every year. How far distant did we stand, it seemed, from the brutalities of the Georgian Age, and of the early Victorian, when whole mobs were sentenced to transportation for the most trifling offences. . . . No wonder the wealthier section of the British community felt justified in toasting itself and in entertaining the world !

Hitherto, in London there had been little for the pleasure-lover to do, little for him to see. The wealth of the great city, unbelievable to those in the street, had always hidden itself behind doors : but now they were thrown wide open. Young men from the prosperous classes, such as my brother-officers and myself, would find themselves invited to as many as five or six entertainments a night. An air of gaiety, unusual in northern climates, prevailed. Music flowed with the lightness and flash of water under the striped awnings and from the balconies; while beyond the open, illuminated windows, in the rooms, the young men, about to be slaughtered, still feasted, unconscious of all but the moment. For a hundred years the social scene had not been so attractive to the eye, and it was not destined to shine with such lustre again for several centuries; because the Age of Private Life, founded on the family, was nearing its end. To women, this was a great age of dress, for, in those final years, the girls of rich families, as well as the middle-aged, had their clothes designed by the famed Parisian dressmakers, of whom Paul Poiret was chief, — though this change was not effected without a battle, for a sudden rebellion of patriotic English sentiment occurred when Mrs. Asquith allowed an exhibition of Poiret's fashions to be given at 10 Downing Street. Further, as a result of the influence of the Russian Ballet, the art of spectacle was again beginning to be understood, and hostesses took a pride once more in the beauty, no less than the costliness of their entertainments: while, in addition, in a few houses, the discovery had been made that life could be more enjoyable if you surrounded yourself with intelligent people, or at least admitted one or two to panic the assembled herds. Night by night, during the summers of 1913 and '14, the entertainments grew in number and magnificence. One band in a house was no longer enough, there must be two, three even. Electric fans whirled on the top of enormous blocks of ice, buried in banks of hydrangeas, like the shores from which the barque departs for Cythera. Never had there been such displays of flowers; not of the dehydrated weeds, dry poppy-heads and old-man's-beard that character- ised the interbellum years, when a floral desiccation that matched the current beige walls and self-toned textiles and carpets was in evidence; but a profusion of full-blooded blossoms, of lolling roses and malmaisons, of gilded, musical- comedy baskets of carnations and sweet-peas, while huge bunches of orchids, bowls of gardenias and flat trays of stephan- otis lent to some houses an air of exoticism. Never had Europe seen such mounds of peaches, figs, nectarines and strawberries at all seasons, brought from their steamy tents of glass. Champagne bottles stood stacked on the sideboards. . . . And to the rich, the show was free.

As guests, only the poor of every race were barred. Even foreigners could enter, if they were rich. The English governing classes, — though still struck dumb with horror if a foreigner entered the room, and albeit, when obliged to talk to him, they still often shouted at him in English baby-language, a result of the Public School System —, had grown used to the idea that foreigners existed and were — well, foreigners. Xenophobia had temporarily disappeared, and we were toppling to the other extreme. If foreigners did not hate us, and were not hateful, they must all love us and be lovable. The eternal innocence of an island race asserted itself again, in a contrary direction. Was it likely that the Kaiser would visit England so often, and so many Germans come to London, and so plainly love it, if they were planning a war against us ? . . . And the Russians, under the guidance of the Tsar, they, too, would prove a progressive, parliamentary people, like ourselves. Our system was the envy of the world, a millionaire's cheque-book lay hidden in every errand-boy's basket. (Among the poor foreigners who had visited London in recent years, however, was one thin little man, whose lips were lightly flecked with foam when he spoke : a curious man, half Tartar bureaucrat, half Jew, for whom ideas were clothed with flesh and blood, and only men and women were spectres : a man destined to destroy much of this luxurious and beautiful world, by offering an alternative to it.) Every foreigner loved and respected England. . . . Occasionally, a brother-officer would mention to me that he believed there was going to be war with Germany, and that it should spell quicker regimental promotion, but the rest of us dismissed it as a phantom called up by professional keenness.

Who could wonder that foreigners loved London ? Though as different from Vienna or Paris as Peking, it was no less essentially a capital, with all the attractions of the centre of an Empire. It remained unique in being a masculine city, as it had been throughout its history, created to the same degree for men as Paris for women. The luxury shops were unrivalled in their appeal to male tastes, were full of cigarettes, and objects made in leather, glass or silver, better than those to be seen anywhere in foreign capitals; solid, plain, unimaginative, but showing the English feeling for material, the English sobriety. As for suits, shirts, shoes, ties, hats, London was acknowledged, throughout the world, by all races, of all colours,[1] to set the fashion for men. And these years, 1913 and '14, were the last when there was a successor to the long line of fops, macaronis, dandies, beaux, dudes, bucks, blades, bloods, swells and mashers, who for so many centuries had given life to the London world of pleasure. To these was now added the *nut*, or, more jocularly, the k-nut, as personified by a young actor, Mr. Basil Hallam, who in this respect both summed up and set the tone, in a song entitled " Gilbert the Filbert, the Colonel of the Nuts ! " : the refrain ran—

> I'm Gilbert the Filbert, the Nut with a K,
> The pride of Piccadilly, the blasé roué.
> Oh, Hades, the ladies all leave their wooden huts
> For Gilbert the Filbert, the Colonel of the Nuts.

Dressed in a grey tall-hat and a morning-coat, Hallam gave a rather languid rendering of this song at the Palace Theatre every night in *The Passing Show*, a revue which was running throughout the summer of 1914 and until after the outbreak of war. It was no unusual greeting for a young man, wearing a new suit, to be told, " What a k-nut you look ! " The nut must be thin, clean-shaven except for a small, cut moustache, and have an air of concave and fatigued elegance, in this taking after his Dundreary grandfather rather than his father the swell. On the other hand, he had to dance with vigour and ease, in the new style. . . . The nut died fighting in the trenches of 1914, and Mr. Basil Hallam, his amiable exemplifier, was killed in the spring of the following year. He was in a

[1] The tradition survived. In 1925, when I was in New York, I asked a negro singer, Taylor Gordon, how he liked Aldous Huxley, whom he had met; and received a rich-voiced reply, " When I think that that man comes from the capital of the world's tailoring ! "

captive balloon with a rather inexperienced observer, and when the balloon was shot down this man had difficulty in fixing his parachute harness. Hallam stayed to help him and was too late to save himself.

Just as the swell had driven his tandem, so the nut essentially belonged, as much as a snail to its shell, to the fast open motor of those days. This vehicle, so modern and of its time, induced in the young man a sense of being heir of all the ages, lord of all he passed by. For the sense of speed flatters the sense of power, raising the rich, and even the humbler lorry-driver, to a new and god-like level, as the houses rush past them, a peep-show, though filled with living people. In this matter, at least, the twentieth-century world had advanced upon the Roman (how greatly would the Romans have enjoyed rushing down their straight roads to the infinities of their Empire). Moreover, mine was the first generation in which the young men were allowed to take their sweethearts for drives — only the fastest of fast actresses had ridden in tandems. . . . They would sit together, the two of them, the man at the wheel, the girl beside him, their hair blown back from their temples, their features sculptured by the wind, their bodies and limbs shaped and carved by it continually under their clothes, so that they enjoyed a new physical sensation, comparable to swimming; except that here the element was speed, not water. The winds — and their bodies — were warm that summer. During these drives, they acquired a whole range of physical consciousness, the knowledge of scents, passing one into another with an undreamt-of rapidity, the fragrance of the countless flowers of the lime trees, hung like bells on pagodas for the breeze to shake, changing into that of sweetbriar, the scent of the early mornings, and of their darkness, of hills and valleys outlined and tinged by memory; there was the awareness of speed itself, and the rapid thinking that must accompany it, a new alertness, and the typical effects, the sense, it might be, of the racing of every machine as dusk approaches, or the sudden access on a hot evening of cool waves of air under tall trees; — all these physical impressions, so small in themselves, went to form a sum of feeling new in its kind and never before experienced. Even the wind of the winter, at this pace snatching tears from their eyes, and piercing through layers of clothes, was something their fathers had not known. The open car belonged to that day. No other generation had been able to speed into the sunset.

In London, in the streets, you still saw a few carriages, but they diminished day by day, and seemed to be part of life's decoration. And decoration was in the air: many busied themselves with it. The currents that showed were mostly foreign, and reached life through the theatre — a new development. Every chair-cover, every lamp-shade, every cushion reflected the Russian Ballet, the Grecian or Oriental visions of Bakst and Benois, or else the vulgar and colossal coloured fantasies of Reinhardt and his aides or of the rebels against his rule — but both dreams equally in the German taste. The galleries in Bond Street and elsewhere, though they could not, in so far as modern pictures were concerned, vie with those of Paris, showed for the most part eighteenth-century English pictures, Italian old masters, and modern English as well as French paintings: for the dealers had struck the Pre-Raphaelite camp, in which they had dwelt for so long, and had moved on. England possessed its own painters again, and a ferment such as I have since never felt in this country prevailed in the world of art. It seemed as if at last we were on the verge of a great movement. Though the exhibitions of French Post-Impressionist painting and the Futurist Exhibition had opened the eyes of the young to the nature of modern painting, in what existed its essence and in what direction future development lay, and though it could be seen that our island painters were not in the vanguard, yet the art of the late nineteenth century was, in a retarded spring, just beginning to blossom within our closed gardens. (It is a peculiarity of our island climate in the arts that painters are apt to appear too early, or too late: Turner fifty years before his season, Steer fifty years after it.) At last, at least, we possessed again artists of a kind new to us, in whose work showed the national qualities, and who were not merely the imitators of Paris goods: men in the full maturity of their gifts. Sickert; Nicholson; Steer; Orpen, supreme Irish carpenter and flashlight photographer; McEvoy with his nostalgic, equivocal portraits of the fashionable dissolving in light, as Cleopatra's pearl in wine, and Spencer Gore, with his lilac-toned town-scapes. . . . And it must have been in the winter of 1912, I think, that I visited the Chenil Galleries, then situated in a little room near the Post Office in King's Road, Chelsea, and saw a collection of small paintings by Augustus John: young women in wide orange or green skirts, without hats or crowned with large straw hats, lounging wistfully on small hills in un-dulating and monumental landscapes, with the feel of sea and mountain in the air round them. . . . By these I was so greatly impressed that I tried to persuade my father to purchase the whole contents of the room; they cost twenty pounds apiece. Alas, I did not possess the authority necessary to convince him. . . . But this was only one out of many exhibitions: for there were many English artists then with a future, who today have no past.

My sister, whenever, too rarely, she was able to escape from her captivity with my family, would come round the exhibitions with me. Fortunately for my enjoyment of art, from the first my approach to a picture was the foreign attitude of " What pleasure is to be obtained from it ? ", rather than the more usual national attitude of " What would Ruskin say; what addition of moral worth can I refine by mental labour from the picture in front of me ? " But I had no desire to obtain virtue by wrestling with angels: I was content to admire them. And if there was anything I did not understand, my sister would help to make it clear for me. No conquest of fresh esthetic territory was ever hidden from her by fog: and her perceptions had an enthusiasm about them I have seldom known equalled. But, alas, under what she thought, as, tall, fair and rather thin, with the lines of her face developing every day into the classic mould of the poet's, she walked round examining the pictures with me, must have been always the feeling, " What sort of row shall I find when I get home ? " . . . For she had not yet left my parents; that was to be next year, by which time she had realised that if ever she was to become such a poet as she hoped — she had already begun to

236

write poems — she must free herself from her state of absolute bondage. It was impossible to do any work at home, in the atmosphere of hysterical violence that prevailed. . . . Just as it may seem strange that a poet of my sister's order should arise out of the circumstances I have described, so it may be unexpected that a paper such as the *Daily Mirror* should be the first to publish her work, in the spring of 1913. But this was due to the perspicacity of the then leader-writer and literary editor, Richard Jennings, the well-known bibliophile : and to him, as will be seen later, I also owe my own first appearance in print. . . . At present, then, she would be staying with Helen Rootham, and going with her as often as possible to the gallery of the Queen's Hall, where they always occupied the same seats. . . . Sacheverell, too, on his short periods of leave from Eton would come round the exhibitions with me : and he was, even thus early, at the age of sixteen, in correspondence with the leaders of the Vorticist and Futurist movements. He was now a boy very tall for his years, well over six feet, and having, with the curls at his temples, his rather tawny skin, and straight nose — with the pinched-in nostrils that are so typical of my mother's family — something of the air of a farouche young shepherd, but a shepherd of lions rather than of lambs. He was already immersed in his lifelong search for knowledge, infused by a passionate love for, and divination of, beauty. His range and depth of learning put me to shame then, as they do now. When he was able to get away from Eton, we would spend the whole time together, and I used to take him with me to the opera and ballet, and in my company, I am glad to say, he saw Chaliapin at the very height of his powers, in *Khovanshchina*. And Sacheverell already manifested very clearly that understanding of music which makes him so comprehending and revealing a biographer of great composers and executants.

There was activity in English music, as well as in painting. The national standard was again being planted. Cyril Scott, echoing French modes with an added plaintiveness of his own, was the most celebrated of the younger composers : and there were others who turned melody to a craft, like making rushwork or Harris tweed. (It is singular, in this connection, to note what an air of cordiality the English invariably extend to their composers, though they have scarcely produced one, of even minor interest, since the death of the great Purcell : whereas poets, of whom the nation has since the earliest times produced an unbroken line, both of major and of exquisite smaller artists, are invariably greeted with howls of derision.) Nevertheless, it must be admitted that in music the English know what they like, jolly bumpy tunes, of a short line of melody, and with the bleat of Southdown sheep never far from their core. The trained part of the audience, however, the band of concert-goers, in the years before the 1914 war, followed with concern, if not with approval, the progress of foreign music. Thus I recall most vividly the first performance in England, at the Queen's Hall, of Scriabin's *Prometheus*, a work in which at the time I was enthusiastically interested. For weeks beforehand there had been announcements in the press concerning the Colour-Organ its composer had invented ; which instrument was, during the performance, to translate the sound into its equivalent terms in colour, by throwing upon a screen these moving tones and shades. Alas, the Colour-Organ did not materialise on that afternoon in February 1913, but this failure did not prevent the piece from having a tumultuous and, indeed, rowdy reception. I have never understood why the melodious and scholarly, if rather arid, *Prometheus* should have evoked such a demonstration, and even Lady Colvin and Sir Claude Phillips, who were present, as they had been at all the chief musical events of the previous quarter of a century or more, and by no means held any brief for modern music, were amazed at this outbreak of feeling. . . . Perhaps the crowd expected a musical genius to appear from Russia. If so, it was right, but as usual gazing in the wrong direction. The following year, *Prometheus* was given again, followed by the *Piano Concerto*, in which the composer was soloist. To look at, he resembled a German professor, of the thin type, grey, careworn, fatigued by calculations. He received with equanimity the boos that greeted his work at the end, unmoved as his nephew, Monsieur Molotoff, shows himself to be at the reception by foreign powers of his aggressive policy.

In the theatre, similarly, there was much to see : new plays by Shaw and by Granville-Barker and by Arnold Bennett in collaboration with Edward Knoblock. There were the unforgettable Shakespearian productions of Granville-Barker, interpreted and mounted with learning and imagination, and with the most consummate skill and tact, the parts played to perfection. Perhaps the most memorable was *A Midsummer Night's Dream*. In the scene in which Titania and Oberon and their court are visible, the stage presented the semblance of a grassy knoll, and the fairies, to separate their race from that of ordinary human beings, were painted with gold. The whole stage picture possessed its own illusion and leafy perspective, and succeeded in making the magic element of the play singularly credible. For this, the late Norman Wilkinson, an artist of original ability in the theatre, was responsible. Very full, too, of character was Albert Rothenstein's mounting of *The Winter's Tale* ; for he succeeded admirably in transferring the quality of his drawing on to the stage. . . . In the winter of 1911 and spring of 1912, the elephantine production of *The Miracle* had filled Olympia (still echoing with the clatter of the expelled roller-skates) with the incense and tenebrous colour of a medieval cathedral as seen by a Jewish impresario : and the years that followed also saw Reinhardt's heavy-footed oriental phantasies of harem life, played with a plethora of turbans, gongs, kohl and henna. . . . But, above all, there was the opera and the ballet. The Russian operas, never before performed in London until these years, relieved one suddenly from the Viking world of bearded warriors drinking blood out of skulls that had been for so long imposed by Germany. They pleased the eye, at last, as well as the ear.

Though, perhaps, those who belonged to my generation never had the chance of seeing pure acting at its best — for Irving was dead, and Sarah Bernhardt was an old woman —, nevertheless, what a privilege we enjoyed in going to hear and see Chaliapin, that rarest of salamanders, a great artist with a great voice ! How fortunate I have been in that I have seen him many times as Boris, have also often watched him ride on to the stage alone, on his white horse, to stare down on Moscow burning, and, in a third rôle of an altogether different character, have applauded his gigantic sense of comedy as Don Basilio, in the *Barbiere*! I have written, earlier in this work, of how he altered his appearance by make-up: but so great a theatrical artist was he that it would be possible to write of him and the numerous aspects of his art for page after page: in the towering and magnificent frame that housed his voice, he seemed to embody the immense spaces of his native country, to be, almost, a god of Russian music. But though like the majority of artists he was without class, admitting the existence of no division but that of talent, it was easy, too, to picture him working with his friend Maxim Gorky, on a barge, as formerly he had done. This man, the most splendid interpreter of Russian music, with all its grandeur and lack of pettiness, had about him, it is true, no conceit, no self-consciousness: but he was supremely confident of his powers.

Thus, one evening, in after years, when I had grown to know Chaliapin fairly well, Lady Aberconway and I went to congratulate him, in his dressing-room, after he had taken the part of Salieri in Rimsky-Korsakov's *Mozart and Salieri*. Mozart had been played by a young Italian tenor, of whom Chaliapin was a warm supporter, having proposed him for the part, and to a certain degree coached him at the rehearsals. The Italian was small — or perhaps not, for one of Chaliapin's attributes was that, though a giant, he never looked over life-size, but merely reduced the scale of others, even tall men. At any rate, on this the first night, this protégé had enraged Chaliapin by the lightness of his singing, and by the airy way he played the harpsichord on the stage, lifting his hand up and down in a fashion against which he had been warned by the great singer. When, therefore, we arrived and opened the door, we found the enormous Russian shaking the young Italian as a mastiff might shake a *griffon*. After we entered the room, he desisted, saying in explanation, " And the plot of this opera is that *I* have to be jealous of *him* ! " . . . And, as an instance of his lack of self-consciousness, I remember, not long before his death, his telling me that in order for a man to keep well, his skin must be used to fresh air, and it was therefore absolutely necessary to go naked for part of the day. For this reason, he made a practice of having luncheon alone in his sitting-room in a condition of Nature, at any hotel where he might be staying. . . . At the time it presented to my mind a strange picture that amused me, but I have often wondered since whether his death from pneumonia may not have been connected with his adoption of this health-habit.

In the same theatre in which Chaliapin appeared, on other nights or at other hours, another art, besides opera, was to be seen in its perfection: the ballet that blooms for a year, it seems, every century, was enjoying one of its culminations. It becomes inevitable, when writing of it at this time, that the word *genius* should recur with frequency, almost with monotony, in these few pages, for no other word can describe the quality of the chief dancers or the influences at work: Stravinsky, Diaghilew, Karsavina, Fokine and Nijinsky. . . . Of all the productions of these years, *Petrouchka* must be mentioned at the head of the list; the music the first work of a composer of genius grown to his full stature (*L'Oiseau de Feu*, wonderful though its music is, was the more derivative work of a very young man); as moving and symbolic a creation of its time as Mozart's *Don Giovanni*. I have seen other great dancers, but never one inspired as was Nijinsky; I have seen other great dancers play Petrouchka, but never one who, with his rendering of a figure stuffed with straw, struggling from the thraldom of the puppet world towards human freedom, but always with the terrible leaden frustration of the dummy latent in his limbs, the movement of them containing the suggestion of the thawing of ice at winter's edge, evoked a comparable feeling of pathos. This ballet was, in its scope as a work of art, universal; it presented the European contemporary generation with a prophetic and dramatised version of the fate reserved for it, in the same way that the legend of the Minotaur had once summed up, though after the event and not before it, the fate of several generations of Greek youths and maidens. The music, traditional yet original, full of fire and genius, complication and essential simplicity, held up a mirror in which man could see, not only himself, but the angel and ape equally prisoned within his skin. The part of Petrouchka showed Nijinsky to be a master of mime, gesture, drama, just as, in pure dancing, his rendering of the Spirit of the Rose, in *Le Spectre de la Rose*, was the climax of romantic ballet.

His profoundly original ballet, *L'Après-Midi d'un Faune*, to the music of Debussy, produced at Covent Garden on 17th February 1913, and his amazing feat *Le Sacre du Printemps*, a ballet that will always stand alone, the most magnificent and living of dead ends, proved his genius as a choreographer, no less than as a dancer. . . . But let us turn for an instant to his less revolutionary creations; to, for example, *Le Spectre de la Rose*. In Nijinsky's *Diary* [1] he relates how, when he was six or seven years of age, his father threw him into the water to teach him to swim, and how he felt himself to be drowning, but perceiving the light through the water above him, became conscious of a sudden accession of physical strength, jumped and was saved. That striving to escape, to live, may account for his miraculous leap across the window into the room in the ballet I have named; something that no-one who saw it will ever forget. This great dancer seemed to hold all physical laws in abeyance and for an instant of time to remain, at the height of his leap, poised and stationary; when asked how he achieved this defiance of the law of gravity, he replied, " It's very simple : you jump and just stop in the air for a moment ". [2] . . . Even as I followed Nijinsky's movements on the stage, I realised that I was watching a legend in process of being born : for he was by nature fabulous, a prodigy. Now the legend is complete, even to the affliction that has fallen on him; reducing him for a time to the status almost of the puppet he so often portrayed, but with occasional chinks of light filtering through into his tragic mind. . . . No less true, though happier, is the legend of his partner in triumphs, his complement, the great Karsavina; in *Le Spectre de la Rose*, as graceful and romantic a spiritual realisation of the flesh as Nijinsky, a being of a new

[1] Edited by Romola Nijinsky. (Gollancz, 1937.)
[2] See *Diaghilev*, by Serge Lifar. (Putnam, 1940.)

creation, born of the rose, was an epitome in flesh of the spirit.

On 23rd June, I was present at the initial appearance of a great new dancer, a man the coming decade was to reveal as no less individual and significant an interpreter of rôles in satirical, grotesque and baroque ballets, and no less remarkable a choreographer of them, than Nijinsky had shown himself to be in the range of classical, romantic and revolutionary; Massine — or Miassine, as his name was then spelt —, in after years a valued friend of my brother and myself. *La Légende de Joseph*, in which he first danced, had been designed as a spectacle, rather than a ballet, to the music of Richard Strauss. In it, figures costumed by Léon Bakst, and such as might have been portrayed by the brush of Paolo Veronese, feasted in an enormous scene, pitched, at a hazard, half-way between Babylon and Venice, and extravagantly furnished with huge twisted columns of bronze and gold, the creation of the fashionable Spanish decorative painter, J. M. Sert. This ballet, the last pre-1914-war production by Diaghilew, was typical of that phase of the Russian Ballet. Lavish, profuse, full of sombre colours, blues and greens, and dripping with gold, like the music, it helped to overwhelm the dancers, even Karsavina, with her great allurement and experience, who played Potiphar's wife. As for Massine, I think only the most expert could have foretold from the timid movements of the young man — timid, perhaps, because it was his first appearance, no less than because the sentiment he expressed fitted the rôle — how fiery and idiosyncratic a dancer, though ever in the great tradition, he was destined to be. Of that period, of his glory, I hope to write in the next volume; and now the reader must picture him as the nervous youth I have described, borne on to the stage in a litter: when he got out, he was seen to be dressed in a white goatskin, and to have the look of a typical Alexandrian portrait of the fourth century; his natural appearance, which he has always retained.

Throughout the three years of 1912, '13, '14, new operas and ballets were continually being produced, until it seemed as if almost every evening brought its own vision, its own experiments in dancing and music. . . . And it would be

profoundly ungrateful not to mention that the man responsible
for these seasons, and for the enterprise they showed, was the
then Mr. (now Sir Thomas) Beecham, greatest of English
conductors and wittiest of musicians. Not only did he make
known to us countless foreign works, but at the same time he
accomplished more than anyone else for English composers.
While thus every week introducing new works at a great
expenditure of money and energy, and receiving little in
return except misunderstanding, coupled with a certain amount
of that deliberate malice which the stupid always have in
reserve for the creative, this most unusual man went on
his way, undeterred by the lack of support he occasionally
encountered. He started life the son of a very rich man, and
has at times, through his work for the English musical world,
been a poor one. Both conditions stood equally in his way :
English people do not expect musical genius from the rich, nor
expensive seasons from the poor.

Let us consider some of the works he brought to the attention of the audiences of 1914. I have already described *La
Légende de Joseph*. A fortnight earlier, on 9th June, *Daphnis and
Chloe* had been mounted, to the exquisite music by Ravel, and
a week before, on 15th June, came the first night of *Le Coq
d'Or*. Here was a production such as none had dreamed of in
the world of opera, and such as had only been brought into the
realms of possibility by the simultaneous presence in London
of the two great Russian companies of opera and ballet, who
were thus able, in a single effort, to combine. The stage was
set between two choirs of singers, dressed in petunia-colour,
and ranged, tier above tier, to the summit almost of the pro-
scenium : and the action part of each dancer was accompanied
by an appropriate solo voice. Besides giving us some of the
most dramatic and haunting music of the past century, *Le
Coq d'Or* constituted a great satire. In its stilted, dream-like
rhythms, displayed against a background of huge flowers and
brightly-hued buildings, was to be felt a mockery of the great,
a kind of joy in the doom of lordship. Fortunately for its
success, the fashionable audience could revel in the beauty and
strangeness of it without concentrating too much on its mean-

ing or implications. I mention it particularly and at length because it was so laden with omen and portent for those who watched it. King Dodon was a symbol to the youth of the world: and who can ever forget the Astrologer and his song ? . . . Three nights after the introduction of *Le Coq d'Or*, we were given another combined opera and ballet, Stravinsky's *Le Rossignol* : a work now rather seldom mentioned, and perhaps in its first version not altogether successful. It did not manifest the miraculous sense of growth, of fullness of the earth, that *Le Sacre du Printemps* possessed, of the blocks of ice bumping and clanging together in the freed rivers, of the furry buds bursting from their boughs with the loud grunts and cacophonies of spring: it had not *Petrouchka*'s drama and pathos, nor the mellifluous enchantment of *L'Oiseau de Feu*, yet it had about it a kind of pure, flat, two-dimensional beauty, very rare and full of delicacy. . . . At the end of the performance I was excited to see the Russian composer, the master of the epoch, walk before the curtain. Slight of frame, pale, about thirty years of age, with an air both worldly and abstracted, and a little angry, he bowed back with solemnity to the clustered, nodding tiaras and the white kid gloves, that applauded him sufficiently to be polite: yet for all their genteel tepidity, how little did the audience comprehend the nature of the great musician to whom they were doing honour, or the often eschatological import of his work!

By one of the most singular paradoxes in the history of art, the tiaras and the gloves at least were *there*, doing him honour from the stalls and boxes; whereas the audience that should have been in their place, the advanced painters and musicians of England, convinced that nothing esthetically good could come from such a quarter, rigorously abstained from being present at any performance at Drury Lane and Covent Garden. Thus, the enthusiasts for beauty missed, for some years, the most vital influence in the art world. Few of them saw Diaghilew's ballet until 1918, and I myself in the autumn of that year introduced the Russian impresario to Roger Fry. To him, and his followers, sumptuousness was always suspect; haunted by the spectre of *l'Art Pompier*. . . . And so it was that the fashionable and, for the most part, inappropriate audience had been the first to be aware of the revolutionary genius of these dancers, decorators and composers. It is always a gamble : no-one can be sure of the direction from which the next development of art, or the next artist, will arrive. Fortunately for myself, I came from the stalls, the wrong side of the house, and at Covent Garden and Drury Lane found the esthetic and musical education that had been denied me elsewhere.

Among the occupants of the stalls, there were, moreover, some genuine patrons and persons of discernment ; chief of whom was Lady Ripon, a memorable embodiment of the old order. Alas, I never knew her well, but I met her sufficiently often to be able to admire her unusual beauty, personal dignity and intelligence. She carried herself with the supreme grace of her generation, and with her grey hair, and distinguished features, of so pure a cut, she remained, though no longer a young woman, the most striking individual to look at in any room she entered. A daughter of Lord Herbert of Lea, and sister of Lord Pembroke, as became a member of her family she was a patron of the arts, as well as a leader of the social world. Perhaps it was her Russian ancestry, so visible in her appearance — for she was a great-granddaughter of Prince Simon Woronzov, brother of the celebrated Princess Daschkow — which may have been partly responsible for her great love of the Russian Ballet. . . . It was at this time that I first saw in her company Serge Diaghilew ; with his burly, tall, rather shapeless figure, he seemed formed, like a bear, to wear a coat of fur, but his clothes were smart and well cut. His black hair carried a badger's stripe of white in it, and he was of an impressive and alert appearance, with a robust elegance pertaining to him. Nevertheless, when he was preoccupied, his massive head, with a nose of the flat, not aquiline, Russian type, had something of a Velasquez dwarf's air of solemn pathos and listless fatality ; but this was quickly banished by the intense energy of his eyes, as they came to life again, and as he gave his very charming smile. . . . The great impresario would never talk English — and, indeed, almost the only time I heard him speak it was at luncheon one day. He was intensely interested in food, and said suddenly and very distinctly, *"More Chocolate Pudding!"* : a dish for which he had a curious foreign mania. French he spoke with wit and ease.

Another continual and perceptive member of the audience was Muriel Draper, as much a portent of the age to come as Lady Ripon of that which was nearing its end. I met her, too, for the first time now, and was destined to know her well in later years, seeing her frequently and taking delight in her company. Her looks at once set her apart. Tall, slight, with her pale, rather high-cheek-boned face, her head was set at an angle of pride and beauty, and the clothes she wore, the pale colours, the turban, the jewel on her forehead, all made her very much a type of some new human being : albeit her breeding was at the same time evident from the shape of her fine bones. In fact, she looked, it seemed to me, as every woman of the New Continent should look. She and her husband, Paul Draper, were the friends and guardians of all visiting foreign musicians ; Thibaud, Casals, Rubinstein frequented her house and caused the sombre air of the London night to be filled, until the latest hour of early morning, with music : but in that I did not share, for we were only acquaintances then, though when we met our conversation was of music, conductors, composers, ballet, but in the usual desultory vein of the polite London world ; whereas when, after the war, we became intimate friends, I found her conversation, fascinating and spontaneous, to be like that of no other person in the world. It opens up whole vistas of understanding of things which, until she sheds light on them, remain dark. Talking to her, indeed, resembles a conversation with some great observer of Nature, such as Fabre, except that this watcher is concerned, not with the ways of insects, but with the behaviour of human beings. Not for a moment, either, does she appear, as Aldous Huxley perhaps used to, interestedly disinterested, aloof; she adheres with passion to the species to which she belongs.

At Covent Garden, the house would contain many foreigners : music and dancing knew no barrier of race. Indeed, the whole world of amusement was international. Similarly, among the people I saw of my own choice, talk turned as much on doings in Paris, Berlin, Rome, Vienna and St. Petersburg as on events at home. There was none of the hatred and dissension that has devoured nations and classes ever since 1914. . . . In June of that year Richard Strauss, for example, came over to London for the rehearsals of *La Légende de Joseph*, and was present at a reception at the French Embassy: (that evening, the only hint of the approaching conflict was when a well-known American hostess went up to the German composer, and remarked to him in a confiding and congratulatory voice, " Monsieur Strauss, in England we think your music very vulgar " : a scene which must have ravaged the heart of that accomplished diplomat, Monsieur Cambon). To show the high place that London held as a music-centre, the *Morning Post* was able to announce on 12th June that the Music Club would give a reception to Dr. Strauss on the 21st, in celebration of his fiftieth birthday, and that besides the guest of honour there would be present Monsieur Igor Stravinsky, Monsieur Chaliapin, Madame Karsavina and Monsieur Claude Debussy; that Mr. Thomas Beecham would conduct Strauss's early Suite for thirteen wood-wind instruments, and that Madame Elena Gerhardt would sing a group of his songs, accompanied by Herr Nikisch. . . . This particular occasion, I believe, never saw the full realisation of the programme designed for it, but that it could come so near fruition shows how far, how deep, how bitterly, we have fallen from the standards of those days.

On the evening in question Strauss did, in fact, join in the performing of his Sonata in E flat for pianoforte and violin, Lady Speyer playing the second instrument. . . . And, as if to return these international compliments in the arts, a few evenings later Debussy went to Lady Speyer's house in Grosvenor Street. Behind a frowning, rusticated Palazzo-Strozzi front, it sheltered the sort of art collection that is seldom seen in England but is more common in America. Many of the items might have been chosen by a magpie who had found himself a millionaire: some were dark in tone, it is true — dark in the manner of oak, walnut, armour, red velvet — yet all glittered and were rich in lustre. There was something in the atmosphere, too, that recalled the public rooms of an expensive liner. French staircases, German wood-carving, Augsburg plate, crystal vases from China, Persian tiles, and some of the furnishing of Marie-Antoinette's boudoir, all these were united by the taste of the owners for objects of luxury. . . . At the back of this mansion, on the ground floor, was a music-room, built at the further side of a small garden-court, in the middle of which stood a Renaissance fountain. And in the summer months, if there was to be an entertainment — and how often there was to be one! — there would appear on the water in this basin, as a sort of mute herald of a party, a large white water-lily tied by a piece of string to a ring at the bottom.

My presence in the house was due to my friendship with Miss Enid Howland, Lady Speyer's daughter by a former American marriage. Her mother was a tall, handsome, headstrong and ambitious woman, lacking, I should say, in the power of self-criticism, and with a process of reasoning that was apt to be influenced by her motives, though of this she would remain unaware. But the predominant trait in her character was her love of music, which made her house a centre of the musical world in London. There the standard of performance was that of the contemporary German musical life, and no higher existed; though in other respects, in painting and literature, the usual outlook of the cosmopolitan millionaire upon the arts prevailed. Indeed, the whole accent of the house, in spite of its affiliations, was more American than German, and for that reason I found the charges levelled against the Speyers during the First World War most difficult to believe. I suppose the general attitude in England at the time towards those of German name drove Lady Speyer, with her headstrong nature and willingness to hit back, into taking up an attitude or making remarks which, though only the result of a temporary mood of exasperation, were unfortunate. Certainly Enid Howland was devoted to this country and the Allied cause, and suffered when her family left for America.

My admiration for Debussy was so enormous that, as I

have mentioned in the Introduction to *Left Hand, Right Hand!*, I remember nothing of his appearance. I shook hands with him: I recall my emotion, I remember clearly Madame Debussy's face — but that is all! . . . By then the first impact of his music had already a little worn off, and he was recognised as the presiding genius of French music, though only a few years before, even to the most musically endowed of concert-goers, his work had seemed as difficult to understand as would be a picture viewed through spectacles that did not focus. His music sounded, it may be, a little incongruous, a little over-pure, between the rich walls of the Speyer mansion ; even the water-lily hardly enticed the breath of Nature into the garden : but it cannot be gainsaid that here it was possible to hear Debussy's music played, and to meet the illustrious composer, and that everything modern and enlivening in music would before long find its way to these hospitable doors.

More in keeping with the surroundings, however, was the music of Richard Strauss, so essentially *nouveau riche* : but, in spite of that, not appreciated by the English world in general — though in no country were *nouveaux riches* more popular. Indeed, Lady Speyer's neighbours entertained no liking for the subtleties of modern music of any kind. In the mean streets that surrounded the back of the house, all that the hard-working populace wanted to hear was *Home, Sweet Home* or, at the liveliest, *Pop Goes the Weasel*. Having to rise early every day, these workers were roused to fury by perpetual musical parties that continued throughout the night, and, by a paradox, their anger reached its climax when an Alpine Band, of which Strauss was the patron, was brought to play in the music-room at the back, and gave a concert of popular Tyrolean and Swiss music. The sounds the band made were, indeed, unconventional, unusual in a city ; the simple music of a mountain people, suffering from iodine-deficiency, and intended to carry great distances from peak to peak, a translation of yodelling into other terms. After a few pieces had been played, assorted objects, chiefly fish-heads — which seemed greatly in supply — began to fall among the startled guests, arrayed in their finery, in the garden-court, and the first casualty was Sir Claude

Phillips, a rotten egg exploding on the large pearl stud which held together his expansive and exquisitely laundered shirt-front, as he lingered outside, by the tethered water-lily. . . . It was the forerunner of many an evening with the Marx Brothers.

It seemed singular that Lady Speyer, devoted to music though she was, seldom or never appeared at the opera : but it was said that there was never a box for her. . . . In the world of opera and ballet, Lady Cunard reigned alone. Her boundless and enthusiastic love of music places all those who enjoy opera in her debt : for it was largely her support, and the way she marshalled her forces, that enabled the wonderful seasons of opera and ballet in these years to materialise. There appeared to be no limit to the number of boxes she could fill. Her will-power was sufficient, her passion for music fervent enough, to make opera almost compulsory for those who wished to be fashionable. She had grasped the fact that in the London of that time, in order to ensure the success of such an art-luxury as Grand Opera, it was absolutely necessary to be able to rely upon a regular attendance by numskulls, nitwits and morons addicted to the mode, even if they did not care in the least for music. . . . Lady Cunard's house was then 20 Cavendish Square, which she had taken from Mrs. Asquith when she moved to Downing Street : it was a late seventeenth- or early eighteenth-century mansion, with a fine, substantially panelled dining-room, a long, blue drawing-room, and a stately baroque, stone-flagged hall and staircase, frescoed by Sir James Thornhill.[1] And much as I loved the opera and ballet I was often sorry when the hour came for us to leave her house, because her airy and rather impersonal alertness, and her wit, which consists in a particular and individual use of syllogism, so that it was impossible beforehand ever to tell to what conclusion any given premise might bring you, made her drawing-room unlike any other, gay, full of life. But she would never be late for the opera, if she could help it, albeit she would find it difficult, I think, in

[1] Though most of this house has been destroyed, the staircase and a few fine old rooms still survive, enclosed in the new building of The Nurses' Association.

other matters to be punctual. Again, whereas the majority of London hostesses love dullness for its own sake, and without hope of reward, and whereas, moreover, one is continually surprised to find how little literary hostesses have read, Lady Cunard loves to be amused, and her passion for books is obvious. She takes the pleasure in a volume that is new to her that a child finds in a toy, and when the talk turns on abstruse subjects, you will find that she has read the most unlikely works on them. . . . On the other hand, though a foe to dullness, she is a collector of people, and sometimes, by means of that very individual, personal logic, visible in all she touches, that she has invented for herself, she may detect in her guests points that are hard for others to see: she will like and praise a politician because he recites Corneille, a great General for some such reason as that " he knows all about butterflies! " or a poet " because he seems to understand fish ". . . . But she tires so quickly of dullness, even of dullness new to her, that she has developed her own method of combating it. She can goad the conversation, as if it were a bull, and she a matador, and compel it to show a fiery temper. . . . In addition to the fashionable near-art world, the eminent of many kinds, politicians, and occasionally a statesman, as well as writers, painters and musicians, frequented then, and still frequent, her drawing-room.

It was at 20 Cavendish Square that I first met Delius, and for him I cherished a feeling of the deepest respect, not only for his music, with its warm, melodious climate, but because he was the one Englishman I have ever met who knew personally the giants of the Post-Impressionist Movement, recognised them for what they were, and was privileged to frequent their studios. He used, for example, regularly to attend the Sunday evening at-homes of the Douanier Rousseau, social occasions that now exhale a legendary quality unrivalled in the art history of a period comparatively near to us. Thus, Delius linked the present day to a fabulous past, and though then still in middle age was as solitary a survivor here as would be the last Blue Man in Tasmania. . . . I do not know that his looks precisely interpreted his nature. He was rather tall and thin, possessed a high, narrow forehead, an aquiline nose, delicately cut, and a finely-drawn face, of the Roman intellectual type. Though it is true that his head showed every sign of distinction, he might, from his appearance, more easily have been a great lawyer than a great composer. In talking — and he was a voluble and delightful conversationalist — his tongue betrayed, not an accent, exactly, but a slight foreign stress and lilt, attractive, and personal enough to make a contrast with the theories and speculations of which his soliloquies were full : for he loved abstract ideas with the passion of a Latin for them — the English hate them — and, though he formulated them with all a clever Englishman's love of paradox, there was, nevertheless, a certain stringency pertaining to them. The most gifted of English composers living at that time, head and shoulders above his bumpy buttercup-and-daisy confrères, a musician of the world, he found himself somewhat of a stranger in London. Indeed, once again, without Sir Thomas Beecham's enthusiasm to support him, his music would have scarcely obtained a hearing in England. The later advocacy of Philip Heseltine, who served the cause of his music with unfaltering devotion, should also be mentioned.

At Lady Cunard's, too, I used often to meet George Moore : though in the first place I had seen him at Mrs. Charles Hunter's Edwardian arcady at Hill in Essex. And before proceeding to write of him, a few words must be devoted to that house and its hostess. . . . Mrs. Charles Hunter, whom the reader of *Left Hand, Right Hand !* will recall as the favourite subject of Sargent's portraits, represented the Edwardian generation, the Edwardian hostess, *in excelsis*. By birth she belonged to a distinguished family of soldiers, and she was the sister of Dame Ethel Smyth. I had first known Mrs. Hunter when I was about twelve, for her husband had once stood as Conservative candidate for Scarborough, but he was unsuccessful. They had taken Londesborough Lodge : but the political worthies of the town understood her interests and methods of entertaining as little as farm labourers would, for the most part, understand Marcel Proust's descriptions of fashionable Parisian life. She belonged essentially to the capitals ; and it was significant that her country house was situated so very near London. To the part she played so well at Hill and in London, she brought a massive and gilded beauty, like that of the Italian and Spanish furniture with which she filled her houses, a power of imagination, her husband's considerable wealth, and, above all, a capacity for organising that was to make her the Kitchener of hostesses. I have never forgotten seeing her sitting out one morning in various corners of the garden at Hill, in order to test where it was warm enough, behind what brake of bamboos, under what oak tree, in the shelter of what loggia, for her guests to have luncheon in the open air. In the highest degree, she was lavish : and if her house was a little over-exuberant, the curves and gilding of table and chair a little over-emphasised, the velvets a little too complicated in pattern, these were faults of taste indicative of her epoch. Hill was almost too luxurious for comfort, but its rooms were beautifully disposed and displayed none of the period-tyranny to be observed elsewhere, though nothing had been inherited, and everything had been bought. But all its objects were united by their rich, massive, and yet rather flimsy character. The two large scagliola pillars in the hall had been painted by Sargent, whose various portraits of Mrs. Hunter and her three daughters hung on many of the walls. This painter was a frequent guest, and even though he was not present in his rather taurine flesh, his influence could yet be felt, and " Mr. Sargent " was a frequent and notable prop of the conversation, as was " Mr. Henry James ". Here, too, I met Tonks again for the first time since he had come to Renishaw to paint my father's portrait when I was a very small boy. But even after this lapse of years, he was easy to recognise ; a type, indeed, for his own most brilliant caricatures. Tall, lean, with something of the aspect of a vulture, he imbued his pungent remarks with an almost aggressive sincerity. Among other regular visitors to Hill was Robert Ross, with his adroit and pleasing company, his tact and cleverness, above all his sympathy and his witty comments on life. In London Mrs. Hunter lived in beautiful, rare, characteristic rooms, painted by a French *Singerie* painter of the early eighteenth century, and situated at the back of the Burlington Gardens Hotel, to which they belonged. They were furnished with her own possessions and it is unnecessary to say that she imparted a decorative intent to all she touched : even her motor-car, modelled on a hansom cab, but with a body painted to resemble wicker-work, had something of the charm of a gondola about it, as it glided about the London streets of which it became so well known a feature. But Hill was more essentially Mrs. Hunter's creation. Here, like the sun, she was setting in splendour ; her flowers growing larger, her food better, her head-dresses bigger, her parties more interesting and typical, and all of them infused with the quality of her own enthusiastic vagueness. She belonged essentially to the world that in the words of Walter Sickert " dined out for Art ".

It was here, then, that I met George Moore, and I watched him delightedly, for, very often, he was out to shock ; and when he had said something that he hoped would appal every-one in the house, or even in the garden, a seraphic smile would come over his face, and remain on it, imparting to it a kind of illumination of virtue, like that of a saint, for several minutes ; the bland unself-conscious smile of a small boy — though at that time he must have been nearly sixty — saying to himself delightedly " I've smashed it ! ", and he would regard his audience attentively, with his eyes of a mild and rather misty blue, peering out of a plump, pear-shaped, pink-and-white face, surmounted by soft white hair. The lines of his drooping mouth seemed a little to contradict the spirit of enterprise he showed. But his voice, fascinating though it was, had an almost aggressive distinctness about it, and its rhythm and stress seemed to proclaim that once he had formed an opinion, on however faulty grounds, he would be unwilling to alter it. . . . At first — or, at any rate, a year or two later — he took a great dislike to me, but in time that passed ; it was based on the fact that I did not support with enthusiasm the idea of an indefinitely long war with Germany : but his own bellicose attitude gained greatly from his ignorance of geography, and his belief, for instance, that Baghdad was in Germany. In time, as I say, he grew friendly, and used to send for me to

Ebury Street. His mind was not large, but its working was most original, and his sayings — and actions — were unexpected, even when he had no desire to shock. If his views were opposed, his voice would rise, as it did when he became angry; as it did, for example, I remember, some years later, when he took me up to the drawing-room in Ebury Street, and found the sun, unscreened by blinds, shining on the rosy and pale-blue splendours of his celebrated Aubusson carpet: or as, again, when one afternoon Ada Leverson, who had been a great friend of his, called at the house, accompanied by William Walton — then only a boy —, who greatly admired Moore's books. She rang the bell, and when the door was opened Moore shouted down the stairs, " *Who* is it, *who* is it ? " Mrs. Leverson cried back, " It's *Ada*, G.M. ! I've brought a great admirer of yours to see you, William Walton the composer ! He's only eighteen ! " " I don't care if he's eighteen or eighty ", Moore replied at the top of his voice. " I *won't* see him. Tell him to go away." . . . As a matter of fact, I think, he did care if a man was eighteen or eighty, for he was inclined to be jealous of, or distrusted, those who were younger than himself, until he became accustomed to the idea of them. As I saw more of him, however, I began to find ever greater pleasure in the personal idiom of his talk, to which the Irish run of his voice, and his startling accentuation of certain words, gave an added point : and those who read his prose can still, if they listen for it, hear his voice beneath its beautiful texture, like the echo of the living sea in a shell.

Youth was not much in evidence at Mrs. Hunter's, but Lady Cunard's intensive hospitality applied to young as well as middle-aged. Being young myself at the time, and not as yet a writer, I was invited for the most part to meet those of my own age. And the young one met at Cavendish Square were usually the same band of young people, with nearly all of whom I became friendly : among others, the daughter of the house, Nancy Cunard, with her ineffable charm and distinction of mind, Edward Horner, Diana Manners, Denis Anson and Duff Cooper. . . . And this, perhaps, is the place to write of Lady Diana Manners, whose beauty and personality placed her alone in the English scene : the only beauty whose looks entitled her to be discussed by those who remembered the celebrated beauties of former days, the Comtesse de Castiglione and Georgiana Lady Dudley, debating whether she should have been half an inch taller or shorter ; in fact the only classic of her kind and generation. For this was not the era of the classic beauty : never before had the ugly woman enjoyed such a run for her ugliness as in these days, and after the war, the uglier, the more " amusing " her appearance was deemed to be ; so that the great beauty traditional in line stood almost at a disadvantage. But fortunately for Lady Diana, though her looks belonged to all the English generations before her own, her spirit was essentially of the time, audacious, enterprising and critical. I have heard it said about her — and about whom else could it justly be said ? — that when she enters a room, it seems to grow lighter ; and her eyes certainly hold an unusual refulgence, blue and grey.

The first time I dined in Cavendish Square, those I have enumerated as the younger habitués of the house were present, and I sat next to Diana, and I remember her telling me in later years of her surprise at meeting a young officer of the Brigade of Guards who insisted on talking of Stravinsky. Our friend-ship quickly ripened — but this was due to her, for she is the most inspiring as well as the most steadfast of friends, quick to seize on character, and to understand the point of those she meets : whereas I, in spite of an air of composure which I believe I possessed — and of some reserve —, was shy. The directions of my ability were unresolved, and my every day's occupation was in conflict with my character and heredity ; hence I was diffident, and it sometimes took me a long time to break through the stage of acquaintance into friendship, except with those to whom I felt immediately drawn. Never-theless, there are many others, many, whom I should write about thus, separately and in their order and context, to give a just impression of those years and what they mean to the present writer, as they meant to his earlier incarnation. To them, whether it was hatred or love I bore them — and in those days I seldom experienced any feeling between the two —,

I owe a duty; but to the law of selection that governs the art of the writer I owe a higher allegiance, and, in consequence, I must ask my friends of this period of my novitiate in life to forgive me for my omissions.

To revert to that evening, after dinner, Thomas Beecham played through some of the score of *Der Rosenkavalier*. I was to hear it many times that summer, superbly sung; but so far I had only been acquainted with the waltz, which for the two years preceding the war had formed the background to every dance, so that if I can ever catch the rhythm of it today, the world is again for the moment peopled with a legion of the young, enjoying themselves, who have long since ceased to exist. . . . Looking round, not even the most sombre-minded of prophets in that flowering summer — for never can England have known a more ideal season — could have foreseen the extinction of the young men as a whole, within so short a space of time. . . . Later that night, we, the younger members of the party, went to a ball in a house, the walls of which had recently been sumptuously frescoed by Sert, with designs of elephants and howdahs and rajahs and pavilions and melons and bulrushes in sepia and gold. Outside, the house was ordinary — a tall, long, brick house with the usual drain-pipes : and I recall that, when one of the girls dropped a glove by accident from a balcony, Denis Anson had, without mentioning what he intended to do, and before anyone could stop him, quickly swarmed down a leaden pipe to the ground, some twenty feet below, picked up the glove, and returned with it in the same manner. This recollection I place here, because it gives an example of his impetuosity and lack of fear, which were two of the many likable characteristics about him, and because this quality of bravura more than bravado helps to explain how he met his death so soon after, on the 3rd of July 1914.

He had been one of a party of fourteen people, all close friends, who had embarked on a pleasure-launch to go up the Thames. They had started from Westminster Pier shortly after midnight, for most of them had attended the Opera at Covent Garden. It was a calm night, cloudy and dark. After supper in the cabin, most of the party went upon deck, where a band was playing. The return journey began at Kew. Battersea Bridge was approached at 3 o'clock. The boat was decorated with lanterns, but the night was still dark. Denis Anson was noticed walking on the seats and balancing himself on the rails : but in him this was nothing unusual. Suddenly he raised his hands above his head and dived into the water. He was never seen again. Nobody had been alarmed at the time, for though the tide flowed strong, it was the sort of thing he had so often done before, and he was a powerful swimmer. His host plunged in after him and was for a long time in the water before being found in an exhausted condition, while an unfortunate bandsman who had also bravely dived to the rescue was drowned. . . . Sir Denis Anson's death at the age of twenty-five caused a sensation, for in him many had perceived brilliant gifts and believed that they would lead to a great future. But beyond that, his death was a symbol to his generation, kind and coterie, as similarly, on the grand scale, the sinking of the *Titanic* had been a symbol of the approaching fate of Western Civilisation.

The great Review of the Brigade of Guards, the year before — on 28th April 1913 —, by King George, accompanied by Queen Mary, on the Parade Ground at Hyde Park, I believe held in it, too, something of the shadow of coming events. I was at Aldershot serving with the 1st Battalion, and the officers, I recollect, were called at 2 A.M. and entrained at Aldershot for the disused railway station at Chelsea : from there we marched to the Duke of York's Headquarters, and were in Hyde Park by 9 A.M. (This was, incidentally, the sole occasion when I wore the scarlet and gold review-belt alluded to in an earlier chapter.) The occasion presented, even for one involved in it, and nervous lest he might make his incompetence plain to the world, a resplendent spectacle, as the most perfectly trained body of men in the world performed the March Past. The King, wearing the uniform of the Grenadiers, as its Colonel-in-Chief, was followed by the Duke of Connaught as Colonel, who — albeit he lived another three decades — already offered a link with the past : for he was the youngest godson of the great Duke of Wellington, who had been a former Colonel of the Regiment. The massed bands of the Brigade of Guards advanced first, headed by the kettledrums and the drum-majors, in their heraldic, playing-card uniforms, with peaked, velvet jockey-caps, this uniform having, it was said, been designed personally by King George IV, greatest of royal impresarios since the Emperor Nero. . . . It was a final salute from the Old Order which was to perish, and constituted for those taking part in it — and how few survived the next two years ! — a sort of fanfare, heralding the war.

We belonged to a doomed generation, and the enlightened Liberal statesmen then in power, men of the highest principles and attainments, and of great forensic ability, presented to it — and it included some of their own sons — the 1914 war as a coming-of-age gift. Even today you see refer-ences to the immense achievements of the Liberal administra-tion of 1906–14 — and admittedly its leaders were men of intellect, and sometimes of imperial vision —, but can any Government whose policy entails such a lack of preparation for war as to make that seeming solution of difficulties a gamble apparently worth while for an enemy, and thus leads to the death or disablement of two million fellow-countrymen : in fact, practically the whole male youth of the country ; can any Government which introduces old-age pensions, so as " to help the old people ", and then allows half the manhood of the country to be slaughtered or disabled before it reaches thirty years of age, be considered to have been either benevolent or efficient ?

That the military element to which I — not of my own choice, it is true — belonged, might be wiped out, was, perhaps, less hard to predict. But even among the particular band whom I have mentioned, Edward Horner, Denis Anson, Duff Cooper, and their friends, men such as Raymond Asquith and Patrick Shaw-Stewart — men sure of themselves, young, full of vigour, with a wit all their own which I take, in essence and origin, to have been a legacy from the old Whig Society — war and accident were to reap a full harvest. Only my friend Duff Cooper survived the next five years, and when one con-

siders the extreme courage and defiance of consequences he continually showed during his career as a soldier, this is, indeed, a
matter for wonder. . . . I always immensely enjoy his witty,
cultivated, irascible, and yet genial company. During the 1914
war, he left the Foreign Office to enter the Grenadiers, and
while we were both young officers at Chelsea Barracks, we
used sometimes to sit for a moment in the corner of the Ante-
Room and grumble together about the rather rigid minds of
the higher military authorities. . . . When, twenty years later,
I was able to write and congratulate him on his appointment
as Minister for War, in his reply he alluded indirectly to this,
with the words, " It is rather a comfort to have all the generals
under me at last ".

As for those friends of mine who were already soldiers,
brother-officers, or those contemporaries with me at the
crammer's who had succeeded in obtaining commissions, and
were in other regiments, they stood, even at that moment, in
the shadows. I attended in 1913 and 1914 many coming-of-age
parties, when we toasted a future which was to have no substance. . . . All these anniversaries were celebrated in much
the same manner — including my own, though that had been
preceded by a twenty-one years' discussion of plans. . . . As
late as 21st June 1913, I find my father writing to me about it;
though perhaps, where this occasion, the subject of so much
fantasy, was concerned, in a — for him — rather subdued and
matter-of-fact tone. " I have been talking this morning to
Hollingworth and Ernest about your coming-of-age. We think
about the sixteenth of June the best time, as the foliage then
still looks so fresh and well, and the evenings are almost at their
longest. We shall turf the lawn beds, so as to have the long
tea-tables against the yew hedges, plant the garden for June,
sow half an acre of sweet-peas and iris for cutting, force grapes
and peaches earlier, and plant early strawberries and vege-
tables. Have you any other suggestions ? . . ." In fact, no
blue-stencilled white cows, no dragons, no reproduction in fireworks of the Sargent group, none of the intended fanfaronade,
separated the dinner-party I gave to some thirty brother-
officers and friends, on the night of 6th December 1913, from

the run of similar occasions that I attended that year. One thing alone removed it into a different category : the fact that the host was alive two years later. I cannot think of a single other host at such a party who outlasted the winter following.

My coming-of-age called forth a letter from the Archbishop of Canterbury, which I here reproduce. In the midst of all he had to do — for, contrary to popular belief, an Archbishop is the most fully occupied of human beings —, it was most kind of him to have found time to write.

OLD PALACE, CANTERBURY
8th Dec. 1913

MY DEAR OSBERT,

I ought to have sent you a word of good hope and congratulation on the years which betoken grown-up life.

May every highest good be yours as these run on.

You have already a rather more varied experience of men and things than falls ordinarily to the lot of man before he is of age. All that will be to the good in giving you grip and force for life's battlefields on behalf of what is good and clean and worthy. You may be very sure that we have you constantly in mind in the best sort of way. God bless you.—I am, Yours very truly, RANDALL CANTUAR.

Now undoubtedly an Archbishop's hieratic office, going back to Tudor times, weighs down the phrases — yet " good hope ", " betoken ", " lot of man ", " life's battlefields " inevitably recall the style of the prayers issued to embitter still further for us those times of national emergency. which now recur with such distressing frequency. . . . " May-every-highest-good-be-yours-as-these-run-on " : repeat the phrase, let it linger on the tongue, and you will soon realise that it has the very lilt of a hymn tune. Moody calls to Sankey — or was it Sankey to Moody? . . . That I had the sense to keep this letter I attribute to my having recently read Samuel Butler's *Way of All Flesh*.

As the nights of 1914 wore on, their splendour increased. There was no sign of anything amiss, no sudden chilling of the blood, unless it were at the single glimpse I obtained of Lord Kitchener, sitting like a pagod shrined in flowers and exotic leaves, beneath wreaths and swags at a ball which I attended, given by the Household Cavalry at Knightsbridge Barracks. He just happened to have chosen this seat, at an angle which commanded the full length of two vistas of rooms; but there was something both intensely appropriate and inappropriate about the place he had selected: moreover, one saw only him, his partner sank into insignificance, since, whatever his faults or his merits, his genius was sufficient to concentrate attention upon him to the exclusion of all others in his neighbourhood, as if he were accompanied by an invisible limelight, with an orange slide; for the colour of his face was tawny beyond sunburn and pertained to the planet Mars. With an altogether exceptional squareness and solidity, he sat there as if he were a god, slightly gone to seed perhaps, but waiting confidently for his earthly dominion to disclose itself at the sound of the last, or, in his case, of the first trump. A large square frame, with square shoulders, square head, square face, a square line of hair at the top of a square forehead, he rested there, with a curious rectangular immobility, enfilading two perspectives of rooms with a slightly unfocused glance, which seemed, almost, in its fixity to possess a power of divination. As well as being the realisation of an ideal of Kipling's — and to that writer, except for his stature, he bore a certain affinity, of head, hair, eyebrow —, he plainly belonged to some different creation from those round him; a rare, distinguished sept such as the Four Marshals of China, vast figures with angry, bulging eyes, daubed faces and drawn swords, who, fashioned of painted wood, guard the entrance to every Chinese temple, or, again, he could claim kinship to the old race of gigantic German Generals, spawned by Wotan in the Prussian plains, and born with spiked helmets ready on their heads. Though his pose offered the same suggestion of immense strength, and even of latent physical fury, yet, just as he could have been nothing but a soldier, and a great soldier, so, too, every trait in his appearance, his blue eyes, and the cut of his features, unusual as it was, proclaimed him to be English: not an English leader of patrician type such as Wellington, but one from the class that had, since the Reform Bill, monopolised power.

And you could, in the mind's eye, see his image set up as that of an English god, by natives in distant parts of the Empire which he had helped to create and support, precisely as the Roman Emperors had formerly been worshipped. Within a few months' time, when from every hoarding vast posters showed Lord Kitchener pointing into perspectives in space, so steadily perceived, if focused with uncertainty, and below this portrait the caption " He wants You ! ", I often thought of that square figure glowering under the wreaths and festoons of smilax, from among the ferns and palms and flowers. . . .

The nights, sumptuous as they were, each with its own bloom of perfection on its surface, wore on. Day and night mingled in a general glow, and sometimes the regimental duty seemed exhausting of a morning : but one must not show fatigue. There was as yet no disturbance in the air round us, no ruffle of wind across the century-old calm. The continuing differences between the Government and Opposition about the Irish Home Rule Bill remained the only subject of political gossip and excitement. . . . And then, in the evening papers of 28th June came the news that an Austrian Archduke had been shot, while performing a tour of inspection, in a town in some rather outlandish portion of the Austrian Empire. Few people, especially among my brother-officers, knew anything, either of him or of his place of assassination : though some there were who had visited this part of the world in order to shoot moufflons. I was total in my ignorance ; except that I was aware that the famous Villa D' Este, perhaps the most beautiful Italian garden in the world, belonged to him, for the Archduke Franz-Ferdinand was heir of the House of Este. . . . A few people I saw seemed oddly perturbed at the murder. It was difficult to understand why. The place, wherever it was, remained a long way off ; and throughout the lives of my generation foreign royalties and heads of states had been murdered with regularity : Grand Dukes without number, King Umberto of Italy, President McKinley, the Empress of Austria, the King and Queen of Serbia, the King and Crown Prince of Portugal, to take at random a few examples in which the attempts had been successful. . . . No earthquakes had occurred then.

For what reason, then, had this minority of anxious persons grown suddenly so acutely worried? . . . There was nothing else unusual; no warning — only one or two signs so slight, so vague, or so tinged with superstitious feeling, that no-one except a person long trained by continual trouble at home to be of an apprehensive turn of mind would have noticed them.

I had observed, for example, a sudden, almost unbearable restlessness, in about the middle of June, filling the hearts and minds of many of my contemporary brother-officers; young men, nearly all of whom had, a week or two before, been content with their lot, but were now experiencing an anguished desire for change, like the sudden wave of restlessness that is said to seize on birds and animals before a volcanic disturbance. One planned to join a polar expedition, another to be transferred to an African regiment, a third to start a ranch in South America, a fourth to go to China. It was as though some wind possessed the air and was scattering them, or as if their souls were growing impatient, still anchored within their bodies. . . . Their plans, however, were not destined to be realised. By the late autumn, they were dead.

Something else that might have been an indication, I recall. Nearly all the brother-officers of my own age had been, two or three months earlier in the year, to see a celebrated palmist of the period — whom, I remember, it was said, with what justification I am not aware, that Mr. Winston Churchill used sometimes to consult. My friends, of course, used to visit her in the hope of being told that their love affairs would prosper, when they would marry, or the direction in which their later careers would develop. In each instance, it appeared, the cheiromant had just begun to read their fortunes, when, in sudden bewilderment, she had thrown the outstretched hand from her, crying, " I don't understand it! It's the same thing again! After two or three months, the line of life stops short, and I can read nothing." . . . To each individual to whom it was said, this seemed merely an excuse she had improvised for her failure: but when I was told by four or five persons of the same experience, I wondered what it could portend. . . . But nothing could happen, nothing.

Other incidents fall more precisely within the scope of my autobiography. . . . I spent Whitsun, 1914, in Somerset, with one of my new friends. From this distance, those few days seem singularly representative of the years to which they belonged. It was an enchanted moment of the spring. My hostess possessed an extraordinary gaiety of spirit, and a power of instilling it into others, even the most dull, and for the brief hours of three days the English climate itself abandoned its usual stolidity and blossomed into the deepest blue skies, flecked, like a vast blue sea, with specks of moving white. Most of the guests I had grown to know well in the antecedent months, with the exception of the Baron and Baroness von Kühlmann — he was Counsellor at the German Embassy — and Captain Schubert, the military attaché. On Sunday morning, the two German men suggested that I should go for a walk with them. . . . I recall the morning as if it were a week ago, the feel of the weather, and the scent of the mimosa, so rare a tree in England, which held golden clusters close against the walls of the old house. As we climbed a hill that ran abruptly towards the sky, the talk of my two new acquaintances — and I noticed that for Germans their manners were unusually ingratiating — veered towards English politics, and then settled, like a bird alighting, on the Home Rule controversy. Suddenly Kühlmann asked me,

" How would your Regiment act if ordered by the Government to oppose the Ulster Volunteers ? " [1]

Though by nature as yet politically unsuspicious, since I believed that nations were governed by wise men, actuated by common sense, and that, therefore, there could be no likelihood of a war — yet this question rather startled me. In any case it was one that plainly should not have been put by a foreigner, more especially a foreign diplomat, to an Englishman, above all not to an English officer, however young and unimportant. Fortunately, I answered, almost before I had had time to think,

" Naturally, we shall obey orders ; that is what we are there for."

[1] The Ulster Volunteers were determined to use force against the enactment of the Home Rule Bill.

But all the same, I reflected, how odd this is : because if I shared the prejudices of some of my fellow-countrymen, I should think the Germans were planning something, and were, in pursuance of it, neglecting no source of information, however slight. . . . But that was impossible ! . . . The talk, nevertheless, had grated on my nerves, imparting to the whole day an unpleasant flavour, and leaving me with a permanent wish to avoid their company.

This incident had taken place, of course, late in the month of May ; some weeks before the shooting in Sarajevo. The other, to which I now turn, occurred about ten days after the assassination. Though but a tenuous indication of the trend of events, indeed so volatile in essence as scarcely to bear the strain of transcription, yet this, too, was somehow tinged for me with the darkness of the future. . . . I was having luncheon at a table alone, when an acquaintance asked me if he might sit at it, as the room was full. Our talk was dull, neutral, with no life in it, but towards the end of the meal he turned to me and said quietly,

" Do you see the man over there, by the window, with a beaky nose, and a white moustache and imperial ? Wearing a pink carnation ? Well, he's a very remarkable man. Look at him carefully, and I'll tell you about him." Glancing in the direction indicated, I saw a rather tall, broadly built man, with a strange yellow face, strongly marked features, and pale, sunken eyes. He was dressed in a well-cut English suit, and had taken trouble, it could be seen, about his clothes generally. It was difficult racially to place him. He did not seem to be a Jew, he was too tall and sturdily built ; but apart from his frame, there was about him an oriental air. He might have been a Turk or a Cypriot — I have since seen money-changers in Cyprus who a little resemble him.

" There must be something up," my informant continued, " or he wouldn't be here ! His arrival is always a sign of trouble, and every European Chancellery makes a point of knowing where he is. His name is Basil Zaharoff."

Certainly there was something both evil and imposing about his figure : and as he grew older, the shell hardened and became more typical. His personal appearance should have put all with whom he came into contact on their guard — it is, indeed, singular that western man, while refusing to place credence in anything that he cannot see, while rejecting absolutely omens, prophecies and visions, should at the same time, as he so often does, deny the evidence of his own eyes. This armament-monger most exactly resembled a vulture, and it is no good pretending, in order to avoid the obvious parallel, that he did not. To some it may cause surprise that a man who traded in weapons of death and the prospects of war, and grew fat-bodied on the result of them, should have resembled the scaly-necked bird; but whether or no it seems strange, depends on one's view of the world, and of the immense and startling range of analogy, simile and image that it offers. There, in any case, the likeness was, for all to behold : the beaky face, the hooded eye, the wrinkled neck, the full body, the impression of physical power and of the capacity to wait, the sombre alertness.[1] . . . In later years, I met Zaharoff several times, and came to the conclusion that though the results of his deeds might be evil, his interests were, in fact, of too material a nature to allow him very high flights of imaginative wickedness. . . . He was in outlook merely a super-croupier. And once, in later years, when he was living in Monte Carlo — where he was said to have acquired a large interest in the Casino —, I heard him introduce himself to a millionaire friend of mine with the startling phrase, " I am Basil Zaharoff. . . . I have sixteen millions ! " — or it may have been sixty ! I felt an interloper in a magic circle, but surely such a man, I reflected, could not be a very subtle wrongdoer. He only wanted power in order to amass more money; not money in order to obtain power — but then, again, the vulture does not want to kill you, only to eat your corpse. . . . Already in every capital, the birds of prey were assembling, hovering, watching : the politicians would supply the carrion, though not in their own persons.

[1] Sir Basil Zaharoff was interested in English politics. It would be a relief to be told by the heads of the organisations of the various political parties that he never subscribed to their funds.

Chapter Four   POTHOOKS IN THE SAND

WITH a sense of amazement tinged with consternation my father, observed that my attitude to life was yea-
saying; that I enjoyed myself, that I had made myself at
home in my new surroundings. Soon his feelings became
stronger and deeper, and he grew alarmed, as he drew from
my attitude the conclusion that I could not be doing all those
disagreeable things every day which he held to exercise so
formative an effect on the character. As a result, his former
anxiety to see me follow a military career was now equalled
by his determination to compel me to relinquish it. . . . The
thing to do, he reflected, was to get me out of it — right out
of it into some other profession that he could be sure I would
dislike. . . . But could one be *sure*, he asked himself, after my
recent conduct? : for if I liked being in the Brigade of Guards,
I might like anything. . . . In his mind, he turned over the
various careers open to me. . . . They all seemed to offer a
regrettably pleasant life. However, one could think about that
later. The great thing was to make me leave now. . . . How
could he winkle me out? It was far from easy. What levers
were there to his hand? . . . Chief of them was my extravagance.

In other generations of families circumstanced as mine,
when a young man lived prodigally for a year or two, the father
would murmur to himself with an air of indulgence " *Boys will
be boys* ", and then, after making an armed demonstration,
would pay up. But my father's genuine sense of the necessity
of thrift for others, mingled with atheistic uplift and a horror of
pleasure, made him resolute in his refusal to contemplate
taking up an attitude of this kind : it would only encourage the
extravagant strain that I must inherit from my mother's family
— and so he fell back on the favourite adage of rich people

(how often have I not heard them use it — and the richer, the more frequently, and with the greater force!) : " The kindest thing to do is not to give them more money, but to teach them how to live within their income". It was no good to help me in any way except by advice and oppression : and the first included indirect, as well as direct, methods. Thus I would be treated to improving tales :

" Dear old Mr. MacTotter is dead, I am sorry to say, Osbert. He was only ninety-three. . . . I had thought he was more."

Mr. MacTotter was the father of the Silver Bore. I preserved my silence. My father continued — for he had hoped to draw me with his opening remark — " A really wonderful old man, I call him ! "

" In what way was he wonderful ? "

" He has left each of his thirteen children a small fortune."

" How did he do that, Father ? "

(With a snap) " By Living Within His Income ! "

After this fragment of conversation, or some other, of an equal cautionary value, he would always stare fixedly at me with screwed-up eyes and an expression of the greatest distaste, though he would quickly flitter his eyes away from me, if I returned his gaze. But the moment I looked away, back they would come again to rest, as if drawn by an irresistible compulsion — or perhaps repulsion. . . . Meanwhile, I was contemplating the virtue of the deceased Mr. MacTotter. To me, his seemed an easy and agreeable way of being wonderful. It all depended on the income.

I suppose I was extravagant, by inheritance, disposition, outlook, and by the kind of company I was obliged to keep. But, on the other hand, my father had told me continually that he wished me to behave in the same way in which others of my age conducted themselves : what he meant by this was that he would not mind my squandering several hundreds of pounds on hunting and polo, for he was certain in his own mind that I should be profoundly bored by these sports, and resent having to spend the money on them : but expenditure on going to the opera was another thing ! I *liked* it ! . . . I repeat, I *was* extravagant — but not nearly so reckless as he pretended : and if the sight of some of the bills I ran up now shames me, yet it must be remembered that the lists of them he sent me were full of small tricks, and the letters he wrote me were couched in such terms as to chill affection and successfully to prevent remorse. He always promised one thing and gave — if he did give — another. He would stop my allowance suddenly, for no reason, and, later, once cut off, restored and cut off again, my brother's allowance three times in a week ! As for his devices, he was fond, for example, of paying in to the bank my allowance for twelve months on, let us say, 1st January 1912 — and the next sum, due on 1st January 1913, he would not pay until December of that year. All the expenditure contracted in 1913 would then rank in his mind as debts, for the sum paid in December 1913 would have to serve for the year ensuing as well. He was a difficult person with whom to argue — I eschew the word reason —, and it was impossible to convince him that by this method he was obliging me to make a year's money cover eighteen months : he would merely reiterate with bland offensiveness, " I paid in 1912, and in 1913 : you've only to look at your pass-book ". . . . Sometimes, again, he would not give me the sum he had promised, but would content himself by saying, " If the bank is troublesome " (a favourite phrase), " let me know ". But when the moment he had foreseen came, and I appealed to him, he would vehemently — or rather, icily — deny that he had ever made such a remark. . . . And I think he genuinely believed what he said. . . . He had treated my mother in the same way. She told me — though such matters seldom remained long in her head — that when my father contested Scarborough at the election soon after they had been married, he said to her, " We won't keep a carriage : if you want to drive, just take a cab, and have the bill sent in to me each quarter. It'll be just as convenient for you, and much cheaper for me " — and it was, for when the bill arrived, he at once denied all knowledge of the arrangement, refused to pay and, instead, deducted the sum from my mother's allowance — called " an allowance ", but, incidentally, her own money. These peculiarities were recognised by all who knew him well: but those persons are fast disappearing — and because of that I place some of these instances of this trait on record. . . . For example, Henry Moat alludes to this very idiosyncrasy in a letter of many years later, written in answer to one from me, in which I had told him of my first severe attack of gout. Some of his letter refers to other matters — which I will explain in a moment — but the whole of it is so illustrative of character, and therefore strictly pertinent to my story, that I cannot forbear to give it *in toto*.[1]

1 Beulah Terrace, Falsgrave, Scarborough
April 21, 1938

Dear Captain Osbert,

It made my heart rejoice to see your handwriting on a letter for me this morning. but was very grieved when I read of your complaint, as I have had painful experience. I would bear it for you if I could, but Sir George told me once my pain was not to be compared with his, has he suffered from *suppressed* gout. he would never tell me the symptoms but told me not to ask. Now your having this hereditary attack, you have the kind reminder that it killed his grandfather at 41, he (G.R.S.) will be pleased in a way he will have much to write in his note books about it.

of course his will be the generation that is given the miss, he always was lucky in most things.

I wonder what he will write down about it, I remember once when I was tidying up his bedroom at Montegufoni I heard frequent loud guffaws from the study next door. I thought he was telling himself funny yarns, but, when he was having lunch, I tidied up his writing table, and the note book was open and I read " Whilst I, accompanied only by Henry, was making expeditions in Sicilia, Lady Ida was giving caviare parties at the *Grand Albergo San Domenico*, Taormina, etc " I know different because before he left he had made arrangements with the manager the number of guests and wine she had to have. no wonder some people leave instructions that their writings are not to be published until 150 years after their death, then there will be no one left alive to dispute them.

I heard that he (G.R.S.) was going to die *this September* in Switzerland, but next year was going to commence on the lake pavilion at

1 Following the practice adopted in the other volumes of this book, the spelling and punctuation of Henry Moat's letters have been left as they appear in the originals.

Renishaw. queer state of affairs. but just like the world at the present day, everything mixed up. I myself sometimes forget whether I am coming or going.

Dear Captain, I am truly sorry you are laid up now the spring is here, it is a tremendous strain on one's patience.

Now with all my heart's best love and best wishes I remain Your obedient servant HENRY MOAT.

The reference in the third line, "as I have had painful experience" needs some additional comment, as its elucidation sheds a light, too, on my own troubles of which I am telling. The reader must once more leap forward with me, this time to an autumn in the middle 'twenties, when my father and mother were installed at Montegufoni, and Henry had come into his own again. By that time, his hair was turning grey, his face was less red, more sunburnt, but he had put on still more weight. . . . Every day, for a fortnight past, Henry's ankle had been growing more swollen, the pain in it more acute. At first his master attributed this to old age — Henry must have been about fifty-six or seven — and I recall one day, while my father sat with me at breakfast — himself break-fasted some hours earlier, at six —, he adopted an almost lachrymose tone of voice, as he said to me,

"Poor old Henry; he's getting an old man! I hope, dear boy, you'll try not to ring your bell too often, as he finds the stairs difficult."

I did not retort, as I might have done, that since there were at that time no bells in the Castle, I couldn't ring a single one, even if I had wished to! — but before I'd time to answer, my father's attention was diverted, and, altogether forgetting his altruistic plea of a moment before, he said,

"Do you have your toast like that? . . . I find it gets cold, and so I make Henry bring each piece upstairs separately from the kitchen, as it becomes ready. It's a far better plan!"

Howbeit, it soon became obvious that old age was not Henry's trouble. Plainly, it was gout: but with his combina-tion of will-power and great bodily strength, he refused to give in, despite the endless, unevenly tiled corridors down which he was constantly obliged to hurry, the stone-paved spiral staircases, hardly wide enough for his bulk, which he was perpetually forced to climb up and clamber down. And — what made the torture worse — he knew that my father was watching him, had guessed what ailed him, and was, indeed, only waiting until Henry was compelled by his agony to surrender, to order him upstairs and confine him for several weeks to a diet of bread and water. My father was, of course, eagerly looking forward to the vicarious puritan pleasure he would derive from Henry's prescribed abstinence: whereas to Henry the two bright spots in the long Montegufoni day were the heavy but excellent meals he had taught Adaouina, the Italian cook, to serve him; with plenty of macaroni, red meat, followed by pudding, and grapes and figs, and accompanied by a whole *fiasco* of very strong Castle wine. . . . Day after day, the duel went on: still my father, though it cost him an effort, would not mention to Henry his lameness: he knew it would be more effective to refrain from saying anything about it until in the end his servant could bear the pain no more and should be constrained to avow it.

At last the moment which my father had been for so long awaiting, albeit with impatience, arrived. Just as he was leaving in the motor, to spend the afternoon in Florence, and while Henry was in the act of putting a rug over his master's knees, this movement of leaning forward, by throwing an extra weight upon his feet, made the poor sufferer give a loud roar.

"It's no good, Sir George," he confessed, "I can't go on. My ankle hurts me terrible. It's torture! I'm afraid I shan't be able to wait at dinner tonight."

My father, though this was the first time Henry's pain had been admitted by the victim, did not betray by the tremor of an eyelash either pleasure or surprise. There was, perhaps, only a faint glint in his eye, as he answered lightly,

"Dear, dear! It sounds to *me* like *gout*! . . . Fortunately, it's quite simple to treat! You just give up all meat and red wine for at least six months, indeed, you'll probably have to give it up altogether for the rest of your life. But one soon gets used to it. . . . Better go to bed for the remainder of the day."

My father pounded on, along the road to Florence, in his motor, well known in Florence as " The Ark " : a second-hand lorry engine, of the 1914 war, which he had bought at enormous cost — it was worth about £70, and he had been persuaded to pay £1800 for it —, and for which he had then ordered a new but still more expensive body. The front of it had been specially built so that he could lie by the side of the driver at full length, and thus " rest " his back, while the remaining space, being by that degree reduced, was made proportionately more uncomfortable for those who travelled behind. (As a consequence of this deal, he always maintained that he knew as a matter of certainty that it was impossible to buy a motor for under £4000.) He was well pleased with the way things were shaping. . . . Henry took himself slowly, and with lamentations, to bed in a small room which he had contrived to make look like a cabin : so that even his trousers and shirts, which for some reason he hung on a line between door and windows, recalled the signals run up on ships. . . . I went out by myself for an hour's walk in the cypress wood. When I returned, I was amazed to meet in the Armoury an old hag I had never seen before, of a curious grey dishevelment, who, with protruding lower lip, gabbled to herself. I said *Buona sera, Signora* : she seemed not to notice me, but went on her way; for at this very moment the cook appeared, and treating her with noticeable respect, conducted her upstairs. . . . The explanation of it was this : the reader will recall that I mentioned that I had only once spoken to the sorceress of the Val di Pesa ; and she it was. Henry had been in such pain that Adaouina, who had helped him to climb the stone steps, had been really concerned for him : what could be done ? She thought for some minutes. . . . Then she had remembered that the witch, as well as possessing the touch that withered, could, contrarily and in addition, heal. Henry was in favour of the experiment of sending for her : many sailor superstitions lingered in his blood. An hour later she had arrived, not by broomstick, but by bullock-cart. Having reached his room, she looked at his ankle, and then, with a ritual flourish of the wrist, touched it. In that instant, the patient had experienced — but for an instant only, since if it had been longer the pain could not have been borne — an intense agony, so unendurable as scarcely to seem real : and so apparently had the witch, for both she and Henry had bellowed and shrieked during that moment without restraint. (I shall never forget the yell, even as it sounded from the other end of the Castle.) Then his pain had vanished altogether, and did not return for eighteen months. . . . I cannot account for it scientifically but that is what happened.

When my father returned from Florence, about six, and drove up in the motor to the outside staircase, with an un-wontedly happy expression on his face, which plainly showed how much he was looking forward to going upstairs to give the invalid advice, there, instead, he found Henry, smiling, waiting to open the door of the car. My father mastered his natural indignation, and remarked,

" Better, Henry, I see ! "

" Yes, quite well now, Sir George, thank you ! It must be due to my giving up all those things you told me to, this after-noon."

My father was not going to take this lying down, so he said,

" The danger is still there ! You'll have to be very careful. Probably it's due to high blood-pressure — and you're not as young as you were, you must remember. I think you said your father died of a stroke. . . ."

" Yes, Sir George."

" How old was he at the time of his death? "

" Ninety-six, Sir George."

My father, seemingly stunned by this answer, said nothing more : nor did Henry inform him of how his own cure had been effected. Perhaps it was as well. His master had had as much disappointment as he could stomach in a day, and with his horror of all forms of superstition, he might have grown really angry, had he come into possession of the truth.

The same state of mind which has formed the theme of the above digression was in evidence now, in 1914. He was looking forward immensely to cutting me off the things I liked, since, besides being extravagant, they must be bad for me. And in addition to the tricks I have described, he possessed his own categories of expense, good and evil, his own ratings. Theatre tickets — for my mother loved the play, and her father had been, as the readers of *Left Hand, Right Hand!* will recall, a patron of the stage, — were a work of Satan — if he had believed in Satan : while what he termed " Hot-House Fruit " was a symbol to him, comparable with the *Whore of Babylon* to the Calvinists. He manifested, in a very fully developed state, the anti-Skimpole complex of Victorian times. A bill of mine he had opened, for £3 3s. 3d., with Solomon's, the famous fruiterer in Piccadilly, was in his view something with which I should have to reckon on the Atheists' Judgement Day. Yet, for him, peaches, if grown and not bought, constituted a reasonable luxury — though not for others, so that when, later, he left Renishaw, having handed it over to me, he proposed to blow up the hot-houses he had built not so many years before. And, again, in the same connection, when towards the end of the 1914–18 war he read in the papers an appeal issued to the public by the Government of the day, urging that peach-stones should be collected, either for making gas or gas-masks — I forget which —, he threw himself wholeheartedly into this novel form of war work, remarking to us, with pride, and with a certain sense as of one dedicated to a task of abnegation, " I've managed to get it up to fourteen today ! " (A story of martyrdom to duty, which soon after it had occurred, I related to a friend of mine and brother author, who, failing to see that the only amusement to be found in it resided in the fact of its being true, incorporated the anecdote without permission in a novel, where to this day the injudicious reader may find it.)

Financial arguments were, as will be imagined, frequent and bitter. In the same way that, in the manner I have just related, he assumed that every motor-car cost £4000, so now he leapt to other similar conclusions, from which he could never subsequently be dislodged. It was impossible to argue with him, once he had made up his mind. When I was eighteen, I had been sent to see the family solicitors on a matter of business, and the head of the firm, an old man who had known my father all his life, said to me, " You will not have an easy time with Sir George. In talking to him, it will be better if you always bear in mind, as I do, that he has never made a mistake in the whole of his life." . . . This parental attitude led up, in part, to some curious, farcical situations, which for the rest were founded on my extravagance and innate lack of respect. . . . Thus, one day, I received the following letter :

I am sorry to say you are again heavily in debt : that is to say £315 on the present figures ; but no doubt it will turn out to be much more. . . . It is better we should know at once the full extent of the catastrophe. In consequence, I enclose a list of the tradesmen with whom you deal. Please write *Yes or No* against each name and return the list to me.

You have not sent me your bookseller's bill, nor any bill for uniforms or military accoutrements. . . . How do you propose to find the money to pay your creditors ?—Ever your loving father, GEORGE R. SITWELL.

I should not, I know, have acted as I did : but I was young, and in spite of worries, in high spirits. And so, impelled by a spirit of revolt, since he seemed determined to treat me as an imbecile, I decided to answer in character. . . . I wrote back, enclosing the list of tradesmen's names, in the manner shown below,

Tootham and Snooker	Tailors	Yes or No.
Matcham	Hosier	Yes or No.
Lee's	Hairdresser	Yes or No.
Bovey and Crawler	Haberdasher	Yes or No.
Wilkinson's	Accoutrements	Yes or No.
Trigger and Trapoon	Tobacconists	Yes or No.
Floreyd and Fludyer	Wine Merchants	Yes or No.
Clinker and Snatcham	Jewellers	Yes or No.
Frimkin and Fusker	Theatre Tickets	Yes or No.

The letter accompanying this document ran,

DEAREST FATHER,

Thank you for your letter. . . . Since I believe in always doing as you ask me, I have accordingly written *Yes or No* against each name in the list—though I do not see what practical purpose it serves, or how it will help you. . . . As until only a little more than a year ago, my allowance was a shilling a day, I have not as yet had much experience of money matters.—Your affectionate son, OSBERT.

My letter did not commend itself to my father. He replied,

MY DEAREST OSBERT,

What I expect from you is a frank expression of regret for having got so seriously into debt, together with a promise to reduce your expenditure. I expect your letter to be respectful, which the greater part of your letter received this morning was not. Very little of the debts date beyond 1912 ; so that your statement that you had only a shilling a day as pocket money — you say a *day*, though perhaps you mean a week, — is not, I think, correct.

I shall require details of all the bills.—Ever your loving father, GEORGE R. SITWELL.

This letter contained some points of interest. . . . It was plain, for example, that my father considered an allowance of a shilling a day generous, and of a shilling a week ample, for a young man of nineteen. . . . Over the details, he would pore for hours, deriving a kind of satisfaction from them in the way they fulfilled his fears. On them he could found assumptions, never henceforth to be cast aside. For example, he captured a bill of mine from an old-fashioned firm of hosiers and haberdashers, which had continued to set out the items of its bills in an elaborate style. Among the details he read,

To one pair Laced Pyjamas 2 : 8 : 4.

These garments, of a type then almost universal, were frogged across the chest, instead of buttoning in the usual way ; and this was what the word *laced* signified technically. My father, however — and nothing would ever subsequently rid him of the idea —, read *laced* as *lace*, and henceforth tenaciously clung to the belief that, arraying myself after the fashion of some of Aubrey Beardsley's figures, I habitually wore pyjamas of *Point de Venise* or *Bruxelles*. . . . Very draughty wearing they would have made in the winter climate of the Tower of London, as I told him : but he would not listen, nothing would shake him in his conviction, and for the rest of his life I used to hear him, from time to time, confiding in acquaintances, " As my son *insists* on wearing *lace* pyjamas, Lady Ida and myself are obliged to economise. . . . It's hard, but young people today seem to think they have a perfect right to everything. I should never have dreamt of wearing lace pyjamas myself at that age ! " — as if it constituted one of the comforts of the old.

Another letter from him foretold, in all seriousness, that I should be £20,000 in debt in a few years' time : a prophecy that was almost a promise he made to himself, and at which he worked busily for years, in the effort to make it true in his own mind. It then would justify the most drastic action he could devise. . . . Of course the tendencies in the family, and my mother's extravagance, coloured his vision to a deeper hue in these respects : but this, in its turn, also tinged the whole of life for his children, as if viewed through the faulty, discoloured lens he supplied, the perspective of which they could see to be untrue, and yet had to accept, if they were to keep up any relationship with him ; although they were obliged equally to fight against it, in order to make sense of the outside world. One had constantly to keep in mind his generosities, his kindness and the quality of his thought. He ends the letter in which he first prophesies my total ruin with a most moving comparison. " What horrifies me is the self-indulgence shown in the accounts, large sums for hosiery, hairdressers, theatre-tickets. . . . While you have been doing this, I have had to exercise the strictest denial, giving up almost every pleasure in order to keep out of debt." . . . And yet during these very same years, he had been spending tens of thousands of pounds on " improvements ", thousands, as we have seen, at Scarborough, and eight or ten thousand at Eckington, on making a fantastic garden, with enormous stone piers, and monoliths — one, with a flaw in it — for the entrance : all this, within the grounds of a little house that had been built as a school for the village by an ancestor of ours in 1720, but for the past hundred years had been a farm. (When he took me to see this, and had asked me what I thought of it, I had replied, without thinking, " The garden seems to me too large for the house " : I should **have** known better than to say it. Even as I spoke, I noticed an expression of delight, and of some sort of calculation, pass across his face; but I did not realise what this portended until, when I returned home about eighteen months later, I walked down with my father to The Folly, as the rest of the family called it, and found that the house had now doubled in size. As my father watched my face register the surprise and annoyance I felt, he remarked, with an air almost too affable, " You told me you thought the house too small for the garden, so you see, I took your advice and built on ! ") He had been spending a good deal on making a dam in the woods, and several thousands on renovations to an old house that belonged to us in Warwickshire, where he proposed, too, to construct in cement a garden cloister of large size — happily, this feature never materialised. The two golf-courses and their pavilions, and the over-sumptuous furnishing of one of them — he had lately designed for it a type of walnut table, with legs like the parts of a jig-saw puzzle, so that one longed to fit them together — and other anomalies of taste, had cost tens of thousands. He was preparing for habitation a vast *castello* in Italy, and buying for it furniture appropriate to the opportunities for spending that the many periods of its architecture offered him. Unfortunately, here his desire for bargains overcame his extravagance, and since he would never pay enough for objects, he would, with a few exceptions, obtain only the second-rate in great numbers, but each worth a little less than he had paid for it. In addition, he lived in two houses, waited on by plenty of servants, and with excellent food. . . . I am sure, though, that, absurd as, when these things are considered, the peroration to his letter that I have quoted may appear, yet when he wrote it he believed every word it contained. And this genuine sense of abnegation in all he did throws light on an incident that occurred later, in 1919, just after the end of the First World War. . . . It was a sparkling, bitter winter early afternoon. My father was walking through Leicester Square, with my brother on one side of him, and with me on the other. We were both in the uniform of the Grenadiers, with large grey great-coats, and my father was wearing a top-hat and a blue heavy coat with a wide fur collar. Suddenly a bonneted Salvation Army Lassie came up, and holding out a wooden money-box towards my father, jingled it, and said to him, very gently and sweetly,

" Give something for Self-Denial Week, sir ! "

My father stopped walking, as if overcome by the shock he had received, and then, after fixing on her for some instants a look of the utmost severity and moral disapprobation, pronounced, in patient saint-like tones, these words,

" With *Some* People, Self-Denial Week is *Every* Week."

Then he proceeded on his way.

The one thing my parents never denied themselves or others was a row. They could not exist in a peaceful atmosphere. Consequently, after many months of freedom, it was with a feeling of the most profound depression that I accepted an ultimatum from my father, and left London for Renishaw about the 20th of July 1914, to take up civilian life. He had made up his mind by now. I must enter the Town Clerk's Office at Scarborough. No profession could afford one a more perfect training for after-life. Start at the bottom, and climb right to the top — the top consisting, I inferred, in being Town Clerk at Scarborough. No more was heard now of Governor-Generalships and Embassies. No, the Town Hall at Scarborough was to be my life : and he repeated with enthusiasm, " right from the bottom " ; for, by one of the innumerable contradictions in his character, a success story was that which he had come to require. Previously the newspapers he read had produced no effect on him, but now that his character had softened, their little propaganda tales of Sir Thomas Lipton as an errand-boy bringing his share of tea — or someone else's, I forget which — to his old mother, and of the eye-moistening exploits of Barney Barnato as a curly-haired child (for in those days the rich were as much and unjustly revered as now they are reviled) had begun to influence him. . . . In addition, his Gothic interest still continued, indeed grew more painful, and since he was really very loosely tethered to the modern world, I believe the Town Clerk's Office at the same time summed up a civilisation so strange to his way of thinking as to fascinate him. Roll-top desks, files, efficiency, tea-shops, red-tape: all these exercised over him the same potent attraction that a top-hat holds for a savage, or the primitive art of the Congo and the Pacific Islands for the sophisticated esthete. . . . Better still, before I entered the Office, I must go right back to the beginning, and learn a good commercial copperplate. As it was, my handwriting — by which, he assured me, people judged character almost exclusively nowadays — would gravely prejudice my career. I should get nowhere. . . . Accordingly, before my apprenticeship at Scarborough began, I was to reside at Renishaw for a month or two, and under his restrictive eye learn from starting-point the whole art of calligraphy, as well as how to read double-entry accounts. Into these mysteries I was to be inducted by an instructor from Clark's Commercial College. . . . I hated these plans, but, though even now I did not realise that war was so near, I fell in with them with a definite and curious sense of fatalism. I knew, with utmost inner conviction, that they were futile, and held no solidity. They remained flat on the paper, like a drawing. I was very tired when I left London, tired from pleasure and not from work. The whole of London had still seethed with a feeling of summer and of gaiety. The children of the rich feasted, and from the ballrooms, wreathed in roses, where they waltzed to the deep-hearted rhythm of the Rosenkavalier Waltz, the sons could not see the ruins, the broken arches and cut and twisted trees which were all their future. . . . No-one mentioned the possibility of war: no-one whispered it, least of all in the Regiment.

At Renishaw there were few alterations, with the exception of one important change in the scene: my father had grown a red beard which joined him in appearance all the more strongly to medieval Italy, of the time when Norman blood still ran in the veins of its nobles. Men with beards are liable nowadays to grow slovenly — the tramp, and not, as in the Victorian Era, the dandy, being the type of the bearded man of our epoch —, but he became, if anything, more scrupulous: the beard was just a red flag that he waved perpetually at the bull modernity, when he was not adoring it. (Meanwhile, this new development rescued Robins from the daily dangers attendant on having to shave him; since my father was wont suddenly to say " No ! ", in a loud, angry voice and to dismiss the whole operation, leaving it half done. In London, on the first occasion that this happened, Robins marched straight out of the room and, without offering an explanation, went down to Brighton for the day. Nothing was said, except that the next morning, when Robins came to call him, my father remarked, " You should pay no attention another time ".)

He looked a little older with a beard. . . . Perhaps the entire world seemed a little older.

In spite of the troubles I expected, I have never known a greater calm to prevail. Silence was once again enclosing me. But this time I was not afraid, and I was not unhappy. I was no longer eighteen, and I had made friends. I had found people who believed in my ability, and told me so — it astonished me, for in what direction could it lie ? — who liked me and let me see it. Every day now brought me letters from them, telling me that they missed my company, and letting me have the news. . . . Obviously, *they* did not think I was never going to appear again : so I shed that fear, just as, in the same way, the sense that I was going to be shut up in my shell for ever had vanished. I knew now that life could be beautiful, even if it was not good, and at last felt entirely in tune with my epoch. Nor did the absolutely blank future which extended in front of me, beyond this sudden break, persuade me that I should ever see the inside of the Town Clerk's Office at Scarborough. The stars were not casting in that direction.

The old gentleman from Clark's College had already arrived. He probably was not really old, but he seemed so to me. He had whiskers which tacked on from his ears to the corners of his mouth, and gave him — as sometimes they do — a curiously dyspeptic look, as of one who for years and years had drunk the strongest tea. He was unassertive and kind, in a tactful but soulless way. I worked in the open air, and so, all day long, while I was learning from him or walking with Sacheverell, he sat in a deck-chair, his head crowned by a billycock, always so inappropriate in the country. It seemed to suggest somehow that its wearer had been implicated in a crime — though the only crime with which in reality he had ever been connected was the conspiracy against my liberty: and his genial if serious Scottish intonation when he spoke acquitted him of any personal share in this. He had just somehow got himself involved in it. . . . A kitchen-table had been placed on the grass, near the marble paving outside the garden door, so that my father could see that I was really working. Almost as if I were captive to a Roman General, or a criminal in the stocks, I was thus made to parade publicly my humiliation as I sat there at the age of twenty-one, practising how to make pothooks.

$$? \quad ? \quad ? \quad ? \quad ? \quad ? \quad ? \quad ? $$

Bitterly I resented every moment of it, as people passed and enquired what I was doing.

"Unfortunately, his handwriting is so unformed and childish that he is having to learn to write", my father would explain, with the familiar condescending, downward flourish of his hand.

The worst of it was, I knew my handwriting *was* bad: (though, as I have explained earlier, this disadvantage in the end brought to me unexpected benefits). For the rest, I do not think my father intended to be unkind: but my native treachery to the average had shattered an ideal of competence that he had formed in his mind. I still think it was a mistaken way to treat a young man full of pride — it would have been much worse for me, though, if it had not been for the friends I had made in the past two years, who considered the whole episode just to be comic, and dissolved it for me in a gale of laughter.

As well as feeling incapable of effort, I was restless, and gradually developed an uneasy sense that things outside were going wrong. The news — we were in the last week of July now — was openly becoming serious. . . . For some time there had been talk in the papers of "ultimatums", a word then new to me, having only lately been re-issued from the diplomatic mint as a reliable method of producing war. . . . Still, there *could not* be a war — no country could afford it. . . . I sat at the table, and gazed up at the skies, trying, because the thought of war was so new and tremendous, therein to read the trend of the future, as many thousands of men have done before me through countless ages in times of crisis, for savages and the most civilised all share, at the deepest level, the same superstitions; only ours reach us by more devious routes. The vast arch above, dwarfing the earth, was as full of clouds as, on a map, the oceans are full of continents: drifting masses of gold and grey that at moments approximated to the familiar shapes of countries in the atlas, defining themselves in the wind that blew there, so high up, in the lofty azure, gold-flecked spaces, though here, on the ground, everything was calm, and no leaf moved. I became so mazed by staring that at times I almost distinguished that marching host — which has so frequently been seen before in times of trouble — armed with spears and lances, carrying banners, woven of cloud and sun, and wending its way endlessly into the infinite, to storm citadels and ramparts all the more difficult to attack because the whole time able to change their shape and nature.

The weather was very hot: the lilies, which grew so easily in the light, leafy soil of Renishaw, were larger and more fragrant than I had ever known them, and Ernest had produced a specimen with a hundred heads. From the open window over the low wooden door to the garden, to which as a child of three or four I used to run the moment I arrived in the house, the same air I always associated with the place came at me; the wafted, commingled scent of stocks and clove-carnations and tobacco plant and box hedges, with the faint acrid harshness of coal-smoke lying under it. It blew in, warmly, steadily, scenting the house. Everything seemed the same, but with a strange, uneasy difference. Except that Henry had gone, and Robins was here in his place, there were the same people: my father, my mother — she was upstairs, ill from the strain of her worries —, Edith, Sacheverell, my Aunt Florence, who, now

that my grandmother was dead, came to stay with us more
often, Helen Rootham — who had arrived for a visit to us —
Hollingworth, Stubbs and Pare. To take the last, Stephen
Pare, old friend of my childhood, had retreated into a misty
land; nothing was clear, nothing. He had somehow with-
drawn himself and, now that I was " a young gentleman " as he
phrased it, would not talk much to me. He seemed to move
in the house through darkness more easily than through light.
To him, the exterior world was as deceptive and cruel as was
the interior world to his poor wife. Mrs. Westby, the house-
keeper who had taken her place, a lightly built, stooping old
woman, grey and thin, preoccupied always with the dust, so
that on each sunny day one saw her in a complete aura, still
fluttered her brushes round the house. Major Viburne was in
charge of the household-books, Miss Lloyd had once more
come to stay. And I found Mark Kirkby in the stables, getting
stiffly out of his cart with his dog. The two of them, and the
old grizzled pony, looked three of one kind, I reflected.

Mark, certainly, had altered little since I first remembered
him, and I listened with the usual pleasure as he began to tell
me of a recent experience which had impressed him. . . .
1914 had been a particularly dry year: for months no rain
had fallen, and so Mark, who, as the reader has seen, always
passed a large proportion of the twenty-four hours in his
woodland territories, was now out there all night, sitting in his
cabin, listening, watching, fearing lest some spark or carelessly dropped cigarette-stub should cause a fire. Two nights
before I met him, at the end of the last week of July, he had
fallen asleep for a few minutes, sitting on a bench in his cabin.
He woke up with a start, thinking he heard some sound, and
moved cautiously to the open door. In the breathlessly hot
night, as he stood there, everything seemed deserted and
silent, except for an owl's thick hootings and snorings down
below, and for the scamperings of nameless night creatures
under the bracken. It was rather dark, but clusters of bright
stars showed the banks of trees stretching for miles each side
of the stream. . . . Suddenly, a flash appeared in the sky, on
the right, at the high end of the hill, and, large as a moon and

287

brighter, a fire-ball — in the folk-mind of man so sure a portent of disaster — swept just above the line of the tree-tops, and sailed majestically down the valley to the distant horizon. As it passed beneath him, he heard a faint, crackling sizzle break the strange silence. . . . Here was something he had never seen before, and it had filled his mind, as it now filled mine when he told me of it, with a certain disquiet. Superstitions, as I have said, lurk in all of us. And the fact remained that the guardian of the woods, himself so securely tied to the material world, rooted in the very soil, had seen what I had looked in vain for, in the skies : a portent — the most ancient omen of war. And who are men, he said to me — though in other words —, to dismiss a sign from heaven because of the titterings of Science or the hissing voice of Common Sense?

This, however, was a solitary occurrence : otherwise, the existence familiar to us from childhood continued, inside the house and out ; a development of the accustomed, traditional pattern. Helen was playing Debussy in the ballroom ; Edith was in her bedroom copying into her notebook a passage from Baudelaire, and trying in general to avoid the trivialities of the day ; Sacheverell was talking to Major Viburne, and then went to see my mother, who was still in bed, the windows wide open, and the air laden with the sweetness of geranium leaf and lemon-scented verbena from the broad window-boxes, painted green. My father was immersed in the usual multifarious tasks to which he set himself. Whatever else had altered in him, there was no sign of any slowing-down of his mental activity, nor any lessening of his desire to create beauty as he saw it. Recent experiences had in no wise deterred him from making his plans for changes in the house and landscape. But this did not induce in him an easy mood. As Henry wrote from Montegufoni, in the days of his return, " and now Sir Geo is annoyed but as you know never satisfied will not leave well alone changes, makes a muddle of things and then blames other people. We are supposed to go to the Castello the 1st of May, but you should just see it now many floors up laying hot water pipes and new drains it will not be ready properly to go into for another 2000 years if G.R.S. has the managing of the works." Especially was he worried now over the subject of a new dam. Half a mile long, this narrow sheet of ornamental water, placed between high, wooded slopes, had not long been completed, and was to carry either a colossal statue of Neptune, rising from the middle of the water, or a leaden ship, he had not been able to make up his mind which. . . . Meanwhile, something had gone wrong with the bed, and, since this building experiment had been paid for out of trust funds, I redoubled my expostulations about it. Eighteen months before this, I find the sub-agent writing to Turnbull, " The new dam in the woods is somewhat of a nightmare to me. It does not fill as it ought, and I am afraid we shall soon hear that the water is finding its way into the colliery workings, though there are none just under it." Sure enough, the water vanished, and the coal company, alleging that it had flooded the mine, refused to pay the rents due for it. . . . When I learnt of this, I could not refrain from saying " I told you so " to my father. But, though concerned, he proceeded to bring an action against the coal company. This lawsuit was pending at the time of which I write, and hung fire for many years, since much evidence had to be collected and sifted. The legal expenses therefore mounted to vast heights, but in the end the warnings I had issued proved unnecessary, for, after a whole decade had passed, the two parties reached a compromise out of court, my father obtaining costs and a large sum in settlement of his claims. Henceforth, I apprehend, he looked on the making of a dam, or, indeed, the creation of any decorative scheme that appealed to his imagination, as a possible source of riches. There was no holding him.

At present, then, neither stone statue nor leaden ship could be proceeded with, but he was in no way dismayed, and he allowed other ideas to occupy his mind. . . . He was planning a new garden terrace, to run the entire length of the hill-top, and was again surveying the site for the Island Pavilion, and spending many hours aloft on a complicated wooden platform erected in and above the lake, at the correct altitude, as if he were on the second storey of his imaginary edifice on the imaginary island — for that, too, had to be constructed, the

existing island not being situated in the perfect position for it —
so that he could decide how to obtain the finest views, and note
how best to make use of them. . . . The Island Pavilion, he
would explain to me in the intervals of my pothook exercises,
was to be built entirely for my sake. It was a great sacrifice
— and he hoped I would bear it in mind — but it should
prove a most valuable asset in entertaining one's friends.
(The great thing was never to see them alone, when one was
obliged to talk and tire oneself out, but always to invite a great
many of them together, so that they could look after one
another.) But though in any case it spelt severe self-denial for
him, the building need not really cost more than a few
thousand : just run up an island — while it was being done,
we ought to drain the twenty-two acres of lake, and grow early
mushrooms under flower-pots in the bed, the soil would be just
the thing, and thus defray part of the cost. Then, becoming
enthusiastic over his new plan, he added that you could
manure the ground with the fish that would be stranded, —
roach, perch, pike and gudgeon. Nothing was so good, he'd
been told, for cultivation as fish-manure. The crop would be
splendid. You could easily make several thousands by this
means and might, indeed, more than pay for the whole expense.
It would be an interesting little experiment. Just buy your
own fleet of lorries, grow early mushrooms and cucumbers,
and send them into Sheffield. You might start your own shop
there and make a fortune. . . . What had we been talking
about ? Yes, it was a great sacrifice on his part, but he was
willing to make it. Just run up an island, and build on it in
the local stone. (It would be delightful opening up the old
quarry — one never knew what one might not find in it, and if
the trees were cleared, it might make a charmin' place for
picnics. . . . You could cut out a Rock Chamber, like the one
he'd seen in Sicily.) Local stone always looked best : a
building of three storeys, diminishing in size from the top at
each stage, so that you could have a terrace or broad balcony
all round, the whole thing surmounted by a graceful tower, in
tiers. To the south, the ground floor would look out on a
swimming-pool, with a stone balustrade round it, enclosed

within a pillared colonnade — Ionic pillars and capitals were the most suitable for a purpose of this sort, Corinthian were over-ornate — and there would be a dining-room and kitchen. (You might line the kitchen with tiles, such as he had seen in South Italy, showing a contemporary picture of how a banquet was prepared in the sixteenth century.) It would be considerate, perhaps, to build a special boudoir for the cook, where she could rest, put her feet up, let her hair down, and feel at home. Just imagine the difference it would make to the life of the servants, nothing they'd love so much as setting out on a fine morning, just before or after sunrise — really the most picturesque part of the day —, and spending the whole day in the delicious fresh air. It would be as good as a holiday. . . . In fact, he should tell them tomorrow, holidays would not be necessary in future. He never took one himself. . . . It was a pity that architects always raised unnecessary points against their own interest, and Lutyens, he was sorry to say, had been in one of his silly moods the other day, and when my father had remarked how much the servants, and especially the cook, would enjoy it all, he had blurted out that he wondered if the cook would enjoy sculling half a mile before breakfast. . . . A great pity to say things like that; which reminded him, he said, of something he'd been meaning to say to me for a long while : I must still be careful about my sense of humour. That joke of mine the other night had been most unfortunate, and might give friends quite the wrong impression.

My father was not getting up so early that summer. First, about nine o'clock every morning, he would walk through the gardens and down the steep hill. Today — it was the 2nd of August 1914 — I watched him as he went. He was dressed in a smart grey suit, and wore the rather pointed brown shoes which he bought ready-made for eighteen shillings and sixpence, and a wide-brimmed grey hat, a little resembling a cowboy's, and was carrying a grey umbrella lined with green against the sun. Hollingworth would meet him at the boat-house — where, too, there would be waiting a man, bearing an ulster and various other paraphernalia —, and would row or sail him to the foot of the scaffolding. There my father would

alight and first girdling himself with a leather strap to which
was attached a pair of binoculars, and clutching, in addition
to his umbrella, an air-cushion, shaped like a life-buoy — a very
familiar object in the Reading Room of the British Museum,
whither it always accompanied him — and carrying, under one
arm, a copy of *The Times*, the *Architectural Journal*, the *Lancet*, the
Athenaeum, and the *Financial News* of the day before, he would
carefully, very carefully, mount the wooden ladder to the platform, furnished with a single chair, and a rug to put over the
knees.   Depositing the cushion, and putting down the papers,
which gave ever and anon a flapping sound in the faint
breeze, as of a dying vulture, he would advance to the wooden
rail, and, hooking the handle of his umbrella on to it, easily
within his reach, glance, first, downward at the lake that lay
like a looking-glass, and showed banks of wood running
deeply to an inverted sky.   Hollingworth crossed it in a
boat — and that recalled to my father's mind : he really
must build those two wings on to the house — a storey taller
than the rest, shaped like square towers !   It would be so much
more convenient for Hollingworth ; he could have a delightful
modern office in one of them.   It was true that he said he did
not want one and would much rather remain where he was —
but that had nothing to do with it.   He'd love it, when it was
finished.

Tiring of philanthropy, he scanned the horizon, and then
turned his gaze to the line of spires and crenellations that
just showed above the hill behind him.   But it was not these he
saw. . . . Who knows what changing scenes may not have
presented themselves to his vision ? . . . There were pyramids
and towers, and a construction of great length, like a ruined
Roman aqueduct, with which he planned to end the garden,
so that a high narrow arch should frame each view ; a cascade
dashed down the abrupt rocky declivity of Brockshill, beneath
the Wilderness, carrying with it a roar of watery music, the
notes controlled by the various stones over which it fell, and
by the angles and position of them, so that you obtained the
elements of a composition ; the torrent came to rest in a wide
basin, wherefrom it poured again through the mouth of a

giant's head in stone, into a stream that joined the lake. An enormous double flight of steps, in a great curve, swept down to the ravine between the beech trees. Turning round, he looked behind him, and the square brick building of the colliery company, the top of which was visible above one of the slopes of the park, had become transmuted into a square stucco arch, after the style of one of the inner courts of the Doge's Palace at Mantua, with great double twisted columns, and to the left, on a hillside, among the burnished forts of the corn, the eye of faith could descry the façade of a mansion, placed there " to give interest to the view ", as he used to explain, or sometimes the broken tower, tangled with ivy, of a sham-Gothic ruin. Eastward, above the dome of the Golf Pavilion — that reminded him, they needed another crystal chandelier and two more marble pillars for the Ladies' Room there (he must write to Brussels directly he got in, about the marble) — lay the old railway-cutting, abandoned now, which he intended to enlarge, deepen, and fill with water, thereby joining the lake to the dam in the woods, so that, when the house was full of guests, they could go on boating-parties, and float or sail the whole way, and avoid crossing the village at any point. Today this watery detour shone for him plainly, and on the surface glided, what one could not call boats, but must term barques shaped like dragons. Once they reached the woods, there would be tea ready in a Chinese Pavilion. He saw that, too : an octagonal building, with inward-curving sides, and a clever little box-hedged formal garden surrounding it — in which there had been much play with the modulation from octagon to circle, and back again to square : a double roof, tiled and hung at the eaves with gold bells, and mounting at its top to a gilded ball ; and, inside, a vaulted room, each of the eight walls having a niche in the centre, containing the life-sized figure in china of an angler with a wide hat, holding a fishing-rod from which depended a lamp. . . . At this point he was called to himself, for he felt or heard a drop of rain fall on his shoulder. He put on his ulster, and touched it carefully, several times, to see if it were damp. Robins should have reminded him to bring out a mackintosh, as well ; too bad of him. It was extraordinary the way people thought only of themselves. It might be very awkward — indeed, grave — if it came on to rain, since the boat was not coming back for another half-hour, and nobody would have the sense to think of it: you could be sure of that. He scanned the sky anxiously, and saw dark clouds where there were none, and smiling blue vacancy where the huge clouds were passing. . . . He sat down for a moment, pulled the rug round him and opened *The Times*. There was nothing interesting in the papers except that they had found some thirteenth-century tiled paving in Canterbury, and an account of a curious mention of Ralph the Belted in a contemporary document. . . . What was that? War? War! There would not be war; how could there be? The Germans could not afford it, and we certainly could not! Besides, the Kaiser, a most gifted man, was interested in medieval times, and had presented a magnificent collection of ancient instruments of torture to the city of Heidelberg — or was it Nuremberg? (in any case well worth a visit!) . . . It *was* going to rain. A few more drops fell, so he stood up again: for you exposed more of your body to the rain if you sat down than if you stood up.

Up at the house, or rather, just outside it, I was back again, with my bowler-hatted mentor, learning to make pothooks. It was a week or two since I had started, and I realised that no progress had been made: it depressed me. Perhaps my father was right, and I never should be able to do anything. . . . While I copied, as patiently as I could, my Aunt Florence was walking up and down the nearer terrace, very slowly, with the look of a musing and abstracted Saint. Her golden hair still had about it the authentic gleam of an aura: but every year, every month, every day, it seemed, she was growing quieter, milder, more vague, almost offensively inoffensive, with the kind of meekness that must have redoubled the rage of lions in the arenas of Rome. Unversed in material affairs, her aim was to do good by stealth; but her arrival to stay with us always caused a flutter among the professional tramps and beggars of the neighbourhood — who must have gained the intelligence of her approaching visit from their brothers-inalms where she resided, for they came to know of it almost before we did —, and coincided with the most vigorous, practical and urgent demands from them for money. Many of them, now elderly, indeed ancient, remembered the charities of her childhood and, having retired from business, only returned to it for the period of her stay, as it were out of compliment to her. She, for her part, scarcely recollected these old men. The Saints, I think, were more real to her than living people, and the missionaries in St. Kilda's and the South Seas and the Congo nearer to her than her relatives. Even the pages of her journal were now losing their buoyancy. She had forgotten to order the *Guardian* to be sent here: above all, she missed the Family Prayers, and, in consequence, did not feel quite at home. Still, it was very dear of George to ask her here. As she walked so slowly, with her long, limp feet, among the things that God had created, the flowers and grass and birds and trees, she, too, glanced at the sky and the horizon. But the vision she saw was very different from that of her brother or of myself. The earth, rich in true faith, was planted thick as a forest with the bodies of martyrs, risen and testifying to their belief, and the wide spaces of the sky were crowded with the flocks of the Saints, chanting their witness to God's Glory. . . . The papers, she reflected, were very sad reading just now; she did not understand how people could bear to look at them, with their photographs of Cowes and Goodwood, and fashions of the day, the theatres, and their lack of spiritual vision. There had, however, been an interesting correspondence in the *Daily Telegraph* on the Kikuyu Controversy, and a most moving letter from the Bishop of Zanzibar — but that only made her miss the *Guardian* more. . . . War, War ? . . . The only war she knew was the great and never-ending battle between Good and Evil, and that went on continually, though the issue was sure. . . . Suddenly she noticed me, sitting just by her as she walked, and making an effort, as her mother had always told her to do, she smiled mousily at me, and observed in her meek, weak voice, so utterly good, " How Nice to be Making Signs on Paper ! " Then she passed on, with the golden glimmer of her hair, into the shadow of the tall yew trees and was lost.

Sacheverell's face appeared at an open window on the third storey, and he called me. In a moment he ran down from the top of the house, three steps at a time, in a rush of young feet, a tall figure, broad-shouldered, thin, with an unusual grace, resembling a little a Saint by Cosimo de Tura or Crivelli. . . . He was worried by the news in the papers. What did it matter if my father *was* angry at my stopping work? We must hurry up and have a talk, before my mother appeared. . . . We hastened to the long walk in the Wilderness, entering between the stone Warrior and Amazon, and walked up and down, out of sight, between the dark banks of holly, where the nettles grow so tall, they sting your hands as you go. . . . Sacheverell urged me to telephone to London. It was an agony of suspense, he said, waiting for news: and, indeed, within a day, the feeling of tension — I realised it now he said it — had inexplicably and intolerably increased. Yesterday had been an ordinary day, with a threat of worry: whereas today was two days — or a day or three days — before the Great War. . . . Someone must know how things stood. I must telephone, he insisted. . . . But it was not easy. We had to telephone without being seen, for no trunk-calls were allowed by my father. But in the evening I managed it. I had thought of just the person of whom to enquire: a very shrewd and politically-minded brother-officer, older than myself, who was with a Battalion which had been moved to the Tower, so as to be in London in case of developments. I knew I could trust his acute intelligence and balanced judgement. I got through to him. "The scare is off," he said; "the news is much better: there is no chance of war."

The nervous tension continued to mount, in spite of what he had said. . . . The next afternoon I left Renishaw, abandoning, as I knew, for ever the prospect of the Town Clerk's Office, and my bowler-hatted friend, of whom I never heard again. I said good-bye to my father — who offered to lend me thirty shillings in silver for the journey, as my allowance had ceased — to my mother, who wept, so that she could not come to the door, to my dear Edith and Sacheverell; and to my

Aunt Florence. She now realised that war was near, but was suffering from what Bernard Shaw has since taught us to call a "time-lag", so that what chiefly worried her was, would the Turks be involved, and if so, would they massacre the Armenians. On this point, she asked several small, meek, pleading questions.

I arrived in London at six in the morning, and reported to the Reserve Battalion, already in course of formation. In the afternoon I went to say good-bye to many friends, who, as it happened, were never to return to England. Two or three of the most confident I heard instructing their servants to pack their evening-clothes, since they would need them in a week or two in Berlin. . . . Later, I called on my Grandmother Londesborough, now grown a very old lady. She was, as I have explained earlier, a great-niece of Wellington's, and perhaps some lingering anti-Napoleonic tradition inspired her parting remark to me, "It's not the Germans but the French I'm frightened of". Still, even then, it was not certain that war was coming. But in the evening, I went to the Mall, and waited. If the Lord Mayor's Coach arrived, it meant war, and presently, after dusk, sure enough it came trundling along through the Admiralty Arch toward the Palace. As it entered the gates I heard the great crowd roar for its own death. It cheered and cried and howled. . . . How many of those voices could have been heard in two years' time?

War hysteria quickly asserted itself. Haldane, the most efficient War Minister of the age, was chivied out of the War Office, and Lord Kitchener, god of the hour, but a deity who had grown stiff in the joints, sat in his chair, turning a stern face to the world. Recruiting songs vied with genuine patriotic appeals. In the music-halls, Miss Phyllis Dare was singing, "Oh, we don't want to lose you, but we think you ought to go". Soon whole mattresses of white feathers were coming out, and being given away; for in 1914 the reactions were simpler, quicker and more direct than in 1939. Fortune-tellers reaped a rich harvest, and *Old Moore's Almanack* reached a new sales-level. By September, the story of the Russian armies in England had begun, and I find Sacheverell, who wrote to me regularly from Renishaw every day, and who was unusually wise and cautious for his sixteen years, announcing the great news. " They saw the Russians pass through the station here last night," he wrote, " and Miss Vasalt telephoned to Mother this afternoon and said trains in great number had passed through Grantham Station all day with the blinds down. So there must, I think, be some truth in it, don't you? "

Several times before I left England, I met Sir Edward Grey, the Foreign Minister, and heard him, to my relief, explain most interestingly that the war could not last more than three months. The Germans could not stand the strain, and must inevitably collapse financially. Under his Roman mask, he was a very humane man and could not face the consequences of his policy. . . . I also consulted a fortune-teller : the only time I had ever visited one. It was not certain when I was to start for the Front : but this was to be expected every day. I lived perpetually on the edge of departure ; and some friends, anxious, I suppose, to know what was going to happen to me, made an appointment for me with a celebrated mistress of the psychic art, an unconvincing little person with an over-eager eye. Her lair, with its screened lights, oriental draperies, its divans and incense, was disconcerting and pitifully counterfeit. Crystal-gazing and hand-reading were her specialities. I plumped for palmistry. She told me many things that meant nothing. At the end, she said,

" You will come back and go on with your career."

" What is it ? " I asked, for I had no wish to be a soldier indefinitely.

She looked surprised, and then replied with conviction,

" That is very clearly marked on your hand. Look, there's the star of fame ! You're a writer, aren't you ? "

I thought of the pothooks and laughed.

APPENDIX A

A DESCRIPTION OF WOOD END IN THE 'SEVENTIES

By Sir George Sitwell

I can remember playing with my tutor in the garden at Wood End in the summer of 1870, in the spring of which year my mother had bought the house, to which she made a few alterations before coming in.

The drawing-room, on the ground-floor, comprised, as well as the original drawing-room, the former ante-room and dining-room, these apartments running into each other through two arches in each of the interior walls, so that now the drawing-room occupied the whole length of the south front. The walls were painted a sparrow's-egg blue, and on the floor, toning in with them, was a French carpet, resembling needlework, also of a delicate pale-blue, relieved here and there by rose-pink shades in the pattern. On either side of the fireplace hung the two finest Chippendale mirrors I have ever seen, bought by my mother from an old house in York, which had once belonged to the famous Duke of Buckingham. Among other furniture in the room was the lovely silver cabinet now at Renishaw, a fine Italian chest, and the four gold and red *seicento* chairs from the Palazzo Buonasegai in Siena. To the east, the drawing-room commanded a view across the gardens of Broxholme and Londesborough Lodge. To the west it opened into the large Conservatory that my mother had built over a yard. At night curtains of dark crimson covered the entrance to it, unless it was lit with Chinese lanterns.

This Conservatory was filled with exotic birds flying at large amongst the creepers and flowering trees : red-tailed *Cordons-bleus*,* Indigo Birds splashed with green, Nutmeg and Zelva Finches, Wax-Bills * of cinnamon with rosy beaks, Budgerigars like little green paroquets, deep crimson and scarlet, Cardinal Birds, Blue Robins of all shades from dark to light, Japanese Rice Birds, Pekin Nightingales,* with the mellow russet tints of autumn leaves. These birds sang early and late throughout the year, the Zelva Finches making a gentle pleasant trumpeting sound, the song of the Blue Robin being something like that of a thrush, of the Cardinal

Bird like a blackbird, of the Pekin Nightingale like the sweet singer whose name it bears. Those birds marked with an asterisk nested and brought off broods of young, though the Pekin Nightingale had not previously been known to do so in captivity. This bird when its young were hatched would take almost any food with honey in it, but strangely preferred it off a pink plate: a fact inexplicable, till it was discovered that in its native habitat the bird feeds from a pink flower. On one occasion, the Zelva Finches having deserted their nest, the eggs were hatched out, and the young birds fed by a Virginian Nightingale which was without a partner. The Whydah Birds are blue-black with silvery breasts and a touch of orange at the throat and have long sheaf-shaped tails. They are attracted by music, and when there was dancing would sometimes fly in and out of the arches to the further end of the drawing-room, passing over the heads of the dancers.

APPENDIX B

A "FATAL GIFT OF SHRUBS" AND SOME ROSES

Being a Short Extract from Letters indicative of Character in
the Estate Correspondence at Renishaw

THE earlier part of the correspondence is, unfortunately, missing. My father was 36 when the letters were written. The letter I give first was addressed to Peveril Turnbull, my father's agent and former tutor. Across it Turnbull has noted in pencil, " This first part refers to a letter of the Rector's complaining that the gift of shrubs had run him into the expense of iron fencing ".

30 BURY ST., ST. JAMES'S
5 March, 1896

MY DEAR PEVERIL TURNBULL,

Re the " fatal gift of shrubs ", the facts were that I only promised Mr. Barber a few forest trees, he assuring me that shrubs had been offered by Mr. Wells or others. He then ran me in for the price of the shrubs, planted them so carelessly that most died and the rest looked fit for nothing, and sent me a bill for the labour, which was to have been paid by the Rector. I declined this last request but I am not sure that you or Hollingworth[1] may not have been induced to pay the amount on my behalf. . . . Of course, I also paid for Mr. Milner, the landscape gardener's advice.

I am afraid Hollingworth is responsible for the £22 : 6 : 3 for roses, and I wish you would ask a question about them. Mr. Soames[2] made, so far as I can remember, no expensive demands, but Hollingworth has probably got a lot in the paddock for my wife.
—Yours very sincerely, GEORGE R. SITWELL.

At the end of a line in this letter against the word *roses*, runs a note in pencil, by Hollingworth, the sub-agent, and father to Maynard Hollingworth, whose name so often recurs in *Left Hand, Right Hand!* The letter, plainly, had been sent to him for his opinion. His first reaction is recorded in the words, " Those roses

---

[1] Turnbull has written at the side of this, in pencil, " Did we pay for planting ? — I think not. P.T."

[2] The tenant of Renishaw. He took the house for two years running, except for the months of August and September.

have been in the Paddock a long time and are large plants. I do not know where from."

Written in pencil by Turnbull across the whole letter — obviously before being returned to Hollingworth for a further opinion — " These roses were from Proctor's Nursery in Chesterfield. Lady Ida had, I know, been over, but I understood you to say that Sir George had agreed to buy them — can you produce any proof? P.T."

Endorsed underneath by Hollingworth in ink, " Letter enclosed and what I say in mine of to-day. W.H."

" Mine of to-day ", from Hollingworth to Turnbull, is headed " Eckington, Rotherham ", dated " March 8 : 1896 ", and runs as follows :

DEAR SIR,

I am very sorry to see Sir George's letter because he is developing into an inveterate grumbler, and much of it is bordering on untruth.

The shrubs for Church Yard were all arranged by Mr. Milner and Sir George asked him to see the church wardens about planting them under my supervision. I loaned them gardeners from the Hall and Ben Widdowson or G. Barber paid their wages and I have told Sir G. so more than once. As to " Forest Trees ", I never heard the term till Sir G. saw the plants planted, he then told me that Mr E. Wells had promised to find shrubs which was the first word heard about them.— They *were* properly planted, and the ground well prepared, but the wind in the Church Yard is so rough as to make it almost impossible for plants to grow. The varieties were such as will *not* grow here, with some exceptions, and *Fisher and Holmes's* foreman said so, when he saw them planted.

The Roses were ordered by Sir G. through Mr. Soames, and I saw the letter to Mr. Soames giving instructions to have them planted. Sir G. was also consulted as to what beds should be planted with roses and gave his consent. I send you the only letter of Sir G's which refers to them, he told me in addition that he had arranged the matter with Mr. Soames, and I was to act in conjunction. The fact is Sir G. gave his orders as clear as noonday, but the bill is too big for him. . . . Your obedient servant, W. HOLLINGWORTH.

P. Turnbull Esq.

The last letter — as usual, the last word — comes from my father : to whom the opinion expressed in the preceding letter, though no doubt more diplomatically phrased, must have been passed on.

30 BURY ST., ST. JAMES'S
10 March, 1896

MY DEAR PEVERIL TURNBULL,

Shrubs were of course intended, as well as trees, but I was not asked to provide the shrubs. I asked Mr. Milner to recommend only those which would really thrive, and he saw the churchyard at his last visit and said they had died because they had been shoved in anyhow. If *Fisher and Holmes's* foreman told Betts[1] that the kinds chosen were unsuitable he should have given you or me a hint in time.

This leads up to the practical point, that if you will kindly look at the churchyard, and recommend other shrubs to be tried, which are sure to flourish, and recommend me that the cost of buying and planting will not be more than £10, I will go to that expense, in another " fatal gift ".—Yours very sincerely, GEORGE R. SITWELL.

[1] Head Gardener at Renishaw.

APPENDIX C

A DEMONSTRATION

Being a Further Extract from the Estate Correspondence

WOOD END, SCARBOROUGH
5 July, 1905

My dear Peveril,

. . . As regards the Hospital, I decline unless a proper apology appears in that local newspaper for rude remarks made on a former occasion. You say you " will agree as usual ", but you had my directions distinctly not to do so in future. . . . Yours very sincerely, GEORGE R. SITWELL.

WOOD END, SCARBOROUGH
11 July, 1905

My dear Peveril,

I am really very much annoyed with you about this Hospital Demonstration.

In 1901 (I think) after it had been held for a series of years in my Park, I declined for a year, and there was a vulgar attack on me and you in the Eckington paper. No member of the committee took the trouble to point out that thanks were due to me for having so often permitted it.

I was approached again in May 1902 and declined, giving my reasons.

Do I understand that you really gave permission in 1902, 1903 and 1904 ?

I cannot accept your statement that you did not recollect what happened in 1901 and my wish that the demonstration should not be held at Renishaw in 1902. You knew perfectly well in 1902, if you have forgotten since, and you had no earthly business to grant permission.

I do not like your assisting what you consider good objects with my property and against my wishes. I disliked your giving Morgan stone for his church without consulting me. The £20 which I suppose was paid will not have paid for the mess and damage, and practically the stone for the new Church was provided by me free of cost by your generosity. Now I was particularly anxious that that church should not be built. The present Rector complains bitterly

304

that it is a white elephant to him, and has taken all the money needed for putting the parish church in repair. As a consequence I shall probably have to find at least £2000 out of my own pocket.

I never believed that the quarry was likely to be developed again, nor did I think you really believed it. It was an excuse for promoting a " good object ".

I dislike that sort of thing intensely, having had bitter experience of the vast number of busybodies who are always seeking to be generous at other people's expense. Lady Ida is perpetually falling into little clerical and charitable traps which I have to pay for, £20 here and £10 there.

Please let me have a complete list of bills paid for 1902, 1903, and 1904. I have had a fortnight's hard work in indexing and arranging bills, but you have got me in a tight place, as I have absolutely no knowledge of what bills you paid in 1902 and 1903. It is really hard on the tradesmen to keep them waiting. I cannot deal with any old or disputed accounts until I have your list.

I have four packets of receipts for every year, and a complete index of cheques and receipts, so that I can tell at a glance what has been paid. But I must have your list to enter up in my indexes for 1902 and 1903. I suppose Lady Ida didn't hand to you my receipts for 1902 and those for 1901 which I had out to consult when my illness began. I have not seen them since my illness, and somebody must have put them too carefully away.—Yours very sincerely, GEORGE R. SITWELL.

WOOD END, SCARBOROUGH
12 July, 1905

MY DEAR PEVERIL,

Of late years I have given you full license to say what you like when I am well. No, there is nothing in your letter which has in the least annoyed me.

When angry, I don't think you can see there is another side to the case.

I should hardly resemble a slave-driver or even the Kaiser if I wished you to consult me before lending my park or letting one of my quarries.

If you contribute to charities in Derbyshire which I do not support, this will of course increase the zeal of the critics who think I ought to have subscribed. It will not help me.

If I have lent the Park for the Hospital Sunday demonstration for six or eight years, and decline (in 1901) for a year this does not show that I wish to obtain " éclat ". But naturally if attempts are made to force me to lend the Park by personal attacks I resent it.

The Park costs me I believe £200 or £300 a year to keep up. What I am lending is what I have paid for, not my farm tenant's property.

I don't think you realise that my personal expenses have for many years been very small, probably less than your own. Public and political and charitable subscriptions at Scarborough have taken up a third of my income, and there has been nothing left for a horse, or a motor car or carriage or for keeping up the shooting at Renishaw, or even for entertaining my friends. Your complaint cannot therefore be that I do not subscribe enough, but that I don't subscribe to the objects you wish to choose for me. But unfortunately you are not the only person who wishes to choose for me : every busybody who is interested in any charity in this part of the world or in Derbyshire seems to be mortally offended if I choose for myself. And as a rule I find these people don't subscribe themselves.

With regard to the quarry, I don't think £20 would tidy up the mess left by the contractor. Had you proposed to me to let it at £20, I should have declined without hesitation, but it was another matter to refuse when you did it without consulting me and I might be accused of stopping the erection of the church.

There are not a dozen people in the parish who do not now acknowledge what wicked folly it was to saddle the living with that building. I should of course prefer your not subscribing to objects of which you know I disapprove, but I should not venture to make suggestions as to what other people in my opinion ought or ought not to subscribe to.

I have replied *seriatim* to your remarks, but you mustn't think that I consider them worth it. I shall now tear up your letter, as if Lady Ida were to see it, it might interfere with the pleasant relations upon which I hope we shall meet at Renishaw. I think you are angry and unreasonable, but your personal feeling towards me is probably not nearly so bitter as your letter would make out. On my side there is nothing but good feeling towards you.

. . . The subscription of £5 to Morgan is quite right, and *I do not object to the Christmas donation.* But please do not consider ever whether I shall be criticized for not subscribing to any object. I would always prefer not to subscribe in such cases, having utter contempt for that sort of critic.

I shall be very glad to have your list when ready, Yours very sincerely, GEORGE R. SITWELL.

APPENDIX C

My dear Peveril,

. . . I am much obliged for the list of bills. I think you should have let me have lists at the end of 1902, 1903 and 1904, as I have had many dealings with many of these people since and did not know what was paid them. Thus in the account you have rather unkindly endorsed " Champagne and Turtle Soup to Christmas 1902 ", and which does contain nearly £5 for those articles in my illness, the bulk £42 odd is for our rooms etc. when we stayed at the hotel, owing to Lady Londesborough not giving up the Lodge as early as agreed. But I had already paid them a cheque for £71 odd in April 1902, and your bill having no particulars and Lady Sitwell (as it now appears) having mislaid my receipts for 1902, I cannot check it at all. It is very unfortunate that you did not file full particulars of all the bills. Can you tell me what were the " 5 bills for Osbert's outfit " for which Miss King-Church had £11-9-3 in February 1903 ?[1] If not, I shall have to pay them a second time if presented again. It is sad to see the waste which went on, for which of course you could not be responsible, especially in 1903, when I did without any new clothes or underwear for the whole year, and didn't even have a new tie or hat. Not a few of the bills in your list are from tradesmen who had orders not to supply except with a signed order, and I presume you would not know this, and therefore would not examine my order book. Several also should have been paid by Lady Ida out of her allowance. But of course one cannot expect that there should not be difficulties, and can only be thankful they are not worse.—Yours very sincerely, George R. Sitwell.

[1] I was ten years of age.

307

APPENDIX D

A VISIT TO RENISHAW

10 St. John's Wood Road, London, N.W.8
2nd May, 1945

DEAR SIR OSBERT,

In common with other readers of *Left Hand, Right Hand!* I owe you a debt for the esthetic pleasure it has given me ; and I have this further excuse for thanking you for it, namely that you have opened the shutters on a fantastic week-end that I spent at Renishaw thirty years ago. My recollection of this has remained vividly detailed but utterly unreal, and I had grown to wonder whether perhaps I had allowed my imagination, in the course of time, to insinuate some phantasies of its own. Now I see that it all really did happen, and just as I have always remembered it. It has even become explicable.

It was in early June of about 1912 or 1913. Lutyens had just finished the Golf Club house, and it was this that brought about my visit. I was then an unknown craftsman-cabinet-maker, and how Sir George came to discover me I have forgotten. But he asked me to design and make the chairs and tables for the dining-room at the Golf Club, and suggested that I should go with him to Renishaw on the following Saturday night, so that I could see the building.

Our quest of a design for the furniture was a piece of high comedy, and I left on the Monday morning with a mass of contradictory ideas which I was somehow to resolve into the harmony of a perfect design. There followed a short, and — as I recollect it — a quite cordial correspondence : and then the whole project slid gracefully into oblivion. But I was the richer by a unique experience, the remembrance of which has pleased and puzzled me ever since.

Renishaw was completely unpeopled but for your Father, his valet (my vague recollection of him hardly points to his having been Henry Moat) and myself : at any rate I saw no other human soul from first to last, except an old coachman who drove us in a governess-cart through the park to the Golf Club. Still, I judged that at least there must be an excellent cook, somewhere behind the scenes.

APPENDIX D

I suppose there could hardly be a greater contrast than that between the Renishaw you describe, busy with all the life of a great country home, and the Renishaw that I remember, which was like nothing so much as the palace of the Sleeping Beauty, on whose silence even its owner (to say nothing of myself) seemed almost to be intruding. And yet, however much *en déshabillé*, there was a noble and distinctive flavour about the house and its surroundings which held my imagination, and it was a delight to encounter this once again in your book.

Your Father shewed me the most courtly hospitality, which gave an added touch of the bizarre to the vast emptiness of the house. Questions of furnishing and decoration occupied much of our conversation, and on these he would invite my opinion with something almost like deference : the opinion having been proffered, however, seemed to vanish into the air, and I would presently find that we were on some quite different topic.

Previous to my visit, Renishaw had been nothing more to me than a name on Sir George's letter-heading : it might have been as romantic as Haddon Hall, or as ugly as Osborne. As we drove through the north park I hoped for the best.

We arrived after nightfall so I saw nothing of the exterior : the entrance doors were open, and my first impression was of a pair of most undistinguished Victorian glazed doors in the vestibule. Behind them the great hall was lighted only from the far end, and at either side of it were masses of nondescript furniture — chairs standing on tables, or upside down on other chairs, rolls of carpet and oddments of all kinds, enough to furnish twenty rooms as it seemed. I dimly wondered whether the old home was on the point of being sold up, or whether some great scheme of refurnishing was afoot. At one end an immense fire was burning (it was one of those chilly English Junes) and in front of this, like a clearing in the jungle, was a carpeted space with luxurious easy chairs in which we sat chatting for an hour or so over whisky and soda. All this time that strange disarray of furniture in the darkness behind was clamouring for an explanation, but I felt it might be indelicate to ask about it, and your Father made not the slightest allusion to it, either then or later, which seemed to me quite the oddest fact of all. And to this day I am none the wiser.

Meanwhile we talked about almost everything else. I remember your Father saying that sooner or later there would be a socialist government — perhaps not in his time, but probably in mine —

and that the Income Tax would go on rising until it reached ten shillings in the pound. With this horrid thought we went to bed.

In the morning, the scale of the house became apparent, and on going down the great staircase I caught enchanting glimpses of the gardens and park beyond. I was shepherded into a small room where Sir George sat at breakfast. He said, " I have had breakfast served in this small room ; I hope you won't mind, but I thought that for just the two of us it would be more comfortable than the large dining-room ". The table gleamed with damask and silver, and the breakfast was admirable. But the walls of the room were of naked brown brick, festooned above with black cobwebs. The mantel-piece was intact, but between its jambs and the wall I could see the back of the fire. This time I must have failed to hide my bewilder-ment, for presently Sir George said, " I see you're looking at my walls : I suppose I ought to do something about them. There was some very nice panelling here, and I had it sent to my castle in Italy. Yes, I certainly ought to do something. Tell me now, what would you do ? " I said that I thought the obvious solution was to panel them again : already my mind was busy sketching out a scheme. He looked at me with an air of pleased surprise. " Panel them ", he said ; " but of course you're perfectly right. Yes, they certainly ought to be panelled : I must really think about this ; I'm very much obliged to you." So that question was settled and it was never mentioned again.

Breakfast was followed by a swiftly conducted tour of the principal rooms — the great dining-room with its ancestral portraits, which I should have liked to study at my leisure, and with its furniture shrouded under dust-sheets ; the drawing-room, where again I could have spent hours in examining the furniture, but we had hurried on : the beautiful little domed ante-room that Lutyens had finished a short while before : and the ball-room, filled with a profusion of Spanish furniture, gilded, silvered and richly painted, but, as I thought, rather too exuberant for the classic restraint of the room itself with its cool, stippled walls. I wondered how it could ever be possible to clear away all that furniture for a ball.

One incident of this tour stands out sharply. Among the first things I had noticed in the drawing-room were the magnificent tapestries : your Father was already heading towards the left to lead me to the ball-room, but I had strayed to the right, admiring some beautiful pieces of furniture and the harmonious richness of the general scheme. Then I turned round, and the harmony was suddenly shattered at the sight of a great bare space on the wall, where some dirty white cotton " bump " shewed that another of the tapestries had formerly hung : and in the middle of that dingy expanse was the Sargent Group, which I knew well by repute and had seen at the Royal Academy as a boy. This was more than I could bear : the rape of the tapestry from its proper setting was bad enough, but that its soiled underclothing should be thought a good enough background for a world-famous picture seemed to me a callous indecency. I must have broken out into some protest, for I remember that your Father shewed momentary signs of compunction. " No," he said, " it doesn't look quite right, does it ? It *was* one of the tapestries that hung there, but I've sent that to Italy too ; it was just what I wanted for one of the walls in my castle. But I suppose I ought — yes, I certainly ought to find something else to put in its place. Tell me, what would you suggest ? " We discussed various possibilities which he pondered a little, and then he said in a cheerful and confidential tone " But, after all, it doesn't really matter, you know ; because when I have people here I always take them straight through into the ball-room, so they never see this part of the drawing-room ".

A little later we walked out on to the south terrace, and my eye was immediately caught by some huge pyramidal packing-cases lining the main vista on either hand. " Those ", said Sir George, " oh ! those are my statues. I generally keep them covered up to protect them from the weather." I must say that for me this rather spoiled the romance, but it could hardly spoil the serenity of that view — the terraced lawns leading down and down towards the dark belts of trees in the distance, the reflecting waters of the lake and the far hills beyond. " How fortunate you are ", I said, " to have a lake in exactly the right place." " Fortunate ? " said Sir George. " Nothing of the kind : there wasn't any lake until I put it there. I diverted the river into a valley, and that was the result. It does help the composition I think ? " It assuredly did.

With that we turned back into the house and the serious business of the day began — a consultation about the furniture for the Golf Club. He said, " I've been thinking a great deal about those chairs, and I believe I have an old one somewhere upstairs that would be exactly right : I daresay you'd like to copy it ? " This was the very last thing I had expected to do, but I did not contradict him. " I wonder if you'd mind coming up with me," he said. " I've quite a number of chairs, and if we don't like the one I have in mind, no doubt we can choose another."

He led the way up the great staircase — two stairs at a time — and opened the first door in a long corridor : the room was full of miscellaneous furniture, but no chairs. We went a little farther and he stood expectantly outside another door : " I think we shall find it here," he said, and we went in. The near side of this room was empty ; the far side was quite full of chairs stacked one upon another to a height of five or six feet. They looked a very ordinary lot — kitchen chairs, bedroom chairs, " occasional " chairs ; most of them Victorian but a few somewhat older. Sir George's eye searched the forest of legs and backs and at last he said, " Ah ! yes, I think I see it. I wonder if you would be so very kind as to help me to get it out ? " Together we demolished one end of the stack and, from the bottom layer in the extreme corner, disinterred the prize. He looked at it affectionately and carried it down in triumph to the hall.

As I remember, it was a country-made chair of a late Georgian or Regency type ; decent and unassuming but quite without distinction to my eyes. Sir George walked round it, appraising it from every angle : I stood by, rather glum and feeling definitely no enthusiasm. " Yes," he said at last, " yes, that's the one. The back is charming ; don't you think so ? Yes, the back is certainly very good. But now the legs ; not quite so good I think, don't you agree ? No, these legs are not up to the same standard, we must do better than that. Now let me think — yes ! I believe I've got a chair that would do perfectly as a model for the legs. Shall we go and find it ? " He rushed up the stairs once more, with myself in pursuit. This time he went still farther down the corridor and paused outside yet another door. " Yes," he said thoughtfully, and again we entered. I could hardly believe my eyes : this room was exactly like the last, one side empty, the other piled high with what looked like the same stack of chairs. The pantomime was repeated and once again we returned to the hall with an inoffensive chair of much the same type as the first. We stood them side by side and your Father regarded them intently. " These legs are very much better," he said. " I'm sure you agree ; but of course you do. That's settled then ; I'm so glad we've found what we wanted. And now, if you'll excuse me, I have to write a letter to *The Times*. Luncheon will be ready at one, and afterwards we'll go and look at the Club House. In the meantime I suggest that you get on with the design : you have your sketch-book with you of course ? And pencils and everything ? Excellent ! The light is very good in here and I think you'll find it quite comfortable. I shall be in my study, and if there's anything more that you want, please don't hesitate for a moment to ask for it."

He disappeared, and I was left alone with my two uninspiring models. We craftsmen took ourselves very seriously in those days, and were nothing if not creative ; hence, as your Father's enthusiasm had waxed, so mine had waned. Here was a piece of copybook work, I thought, which any hack draughtsman out of the Curtain Road could have done as well as I. Moreover, although my sympathy embraced many different styles, this particular period was outside it. However, your Father was not only a prospective customer but also a most considerate host, and I felt that it would be churlish indeed not to do my best to fall in with his humour ; so I spent a dispirited hour making drawings of those two chairs and then trying to beget a bastard of them. I think I hadn't much to shew for my efforts by lunch time.

After lunch we drove through the park on grass roads and among lovely glades. I had a fancy that at any turn in the path we might find ourselves face to face with Jaques and the banished Duke. Then, on breasting a ridge, we had come upon a small pit-head in the dip beyond it, and I learned to my astonishment that all this time we had been driving over a coalfield. As a southerner, coalmining to me was synonymous with the Black Country, and it was pleasant to find that it could exist without laying waste the countryside.

When we arrived at the Golf House the weather had turned grey and drizzling. The clubhouse was barely finished and smelt of builders' materials, and I could not by any means reconcile the spirit of its design with that of the chairs.

From that point onwards my memory fails me completely : I cannot remember the drive back to Renishaw Hall nor how we spent the rest of the day. I cannot remember what sort of design I ultimately produced, nor whether the project was formally or merely tacitly dropped.

It is curious that, while the incidents I have described remain so sharply focused in my mind, the rest of the week-end should be such a misty blank. I have a vague and dream-like impression of good food, good wine and stimulating talk, but I cannot conjure up the faintest picture to substantiate this.

What does remain is a vivid portrait of your Father, which our few subsequent meetings, at long intervals, did nothing to disturb.

The portrait is wholly sympathetic, but linked somehow with that of the White Knight in *Alice*. Perhaps it was that he seemed to carry about with him something of the same sort of paraphernalia — his rather naïve love of contrivances ; witness those gigantic extinguishers on the statues (" it's an invention of my own ") ; his faculty for collecting and retaining all manner of curious pieces of information on the most diverse subjects (" it's as well to be provided for everything ") : and a certain absent-mindedness ; though this last was perhaps a form of protective colouring. I was always conscious, however, that his was a many-sided personality, of which I had had the opportunity to see only one aspect. A great part of the pleasure of encountering him once again in your pages has been that of seeing, for the first time, a full-length portrait of him by another hand.—Yours sincerely, HAMILTON TEMPLE SMITH.

APPENDIX E

JULIAN FIELD

FIELD's death certificate records that he died at 84 Tennyson Road, Kilburn, at the age of seventy-six, on the 7th of August, 1925. An account of the inquest held three days later gives the following details. Field was living in one room. He was apparently in good health and had not seen a doctor for some time. At 11.30 A.M. on the 7th, he had left home and met a friend at Charing Cross for luncheon. He had returned home in the afternoon, and at ten minutes past seven o'clock in the evening, was found lying on his bed, with a paper on his arm, as if he had been reading it. As he did not answer when spoken to, a doctor was fetched, and pronounced him to be dead. The Coroner certified death as being due to fatty degeneration of the heart.

The former warder at Wormwood Scrubbs, who, while Field was serving his sentence of eighteen months' hard labour there in 1915, had witnessed his will, and who now identified it as his, still described the dead man as " an author ".

Field bequeathed everything he possessed to his foster-son. The gross amount of the estate was £13 : 2 : 6, little enough when it is remembered to what lengths this man had gone to obtain sums of money.

The following account of Field's activities appeared under the signature " Scrutator " in the issue of *Truth* for 11th November 1914 : " The Frauds of Julian Field ".

" In his fascinating sketch of Captain Rook and Mr. Pigeon Thackeray sarcastically claimed that the production of blacklegs was among the many things in which our country excels the rest of the world. He was referring, of course, to blacklegs of the class who by reason of their birth, education, manners, pass superficially for gentlemen. I do not know whether we have kept our lead in this line, but certainly we can still boast of some remarkably accomplished and successful practitioners among the Rooks who pluck Pigeons in the West End. Two of the predatory tribe whose characters have long been familiar to my readers figured in the courts last week. . . . Last week, Julian Field was sued by Lady Ida Sitwell under circumstances which form a remarkable illustration of his unblushing rascality. Like others of her sex (and the same infirmity is not unknown amongst men), the plaintiff has little appreciation of the value of money and no knowledge of business matters. By an unlucky chance in 1911, she was recommended to write to Field as a person who would assist her in raising money to pay off debts she had incurred. An interview followed, and for a period of nearly two years the unfortunate lady was the dupe of this plausible-tongued rogue. He represented himself as a person of independent position, a public-school and university man, who had nothing to do with money-lenders, but would be glad to help her out of her difficulties. The story of the transactions in which the lady was involved is too complicated to relate in detail ; but as an example it may be mentioned that one loan of £600 was obtained from the blood-sucking firm of R. Leslie, Limited, at interest working out at the rate of 100 per cent. per annum, and that £500 was appropriated by Field. The latter did his plundering in a way that showed the hand of the expert in his profession. Having received the lady's confidence in his good faith and persuaded her that he was paying off her debts and extricating her from all financial troubles, he not only swindled her (and incidentally other people from whom money was procured by the use of her name), but with an eye to his own protection in the event of trouble got her to write letters making gifts to himself which he had drafted. The net result of the transactions was that the plaintiff incurred liabilities to the amount of about £12,000 in return for advances of the amount of £8,350 of which £7,775 went into Field's hands. The debts he had promised to settle for the lady amounted to about £2,000, but he actually disbursed on her account less than £100 out of the £7,775 he received. Clever and cunning as he is, however, Field was unable to cover up the tracks of his fraud, nor could he face cross-examination. Accordingly, though fraud was charged against him in Lady Ida Sitwell's action, he submitted to judgement for the sum claimed — £7,775 — with costs.

" The judgement against Field in the civil suit ought not to be the end of the case. Such a harpy is a danger to society, and Field has too long been allowed to snap his fingers at the law. He first came under my notice some ten years ago as a money-lending tout and commission-snatcher. He was in the habit of advertising in the newspapers from West End addresses under such aliases as ' Ellis ' and ' Ralph Vivian ', describing himself at one time as an Eton and Oxford man, at another as an Eton and Cambridge man, and yet again as a Harrow or Rugby and Oxford or Cambridge man. He exhibited a touch of humour, in his lying. ' Beware of usurers under misleading names ' one advertisement ran. ' See them and be enlightened. Et Nasis et Conditionibus.' The employment of ' Ralph Vivian ' as an alias was a particularly offensive false pretence, inasmuch as there happened to be an old Etonian of that name. Field never was at Eton, but there is, I regret to say, some reason to believe that he was at Harrow. People who replied to these advertisements got a letter from Field in which he stated that in the absence abroad of the mythical ' Ellis ' or ' Vivian ' as the case might be, he would personally attend to the business. His procedure varied according to the circumstances of the would-be borrowers. Almost invariably his first move was to persuade the victim to take out a policy with a certain life insurance company, from which Field then drew a heavy commission out of the first year premium. The victim was led to expect that a loan could easily be raised upon the policy, but of course, when no other security could be provided, this representation was untrue and Field's interest in the matter began and ended with the pocketing of the commission. On the other hand, if it was a case in which an advance could be procured Field would take a further fat commission for leaving the borrower to the tender mercies of some such bloodsucker as ' R. Leslie '. Field always posed as a man of means, and for some three years he occupied a furnished house in Park Lane at a rent of £900 a year. He left in 1909 owing about £200 for rent and when Lady Ida Sitwell fell into his clutches he was living at the Grosvenor Hotel. No doubt it was his plunder from that source which enabled him to remove to his present somewhat luxurious flat in Belgrave Mansions.

" Prior to his embarkation on the career of a money-lender's tout Field had dabbled in literature. About 1898 an eminent firm of publishers issued a book of his. . . . It would seem, however, that the profits from the employment of his pen in that way were not sufficient for Field — at any rate, it was found not long afterwards that attempts were being made to procure loans on the strength of two forgeries which purported to be contracts between the publisher and Field. No proceedings were instituted in respect of these documents, but there were others, and on 22nd July 1901 Field was convicted of forgery at the Central Criminal Court, and sentenced to three months' imprisonment. Just before that he had been made a bankrupt, and from that bankruptcy he is still undischarged. Between the middle of 1909 and the middle of 1912 about a dozen petitions in bankruptcy were presented against Field.

" In past years I have more than once suggested that this old-established rogue should be brought to book in respect of different offences under the Money-Lenders' Act. Field has always set at defiance the requirements of the Act as to registration, and I think he might also have been successfully prosecuted under the section relating to the use of false representations. It was apparently not thought worth while to proceed against him on such grounds as those, but now that evidence of his nefarious operations has been brought to light in the case of Lady Ida Sitwell I hope that Julian Field will at last receive the attention he deserves at the hands of the Public Prosecutor."

INDEX